EXPLORING CATHOLIC LITERATURE

EXPLORING CATHOLIC LITERATURE

A Companion and Resource Guide

MARY R. REICHARDT

A SHEED & WARD BOOK

ROWMAN & LITTLEFIELD PUBLISHERS, INC.
Lanham • Boulder • New York • Oxford

*52031479

A SHEED & WARD BOOK

ROWMAN & LITTLEFIELD PUBLISHERS, INC.

Published in the United States of America
by Rowman & Littlefield Publishers, Inc.

An Imprint of the Rowman & Littlefield Publishing Group, Inc.
4501 Forbes Boulevard, Suite 200, Lanham, Maryland 20706
www.rowmanlittlefield.com

PO Box 317
Oxford
OX2 9RU, UK

Copyright © 2003 by Mary R. Reichardt

Quotations from Mark Musa's translation of *The Divine Comedy* in *The Portable Dante* (New York: Penguin, 1995) used by permission of Indiana University Press (Bloomington and Indianapolis).

An excerpt from "Little Gidding" in *Four Quartets*, copyright 1942 by T. S. Eliot and renewed 1970 by Esme Valerie Eliot, reprinted by permission of Harcourt, Inc.

British Library Cataloguing in Publication Information Available

Library of Congress Cataloging-in-Publication Data
Reichardt, Mary R.
   Exploring Catholic literature : a companion and resource guide / Mary R. Reichardt.
      p.   cm.
   "A Sheed & Ward book."
   Includes bibliographical references.
   ISBN 0-7425-3173-2—ISBN 0-7425-3174-0 (pbk.)
   1. Catholic literature—History and criticism 2. Catholic literature—Bio-bibliography
I. Title.
   PN485.R45 2003
   809'.9338282—dc21   2003007809

Printed in the United States of America

∞™ The paper used in this publication meets the minimum requirements of American National Standard for Information Sciences—Permanence of Paper for Printed Library Materials, ANSI/NISO Z39.48-1992.

This world of ours has some purpose; and if there is a purpose, there is a person. I had always felt life first as a story; and if there is a story there is a story-teller.

—G. K. Chesterton

CONTENTS

INTRODUCTION

This book is an introductory guide to twelve masterpieces of Catholic literature. Designed for students of all ages, it may be adopted for use in the undergraduate literature, Catholic studies, or theology classroom, or used as a guide for self-study. Each chapter, focused on a single literary work, presents a brief biography of the author followed by an extended critical essay on the work's themes and techniques, especially in terms of its Catholic content. Essays draw on a wide selection of secondary sources, thus bringing in a variety of influential critical voices that contribute to the discussion. Suggestions for further reading of related texts, questions for discussion or papers, and a selected bibliography complete each chapter.

One might question why such a guide is needed at this time. In these first few years of the new millennium, interest in all things Catholic is on the rise. Statistics indicate that Catholicism, unlike other mainstream religions, continues to grow steadily in the United States: a third of all Americans now call themselves Catholic. New waves of the Spirit are spreading throughout parts of traditionally Catholic Europe, both east and west, reinvigorating dormant faith in that continent. And elsewhere in the world, in parts of Africa, Asia, and Latin America, for example, the increase in the Catholic population over the last few decades has been nothing short of staggering. A new generation of young people in particular is eager to learn more about the faith's teachings, culture, and traditions. As testimony to this fact, one need only witness the astonishing crowds Pope John Paul II has drawn to recent World Youth Day events as well as the proliferation of interdisciplinary Catholic studies programs in colleges and universities across the nation.

With the rise of interest in Catholicism comes the demand for updated educational materials. In the area of literature, the need is particularly acute. For more than a generation now, literary studies in both secular and private institutions have been dominated by postmodern critical theories that, with their emphasis on deconstructing literature and thoroughly politicizing its content, are largely antithetical, if not downright hostile, to Christian thought. In depleting texts of meaning or reducing them to the mere sociological study of power differentials, such theories, in their purest form, negate even the possibility of the supernatural and thus have no use for the transformation of reality by grace. From a Christian point of view, such deterministic thought saps literature of its ability to do what great literature does so well: evoke the spiritual and thereby expand the spirit. Even in English departments at Catholic institutions, it has for years now been rare if not impossible to find courses that examine texts from a religious, much less Christian or Catholic, perspective. Catholic literature, a long and rich tradition indeed, has been ignored precisely because it *must* be examined from a Catholic perspective in order to comprehend it in its totality. Trained in critical methods that deny or discount the existence of God, lacking a scholarly understanding of Catholic teaching, or simply embarrassed to talk about faith in the classroom, many faculty simply choose to ignore Catholic literature. And if included in a course at all, a literary work has often been so distorted as to render it virtually incomprehensible. A case in point is the contemporary American author Flannery O'Connor. Never more popular, her fiction has generated an enormous amount of criticism over the last two decades, most of which gives but a cursory nod to or dismisses altogether her deeply Catholic themes. When studied in a literature classroom where discussion is ruled by the "race/class/gender" mantra, her stories become merely senseless, grotesque studies in the pathology of victimization and violence.

By no means am I suggesting here that poststructuralist theories have no value as literary tools. All critical methods are simply different angles, or lenses, that can help illuminate parts of a literary work. In emphasizing how deeply literature is embedded in and springs from culture—its essential "contingency"—modern theories have contributed an understanding of the many subtle yet insidious factors that serve to marginalize or oppress certain segments of society. At best, such theories can have a laudable ethical dimension. But any approach to education that does not consider the whole person, and any approach to literature that is closed off from even the possibility of the spiritual is woefully deficient. If literary works have no foundation in truth or ability to address ultimate concerns, the study of literature and the endless production of literary criticism become only a rarified, elitist game, yet another interesting rearrangement of deck chairs on the *Titanic*.

This book, by contrast, proceeds from the point of view that the best literature not only invites us to explore the intersection of the natural and supernatural realms, but also that a certain subset of that literature—Catholic literature—allows us to roam imaginatively through the greatest and most profound mysteries of Catholic truth: incarnationalism, sacramentality, God-with-us in the Real Presence of the Eucharist, the profound meaning and worth of suffering, the ties of charity that unite the living and dead in the Body of Christ. It takes as its starting point the belief that reason and faith are not oppositional paths to truth—the one legitimate, the other suspect—but complementary. A Christian understands that while we gain tremendous amounts of knowledge by reading, study, and analysis, that which comes through faith and prayer unfailingly supercedes that achieved by intellectual endeavor. Approaching literature from a Catholic/Christian point of view, one that proceeds from both faith and reason, is as valid a type of criticism as any other. In his influential article "Religion and Literature," T. S. Eliot correctly stated, "literary criticism should be completed by criticism from a definite ethical and theological standpoint."[1] A religiously based criticism, therefore, does not cancel out the use of other forms of criticism but rather builds on their foundation. While drawing on a variety of critical methods, the essays in this book are designed to contribute the "last layer" of interpretation called for by Eliot. This guide thus fills a gap in literary studies by focusing on Catholic literature *and* being written from the seamless unity of both a scholarly and faithful point of view.

But what exactly is "Catholic literature"? A broad category, no precise definition exists. Written by persons of all backgrounds and cultures over its two-thousand-year history, Catholic literature conforms to no single pattern. It has been produced in all possible genres: fiction, poetry, autobiography, children's works, plays, essays, and more. Some Catholic writing is distinctly sentimental and pious. Some is didactic, written with the express intent of converting the reader. Some use Catholicism in ways that purposely distort or disparage the faith. Catholic literature has been written by baptized, believing Catholics, by lapsed Catholics, and by non-Catholics. For the purposes of this book, we can propose the following definition: Catholic literature is good literature that employs the history, traditions, culture, theology, and/or spirituality of Catholicism in a substantial, informed, and meaningful way. By "good" literature I mean those works of art that present the human situation in complex ways and on various levels that can be pondered, analyzed, and discussed. Such literature never lends itself to black-and-white thinking but rather concentrates on exploring the gray areas of paradox, ambiguity, and moral dilemma. Good literature is serious literature: it may entertain but more often disturbs, raising more questions than it provides answers. Moreover, while the works encountered here use Catholicism in a substantial, informed, and meaningful way—that is, they are grounded in a deep and accurate understanding of the faith—as good literature they do not aim merely to soothe or pacify the hyperpious or religiously complacent. These works never attempt to dismiss the struggles and doubts inherent in the human situation for a naïve, sentimental, or "feel-good" religion. Rather, each work here examines profound Catholic issues through the expansive freedom of the imagination, pushing borders, crossing boundaries, penetrating mysteries, and exploring the many astonishing paradoxes inherent in the Christian faith.

As a humanity, literature makes us more humane, widening our contacts with lives, experiences, and events unlike our own. It allows us to observe actions and their results over a short period of time and to empathize with characters whose inner lives and motivations are revealed. Any person who maintains a steady diet of good literature knows its power to broaden experience and expand the mind and heart. Writing in *Literature and the Christian Life*, critic Sallie TeSelle goes one step further, suggesting that literature can play a significant role in the Christian life precisely because it aids vicariously in the widening of the kind of empathy necessary to growth in charity, the goal and summit of Christianity. As she states,

> Literature with its concrete, varied, and creative depictions of the basic structure of human experience, in both its cosmological and anthropological aspects, offers to the Christian invaluable acquaintance. It gives to the Christian, who is called upon to adhere totally to God in spite of the negative powers that appear to rule the world, an understanding of the depth and breadth of powers that his response must embrace if it is to be realistic. He must take into account those diseased and dying infants who troubled Ivan in *The Brothers Karamazov* (and feel for them as Ivan does) and that white whale which embodied all evil for Ahab in *Moby Dick* (and know in his heart the extent of that whale's rule as Ahab did). Literature also offers to the Christian, who is called upon to love his fellows with a profound and appropriate love, an entrée into the crannies of the human heart that

a realistic love cannot do without. What one can learn of the human heart from James or Faulkner or Tolstoy cannot be gained from history, psychology, or sociology books, or even, unfortunately, for most of us, from our own experience with our fellows, which is so stereotyped and patterned that we seldom see beneath the clichés of surface relationships.[2]

TeSelle's point is that the vicarious empathy we gain by reading literature can help us to understand and sympathize more fully with our fellow humans in real life.

One hallmark of the Catholic faith that has strongly affected its literature is its insistent incarnationalism. Because Jesus chose to save humankind by becoming a person and going through life in this world, from birth to death, he sanctified all aspects of our existence on earth. Salvation is not to be found or holiness achieved, therefore, by scorning reality or attempting to close one's eyes, Buddha-like, to all that is human. In Catholic thinking, there is thus no glossing over of the difficulties, evils, and sufferings of life: as St. Paul puts it, all creation "groans" as it awaits the fullness of redemption. The notion that material success or other visible signs of personal well-being are marks of God's special favor is alien to Catholic thought because it has nothing to do with imitating the Christ who lived in poverty, was despised by many, and suffered. The most important symbol of the faith is, therefore, not an empty cross but one with a suffering corpus on it, a constant reminder of God's mysterious connection of suffering and love in his plan for our salvation. By embracing all that is human, the good with the bad, with the intention of loving God and imitating Christ, all things are transformed by grace and become a means to our redemption. As William Lynch puts it, "there are no shortcuts to beauty or to insight. We must go *through* the finite, the limited, the definite. . . . *The way up is the way down*."[3] This Catholic emphasis on incarnationalism resonates powerfully with writers in the Catholic tradition who find in it great impetus for their art. It encourages them to describe life just as they see and experience it, warts and all, without any artificial need to, as Flannery O'Connor once stated, "tidy up" reality for the sake of a positive or uplifting story. It is this life, just as it is here and now, that God loves, transforms, and redeems.

A second and related characteristic of Catholic thought that has deeply influenced its literature is its stress on sacramentality. If all things that exist do so because God has created them, loves them, and sustains them, all things are not only good to at least some degree in and of themselves but also have the ability to communicate the power and goodness of God. Catholics formally profess seven sacraments, each "a sign instituted by Christ to give grace": baptism, confirmation, penance, Eucharist, matrimony, Holy Orders (the conferring of the priesthood), and anointing of the sick. Among these, the Eucharist, a sacrament that may be received every day, is especially significant. Hidden behind the humble, natural elements of bread and wine is Jesus himself, the complete God-Man in his Body, Blood, Soul, and Divinity, not only physically present but taken into the communicant in an act of total unity and intimacy. Like nothing else, the Eucharist powerfully conveys the essential Catholic belief that God is with us in all circumstances and at all times. By contrast, by reducing the communion service to a mere symbolic gesture or ritual, Protestantism has not only significantly emptied it of its meaning but also puts more stress on God's absence from us than presence among us. This vital Catholic sense of Jesus dwelling with us on earth, animating and transforming everything that exists, and the consequent sacramentality of all creation, permeates Catholic literature. All things, events, and experiences "tell" of God and can lead us to God if we have the eyes to see and the ears to hear. By grounding their work in the concrete, material world, literary artists in the Catholic tradition can reveal the supernatural and convey spiritual truths. Thus literature, too, can serve as a sacramental, a vehicle of grace for those disposed to receive it.

It is precisely because of its emphasis on incarnationalism and sacramentality that the Catholic Church prizes artists. The vast collection of art and literature produced by persons of every era and culture contained in the Vatican museums and libraries more than testify to this fact. The Catholic liturgy, too, is permeated with art: music, color, incense, church décor, and pageantry are employed to stimulate the senses, engage the emotions, and lift the spirit to the beauty and wonder of God. In a remarkable letter to artists written for the 2000 Jubilee Year, Pope John Paul II stated that the Church needs art: not just acknowledges it or tolerates it but *needs* it. "Every genuine art form in its own way is a path to the inmost reality of man and of the world," the letter states. "It is therefore a wholly valid approach to the realm of faith, which gives human experience its ultimate meaning."[4] As all art is the creation of something new, a unique entity in the world bodied forth from the mind, heart, and imagination of the artist, so art in a small way imitates the work of the Creator and thus participates in the constant unfolding of the creation. Art is often prophetic, pointing the way toward what is to come. It makes us pause in our daily routine, become meditative, and refresh our spirits in the contemplation of beauty and truth.

An understanding of imaginative literature as an art form has been slow to develop in the Church, however. The case of Graham Greene's *The Power and the Glory*, discussed in more detail in the chapter to follow, can serve to illustrate this point. Greene's novel portrays a fallen priest, a man who, persecuted, lonely, and weak, has slipped from his vows. Yet the story clearly suggests that the priest's very sins and failings paradoxically allow him to achieve a high degree of sanctity. When the book was published in 1940, it was censored by Vatican officials precisely because it fails to depict the Catholic faith in an unambiguous or positive manner. But twenty-five years later in the atmosphere of Vatican II, the novel was exonerated by Pope Paul VI, himself a scholarly man, with the result that today it is considered a central text in the development of modern Catholic literature. Fully comprehending a Catholic view of incarnationalism and sacramentality means that one can embrace without reservation any work of art that represents life truthfully—its goodness, beauty, and joy along with its evil, sin, and misery.

We now turn to a brief tour of the twelve literary works you'll encounter here. Written in several different genres and by authors from a variety of eras and cultures, together they provide representative samples of the wealth of the Catholic literary tradition. Any study of this tradition necessarily begins with Saint Augustine's fourth-century *Confessions*, the classic tale of one man's journey to God. Augustine's passionate account of the myriad internal and external obstacles he battled on the road to conversion coupled with his engaging prose style has captivated readers of all generations and, in fact, set the model for modern, introspective autobiography. Next, we explore the flowering of mysticism in the medieval period through two major fourteenth-century spiritual narratives. Written by an anonymous Englishman, *The Cloud of Unknowing* focuses on the "negative" approach to God through prayer. In this book of spiritual instruction, the *Cloud* author leads readers firmly but gently to the practice of mystical contemplation, a mode of apprehending God that is often misunderstood in Western religious practice. Julian of Norwich's *Revelations of Divine Love* is also a masterpiece of medieval mystical thought. Near death from an illness around the age of thirty, Julian received a series of visions centering on Christ's Passion, the role of suffering in redemption, and God's tender, maternal-like love and care for all his creation. Her message as relevant today as in her own time, Julian's work has influenced a number of major twentieth-century writers. We then turn to one of the world's greatest literary masterpieces of all time, Dante's *Divine Comedy*. This long, intricate poem, a fantasy journey through the three realms of the Catholic afterlife—heaven, hell, and purgatory—combines in an extraordinary manner the author's soaring imagination, powerful technical skill, and deep religious faith. Packed full of theology, history, politics, and culture, the *Comedy* truly serves as an epic of the medieval world.

Approaching more modern times, we next encounter the remarkable poetry of the nineteenth-century British Jesuit priest Gerard Manley Hopkins. Although he often chose to compose his works in the traditional form of the sonnet, Hopkins's poetry is utterly unique, especially in his experimental use of language. In his sonnets celebrating nature, Hopkins discovers the beauty and energy of Christ in all things, and his dark poems of inner anguish equally serve as a vehicle to spiritual truths. Sigrid Undset's trilogy of books set in late medieval Norway, *Kristin Lavransdatter*, opens to readers an entire historical world of lives fully lived in a culture of belief. As child, wife, mother, and widow, Kristin is one of the most fully conceived fictional characters of all time and her saga that of every person struggling to balance the things of this world with the things of God. Graham Greene's dramatic tale *The Power and the Glory* takes us to persecuted Mexico of the 1930s where we accompany the last remaining priest in the state of Chiapas as he flees not only from the authorities of the socialist, totalitarian regime bent on eradicating religion in that country but also from his own duty to God. Greene provides us with a compelling portrait of a flawed man whose very failings serve to increase the humility and charity that alone can purify the soul. We then explore Evelyn Waugh's *Brideshead Revisited*, a beautifully told, complex novel set in England between the two world wars. A budding artist and an agnostic, Charles Ryder meets the charming young lord, Sebastian Flyte, as an undergraduate at Oxford and is soon taken into the circle of Sebastian's eccentric Catholic family. At times both attracted to and repelled by members of that family, Charles finds himself inexorably drawn to their faith in the midst of the privations of war and the emptiness of his own life.

Contemporary American author Flannery O'Connor, who died tragically young, brings us to an odd landscape for Catholic literature: the Protestant fundamentalist south of the 1940s and 1950s. Her blend of dark satire and broad comedy coupled with her deeply held religious convictions results in sometimes rollicking, sometimes horrific stories that take a hard-eyed look at the modern-day Pharisees all around us. Next, the genre of metaphysical nature writing is represented by Annie Dillard's *Holy the Firm*. This slender yet rich volume, full of unforgettable images, leads readers to meditate especially on the thorny issue of how we can understand a God who allows the innocent to suffer. A profound sense of the sacramentality of the natural world informs Dillard's vision. Japanese novelist Shusaku Endo's *Deep River* takes a provocative look at several modern-day, thoroughly secularized characters each of whom is confronted by one or more of life's greatest problems: the death of a spouse, the inability to truly love others, persistent inner loneliness and emptiness, the horror of war, the anxiety of guilt. Endo takes his characters on a trip to India, one of the most culturally and religiously pluralistic nations in the world, where each comes to some degree of insight or resolution. One tourist, Mitsuko, struggles in particular to understand the countercultural lifestyle of a young Catholic man to whom she is mysteriously attracted. And finally, we encounter poet Denise Levertov's *The Stream and the Sapphire*. A prolific author whose career spanned nearly sixty years, Levertov converted to Catholicism late in life. This collection, assembled by Levertov in her final year of life, brings together poems that illustrate her pilgrimage to faith through many fits and starts, trials and doubts, tensions and paradoxes. It is a moving account of a sensitive life lived before God, the mind watching itself as it approaches the fullness of belief.

These twelve works represent some of the best Catholic writing of all time. But they are only a fraction of the tremendously long and varied Catholic literary tradition. Should they whet your appetite for more, as I hope they will, you will find an additional list of recommended books in the appendix.

NOTES

1. T. S. Eliot, "Religion and Literature," in *Essays Ancient and Modern* (London: Faber and Faber, 1936), 93.

2. Sallie TeSelle, *Literature and the Christian Life* (New Haven, CT: Yale University Press, 1966), 114.

3. William F. Lynch, *Christ and Apollo: The Dimensions of the Literary Imagination* (Notre Dame, IN: University of Notre Dame Press, 1975), 7, 13.

4. "Letter of His Holiness Pope John Paul II to Artists," April 4, 1999.

AUGUSTINE OF HIPPO
THE *CONFESSIONS*
OF SAINT AUGUSTINE

BIOGRAPHY

Aurelius Augustinus was born in Tagaste in Numidia (now Souk-Ahras, Algeria), on November 13, 354, to a family respectable enough, but of modest means. His father Patricius, a town councilor, was a sociable and worldly man who spent more than he could afford to give his son a better-than-average education so that he might rise in the world. Patricius died when Augustine was yet a teenager. A pious Christian, Augustine's mother Monica was also ambitious for her son. Monica came of Berber stock and was many years younger than Patricius. We know from Augustine's writings that there were at least two other children in the family, a son and daughter.

At the time Augustine was born, North Africa was part of the crumbling Roman Empire. Only a generation prior to his birth, in 312, Constantine the Great declared Christianity to be the official faith of the Empire, ending Christian persecution. Augustine was born in the first century of Christian government, a time when the Roman Church, now legal and integrated into the culture, faced a new assessment of its temporal and spiritual state. In this period, as Peter Brown astutely observes, "The Christian's worst enemies could no longer be placed outside him: they were inside, his sins and his doubts; and the climax of a man's life would not be martyrdom, but conversion from the perils of his own past."[1] Augustine's *Confessions* is the classic reflection of such a new spiritual interiority.

After schooling both locally and in the nearby town of Madauros, where the secular, classical curriculum consisted mainly of Latin and

Greek language and literature, Augustine pursued higher education in rhetoric at Carthage. In that city known for loose living, the teenager entered into a relationship with a local girl that produced a son, Adeodatus. As his formal education ended and the student turned teacher, the brilliant Augustine was, by his own account, consumed with ambition, confident in his talents, and on fire with sexual lust. At the age of nineteen, however, inspired by his reading of Cicero's *Hortensius,* the worldly young man found himself increasingly attracted to religious and intellectual ideas. Over the next decade, this quest, pursued side by side with his rising career as a rhetorician, led him to study the teachings of the Manichaeans, the astrologers, the academics (or skeptics), and the Neoplatonists. Finally, in Milan, where he had relocated to accept a position as *rhetor* after a brief hiatus teaching in Rome, Augustine turned back to his mother's faith, Christianity. At the age of thirty-one, he became a catechumen in the Catholic Church.

Even as his intellectual quest for the truth moved toward resolution in Catholic Christianity, however, Augustine's internal suffering increased. Sensing that a commitment to Catholicism demanded for him total self-giving to God, he yet clung to worldly ambitions and pleasures. But upon a crisis brought on by hearing stories of heroic converts to the faith, Augustine experienced a powerful moment of grace that brought peace to his divided heart and filled him with conviction and joy. The year was 386. A lung illness he considered providential soon led him to abandon his career, and he and several companions moved to the nearby country estate of Cassiciacum (perhaps modern-day Cassago), owned by a Milanese friend. After completing his period as a catechumen, Augustine was baptized in 387 by Ambrose of Milan, the bishop whose preaching had greatly influenced his conversion. Shortly thereafter, Monica, who had joined her son, died and was buried in Ostia, near Rome.

The next year, Augustine left Italy for his hometown in Africa, hoping to fulfill his dream of living a quasi-monastic life of contemplation and philosophic writing. However, while visiting the port city of Hippo Regius (later Bône, now Annaba, Algeria) in North Africa in 391, he somewhat reluctantly accepted ordination to the priesthood. In 396, he became bishop of Hippo. For the rest of his life, Augustine performed episcopal duties of preaching and administrative work while also engaging actively in discussions against the several major heresies of the day, including Manichaeanism, Donatism, and Pelagianism. He somehow found time to write a staggering number of works, his extant corpus amounting to nearly one hundred books, five hundred sermons, and three hundred letters. On August 28, 430, the seventy-six-year-old bishop died while reciting the penitential Psalms.

Theologian, author, bishop, saint, and Doctor of the Church, Augustine has exerted tremendous influence on the history of Christian thought, both Catholic and Protestant. For nearly sixteen hundred years, his works have played a major intellectual and spiritual role within the Church.

CRITICAL OVERVIEW

A work of theological complexity, deep psychological insight, and poetic beauty, Augustine's *Confessions* is equally at home in the theology or literature class. Our focus is on the work as a literary text, and so it will suffice to consider only books 1 through 9, the autobiographical section of the text that traces the workings of divine grace in the author's past as he is led by God on a tangled route up to his conversion. Books 10 and 11 provide extended commentaries on the nature of memory and time, subjects important to the *Confessions*. The final two books delve into a theological interpretation of Genesis, also of significance to the overall intent of the narrative. This biblical book so intrigued Augustine that he later penned a number of full-scale theological commentaries on it.

Before considering Augustine's story, it is important to reflect on some of the unique challenges that the study of autobiography presents. Three matters, those of intended audience, purpose, and point of view or perspective, come immediately to the forefront. Who is the writer addressing and why? From what vantage point of time or experience does he or she relate the story? In turn, establishing audience, purpose, and point of view leads to the question of selection. Not merely a blow-by-blow account of events, a literary autobiography poses a larger pattern or metaphor around which the author shapes the story of his or her life. The fact that the author begins with an overall intent and then selects and "tweaks" events to illustrate it raises the fascinating question of truth telling in autobiography. Did the events happen just as they are described or have they been manipulated to illustrate a point? Both the perspective and purpose of the author come into play as we consider the truth value of an autobiography.

Turning to the *Confessions,* we see that Augustine, in looking back on his youth, carefully chose those incidents that best form a discernable pattern of spiritual growth and by means of which he could argue certain theological and philosophical points suited to his purpose and audience.

Readers, therefore, must be prepared for a personal story that moves only in fits and starts and is heavily interspersed with digression, analysis, and speculation. As do all autobiographers, Augustine also made decisions about point of view. As Frederick J. Crosson states, "The problem confronting Augustine may be posed in the following way: to tell the story of one's life in such a way that the sequence of events related is adequately accounted for and yet to tell that story in such a way that those events are not adequately accounted for."[2] That is, the converted Augustine who now possesses the "new sight" of faith that transfigures his past must remember how it felt to be the younger Augustine who experiences only blindness and confusion. Augustine writes his life story, then, on two levels operating simultaneously.

In terms of audience, the situation is more complicated. Augustine's putative listener, as we see from the first sentence, is God, and this renders the whole of the *Confessions* a prayer, a sustained dialogue with the Creator. But Augustine is also writing for several distinct human audiences. For one thing, the bishop is addressing his Catholic congregation at Hippo, enjoining them to resist the pernicious influence of secular culture. Yet another audience is his detractors, those who at the time were doubtful about his suitability as a bishop because in the not-so-distant past he had both championed Manichaeanism and earned a reputation for disreputable living. Augustine designed the *Confessions*, therefore, in part to defend himself against his critics. As a newly ordained bishop in his early forties a decade after his conversion, Augustine also composed his autobiography to come to terms with his past. In writing the *Confessions*, he worked toward an understanding of how that past was directed by God and was thus meaningful to the present. He strove to comprehend how, in the mystery of time and memory, the continuity of the past was intimately connected to both the present and the future. Not a book of reminiscences, therefore, the *Confessions* is rather an earnest scrutiny of God's action in his life over the broad sweep of time.

And lastly, another audience of the *Confessions* is all of humankind, including ourselves as we read the work many centuries after it was written. Raised by the author's skill to the level of an epic, each individual incident Augustine recounts assumes meaning for the whole human race. Augustine appeals to all who are discontent, all who feel their lives lack meaning or are hopelessly caught up in a rat race. "Is not the happy life that which all desire?" he queries rhetorically (10.29), and he writes the *Confessions* with the passion of one who has discovered what he long sought. Moreover, in Augustine's experiences we recognize our own: we can all recall childhood fears, the thrill of doing wrong for wrong's sake, and the uncomfortable sense of a disconnect between our outer, social selves and our inner, deeper selves. We are, in short, all *peregrinati*, Augustine's well-chosen word that indicates both "wanderers" away from God and "pilgrims" struggling to find the way back.

Augustine's *Confessions* sounds familiar to us in another way as well. We need only read a few pages to get a sense of why the book is considered the first modern autobiography in the Western tradition. In his minute self-scrutiny, intense introspection, and great sensitivity to nuances of mood and emotion, Augustine strikes the reader as astonishingly contemporary. Furthermore, the *Confessions* anticipates modern psychology in its protracted study of such complex human phenomena as the process of grief, the acquisition of language, the development of conscience, and the divided will.

The book's title is carefully chosen. To Augustine, *confessio* did not simply mean owning up to sin, although such a definition is important to what he has to tell us. *Confessio* is, first of all, a profession or a declaration of belief. *Confessio* is also praise of God, a glory given that testifies to God's overarching role in human life and thereby puts humans in proper relationship to the Creator. At its essence, therefore, *confessio* is an acknowledgement of the human condition of weakness and fallenness before the power, glory, and truth of the Almighty. Throughout the *Confessions*, Augustine thus assumes the stance of the pious seeker, humbly examining his life in the light of God. "Augustine thinks in questions," Karl Jaspers has stated, and only by such reverent inquiry into God's ways is dialogue with the Creator of All Things possible.[3] From a position of faith, the humble inquirer seeks understanding.

Trained in the art of rhetoric, Augustine tells his story in patterns of recurring images, symbols, and metaphors. He weaves together carefully reasoned argument, vivid moments of heightened emotion, powerful drama, and exhaustive biblical references. "Quite literally a symphony," as Robert J. O'Connell has called it, the *Confessions* suggests strains of thought only to swell them into fullness later and then advance them toward a triumphant crescendo at the end.[4] Such incremental repetition reinforces the author's ideas and unites the work artistically and thematically. Augustine was acutely sensitive to the power of language to nourish the soul with truth or starve it with falseness, to convey the things of God or merely tickle the ear. He composed his book in a rich Latin oratorical prose that many times approaches the heights of lyrical poetry. Favoring oxymoron, paradox, and antithesis, he fills the work with such intriguing phrases as "in the agony of death I was coming to life" and "you recover what you find, yet have never lost." In fact, so nuanced and artistic are his choice of words and turns of phrase that the *Confessions* has proven to be exceedingly difficult to translate.

Upon opening the *Confessions*, we initially encounter several pages of direct address to God. Here, in the *Proemium*, Augustine accomplishes several important things. He establishes his primary audience as the Almighty, and the process of colloquy begins. God's omnipotence is emphasized, and, by contrast, humankind's insignificance. Augustine here performs the "sacrifice" of praise that throws down human pride before the Godhead. As he will insist, only by adopting such a position can we begin to understand the truth about ourselves. Now, in the loving presence of God, he can review each incident of his life without fear, observing how God, in his secret providence, has led him step by step to salvation. This indeed will be Augustine's most urgent theme: that despite our blindness and ignorance of his ways, God is supremely at work in all things, including all of the smallest details of our lives. In God is the satisfaction of all our needs and desires and of all life's paradoxes and contradictions: he is at once both deeply mysterious and profoundly intimate to us. "Our heart is restless until it rests in you," Augustine sings in the book's first paragraph.

Now, the autobiography picks up in a more traditional manner as Augustine tells us about his infancy and childhood. Note that he dwells longer than we might expect on his infancy although, of course, he can't remember much about it. He describes infant behavior he's observed (no doubt remembering his own son) and assumes that his own development was similar. For example, he states that at some point he began to smile and express himself through bodily motions, as all babies do. Well and good. But suddenly we are caught up short for the discussion has switched to the sin of infants: greed, anger, jealousy. Infant sin! Such a concept strikes our ears as unduly harsh. But Augustine is quite conscious of what he's doing and proceeds very deliberately to make a point. By observing behaviors common to all babies, he equates himself here with every infant, every human being. Furthermore, he proves to us that infants are not all-good at birth (as the romantically inclined might believe), nor merely *tabula rasa*, blank slates poised to receive the impressions of training and nurture. Rather, he discovers in babies traces of primordial evil, of turning away from the good and the perfect: that is, of original sin. Thus in deft strokes, Augustine not only universalizes his life story, viewing himself as everyman, as Adam, but he also makes the profound statement that the human condition is, from the beginning, a fallen one. In addition, he points out that from the moment of our birth it is God who nurtures us through the human agents of mothers and nurses; God works continually in all things and through all human beings for our welfare. Finally, Augustine's prolonged dwelling on the state of infancy has much to do with his thoughts on conversion, as we shall see later.

In this first book, then, Augustine establishes the fact that turning away from God (what he calls "fornication") is inherent in the human condition. Now, he recalls how his secular, pagan education fostered this natural inclination to do wrong even while it developed his intellect and refined his skills. Led by teachers themselves eager for worldly success and glory, Augustine grew into a young man burning with ambition and proud of his considerable talents. However, as he points out, his most besetting sin was sexual lust, a habit formed early by his school reading of pagan literature. "R[unning] wild in the shadowy jungle of erotic adventures," "burning to find satisfaction in hellish pleasures," and blinded by "clouds of muddy carnal concupiscence," Augustine remembers himself as consumed by a hypercharged libido (2.1–2). Opening with such strongly sensual language, book 2 appears to be careening toward a scene illustrating the consequences of such intense lust. But here again the author defies our expectations. Midchapter, the discussion suddenly changes to a detailed account of an adolescent prank, the stealing of some pears from a neighbor's tree. Why such an abrupt transition and elaborate analysis of what was evidently merely a petty crime? The answer lies in the fact that Augustine has already established himself as every person born with a tendency to turn from God. Now, he universalizes the deliberate act of sin by relating an incident meant to remind us of the story of the Garden of Eden in Genesis. Fascinated by the human will and its motivation, Augustine selects a minor infraction in order to probe deeply into the reasons behind our wrongdoing. Through a series of rhetorical questions and tentative answers, he arrives at the conclusion that while we most often sin in order to obtain a seemingly good end (for example, we steal an item because we really desire it), in this incident at least he stole the pears for no other reason except that it was forbidden. He didn't even want the fruit, for there was plenty of better quality at home. Truly, he finds himself an "extremely twisted and tangled knot" at this point (2.18). Augustine concludes his analysis by observing that all sin—whether it be lust, or envy, or deceit, or greed, or hatred—consists at its essence of a type of pride that seeks to set itself up as a rival to God. He also realizes that he probably wouldn't have committed the act if his friends hadn't been with him. Sin, he therefore concludes, is communal, common to the entire race. Thus, in this scene, Augustine once again moves from individual experience to universal significance, and "exposes the root of all his evil, so that God in his mercy, hearing his confession, can heal him in the depths of his being, in his memory."[5]

In two short books, then, Augustine has accomplished some remarkable things. He has skillfully elevated events from his own life into the larger pattern of every human life. He has made a strong case for the existence of original sin, and he has scrutinized the deepest motivation for willful acts of sin. Now, as he recalls himself as a young man in Carthage desperately searching for love yet finding only "the red-hot iron rods of jealousy, suspicion, fear, anger, and contention" (3.1), he relates a dramatic turning point. Assigned to study a now-lost book by Cicero, *Hortensius*, for its rhetorical style, Augustine finds himself unexpectedly affected by its content. In the book, Cicero praised the beauty of a life devoted to the contemplation of wisdom and exhorted his readers to search for the truth "wherever found" (3.8). For the first time, the nineteen-year-old Augustine is struck by the notion of a higher purpose to life than just the attainment of a successful career, material goods, or worldly loves. So captivated was the young man by this ideal that it redirected his life's course: now, he launches onto an intense intellectual quest for the truth about God, human nature, and the origin of good and evil.

Inflamed with this new sense of purpose, Augustine first turns to the Scriptures as a potential source of the wisdom he seeks, for his childhood memory of his mother Monica's Christianity ran deep. However, the budding rhetorician finds that the Bible's simple style contrasts poorly with the elegant prose he has learned to imitate. It is of little surprise, then, that he next turns to Manichaeanism as a possible source of the truth he avidly seeks. Trendy and countercultural, the Manichaeans of Augustine's day attracted young men with intellectual and social ambitions. Founded by the third-century Persian prophet Mani (or Manes), Manichaeanism offered a seemingly rational faith based on a deterministic universe. Believers in a material dualism, the Manichees viewed the cosmos as radically divided between two primal powers, the realm of light, controlled by God, and the realm of darkness, controlled by Satan. Because God could not conquer Satan's forces, good and evil were engaged in continual warfare. Furthermore, according to the Manichees, Satan had created humans to entrap evil particles and keep the race from rising to God. The conceiving of children, therefore, was deemed a great wrong as it meant that the evil particles would remain in the human race for another generation. Although he later came to view the Manichees's cosmology as absurd, Augustine remained with the sect for nine years, perhaps, as Garry Wills has noted, because the "element of psychodrama [in Manichaean beliefs] fit Augustine's sense of his own internal contradictions."[6] Another reason was that his rising career in the Roman Empire was partly funded by wealthy Manichees. Yet when the answers of the long-awaited Manichaean bishop, Faustus, failed to satisfy his questions, Augustine finally broke all ties with the sect. Still, long influenced by Manichaean teachings, his struggles to grasp the truth about certain basic matters of faith continued. Three issues especially haunted him. First, he was unable to conceive of an immaterial and omnipotent God (the Manichees believed in a God who was a material substance and who was limited in power). Second, he struggled with locating the origin of evil in the human will and accepting personal responsibility for sin (the Manichees believed that evil substances were at work in humans and that humans therefore had no free will). And third, he could not conceive of Jesus as both God and man (the Manichees viewed Jesus as a prophet but abhorred the idea of the Incarnation because they believed human flesh to be utterly corrupt). After briefly entertaining and then dismissing the astrologers' claims, Augustine entered a period of skepticism, preferring for the time to believe that truth was unattainable.

Meanwhile, a second turning point for Augustine occurred when a close friend died. Augustine describes how this unnamed friend who received baptism upon falling ill rejected Augustine's mockery of the Catholic sacrament and then suddenly died. Augustine's profound grief upon the friend's death was intermingled with feelings of confusion and guilt. A dizzying disorientation ensued as he experienced himself fragmented and insecure: "everything on which I set my gaze was death" (4.9). A certain terror of his own death overwhelmed him. Understanding now that earthbound love must necessarily result in such loss, the older, converted man vividly recalls here his first major confrontation with the ultimate human problem, that of death.

In 383, Augustine moved from Carthage to Rome in search of a better teaching situation, but he did not find it. After only a brief stay in that city, he accepted a civil position as *rhetor* further north in Milan. Here, he met Bishop Ambrose, probably at the instigation of Monica who had joined him in Italy. He began to attend Ambrose's preaching, although, as he states, only to observe the bishop's rhetorical style. In Milan, Augustine was also introduced to some of the writings of the Neoplatonists, including Plotinus's treatises recorded in the *Enneads*. In these works, Augustine discovered evidence for a God who is pure spirit. He also learned that the Platonists conceived of evil as "nothing"; that is, not a substance but rather a privation of the good, a turning of the free will away from God. These ideas brought about a radical and electrifying shift in his thinking. With a new belief in God and a new understanding of free will, Augustine strove mightily, as the Platonists recommended, to turn inward and ascend in spirit from earthly things to the transcendent God, from the Many to the One. "I entered into my innermost citadel," he recalls, but no sooner did he glimpse the light of truth within the recesses of his own soul than he realized the frustrating impossibility of sustaining such vision (7.16). It was, consequently, but a short leap of faith to embrace he who mediates between the divine and the human, the God-Man Jesus Christ. While the Platonists could point to the destination, only Christianity provided the way there in the person of Jesus. Eagerly now, and much in contrast to his previous attempt, Augustine returned to the Scriptures and found his state of soul fully echoed in the words of that other famous convert to Christianity, St. Paul, especially in Romans 7. Finally, Augustine affirms, "all doubt left me" (7.16).

Augustine's intellectual dilemma was now satisfied; he had found the truth for which he had long quested. But intellectual understanding, he soon discovered, was not enough. Internally, a battle still raged between his body and soul, his "two wills" torn between love of worldly pleasure and the gleaming "pearl of great price," his newfound love of God. In his early thirties, Augustine was poised on the brink of a brilliant career. As court *rhetor*, he prepared and delivered high-profile speeches for public occasions such as state banquets and funerals. Moreover, Monica was in the process of arranging for him a wealthy marriage that would enhance his ability to move up socially. Yet the dream of living a life solely dedicated to wisdom and contemplation, inspired by his reading of *Hortensius* so many years before, still beckoned. In fact, it was dawning on him that no matter what successes he achieved, he still wasn't happy—not even as happy as the drunken beggar he saw one evening as he hurried by with his well-placed friends, nervous about delivering a speech full of lies and hypocrisy. In immense frustration, he finds himself enslaved by the flesh, bound tightly by the "chain" of perverse habit. His pain is all the more excruciating for he now knows and loves the truth but is simply unable to commit to it. Like a sleeper reluctant to answer a wake-up call, he pleads, "Just a little longer, please" (8.12). Having rejected the dualism of the Manichees, Augustine now understands that this sense of inner conflict is in his will. At his wit's end, he begins to realize that his own struggle to unite the divided will cannot suffice, that conversion only comes through God's gratuitous grace. Gradually, self-reliance gives way to trust in God; in a telling phrase, he observes that when he "relaxed" a bit from the exertion of effort, he "woke up" in God (7.20). As one critic cogently puts it, Augustine "learn[s] that for the slavery of doing evil the human will sufficed, but for the freedom of doing good both man's consent and God's grace are needed."[7]

Uncertain how to proceed, Augustine now seeks the counsel of Simplicianus, a Christian Platonist (he later succeeded Ambrose as bishop of Milan). Understanding that Catholicism upheld the vocations of both marriage and celibacy as good, he wished to glean advice on which course of life was appropriate for him. Then as now marriage brought with it the necessity of making money and supporting a family. Yet Augustine strongly sensed that he was being called away from the world to focus all his energies on God. Simplicianus takes an indirect approach in reply, telling Augustine the story of the famous *rhetor* Victorinus, a prominent defender of paganism (a statue even honored him in the Roman forum!) who in his seventies not only converted to Christianity but also insisted on making a public profession of faith. Far more than Augustine, Victorinus had much to lose by his bold act. In relating this tale, Simplicianus wanted to inspire his listener with an example of humility and moral courage. Not long thereafter, Augustine hears a second story that also sears his conscience, this one related by a visitor to his home, Ponticianus. Ponticianus tells of two government workers who, having come across the writings of Antony of Egypt, the founder of the recent movement of monasticism, were instantly converted to that way of life. Augustine is astonished to learn that a monastic community exists nearby and is, in fact, under the pastoral care of Bishop Ambrose. Galled by the fact that others were heroically "rising up and capturing heaven," while he yet wavered in indecision, he is forced to a crisis (8.19). As he flings himself, convulsed with tears, under a fig tree in his garden, he is suddenly quieted by a sing-song child's voice repeating, "*tolle, lege; tolle, lege*": "pick up and read." Recognizing in the voice a divine command, he obeys and reads from the Bible Romans 13:13–14, a passage that speaks directly to his heart. In an instant, grace accomplishes in him what he was unable to do for himself, and he is filled with peace and conviction: "it was as if a light of relief from all anxiety flooded into my heart" (8.29).

It is important to consider just what Augustine was converted to in the Milanese garden. He was not converted to Christianity, for he had already been a catechumen in the Church for some time and was fully convinced of Catholicism's truths. Rather, Augustine's long battle, as he now understands it, was primarily with pride, a reliance on his own abilities that, as he minutely analyzes in the pear-stealing scene, set himself up as a rival to God. Failing to acknowledge God's omnipotence, such pride causes us to exalt ourselves as independent entities in life. For many years, Augustine believed he could attain conversion on his own terms. He thus had to come to the limits of his powers, to an agonizing sense of helplessness, before he could accept God's transforming grace. His conversion, therefore, was to a humble acknowledgement of complete dependence on God. And now Augustine reminds us of why he earlier displayed such interest in the state of infancy. Only by reverting spiritually to the trust and dependence of a baby can we "come to suck milk from [God's] wisdom by which [he] created all things" (7.24). "When all is well with me, what am I but an infant sucking your milk and feeding on you," he asks the Almighty (4.1). It is not surprising, therefore, that he describes the moments just before the garden conversion in childhood images: throwing himself under a tree, uncontrolled weeping, spasmodic body movements, a child's game. We have come full circle here, for the stance of humility before God is at the heart of *confessio*. Only the Creator can solve the "vast problem" that is ourselves (4.9).

While he viewed a celibate life in the pursuit of wisdom as an ideal, Augustine was long convinced that attaining chastity was impossible. He simply couldn't achieve it, for his addiction to sex had become a strong force of habit. Yet in the garden, just prior to his grace-filled reading of Scripture, a vision of a "serene and cheerful" Lady Continence admonishes him, "cast yourself upon [Christ], do not be afraid" (8.27). Augustine's humble surrender to God gives him the grace to overcome the hard chains of this habit. For Augustine, conversion, then, is also the "reassembly" of the scattered, fragmented self, the reigning in of all the faculties and directing them toward a single purpose, the love, praise, and contemplation of God. "By continence we are collected together and brought to the unity from which we disintegrated into multiplicity," he explains (10.40). And in embracing chastity, Augustine in no way demeans human sexuality, as some have accused him. He had, in fact, rejected the Manichee belief that the body was corrupt. Rather, in keeping with the Church, he views chastity not as a negative "giving up" but as a positive orientation toward a higher goal. Celibacy allows a person to concentrate totally on the things of God, free from many of the cares of domestic life. Moreover, it implies a certain trust in God, a confidence that what we deny ourselves for his sake in this life will be amply satisfied in the next. "Clearly, Augustine's idea of continence is not that of an austere renunciation of delights, but their direct exchange for greater, more trustworthy, lasting delights," writes Margaret Miles.[8] In Augustine's day, celibate living for the sake of a higher purpose was not unusual: asceticism was advocated by the Neoplatonists and other pagan philosophers. As we have seen, Augustine was amazed to hear of this practice adopted by Christians in the formation of a new type of religious community, the monastery.

In conceiving of himself as "every person" who turns away from God and who struggles to find the way home again, Augustine patterns his *Confessions* not only on the story of the Prodigal Son returning to the Father but also on that of the Israelites crossing the desert to the promised land and on Ulysses's perilous voyage home to his wife, Penelope. Augustine thus uses the age-old journey motif at the core of our earliest tales to shape his life story. But he also perceives his conversion in terms of a child's return to the mother. As he makes evident in his story, Monica exerted a strong influence on her son, an influence the bishop now believes was highly instrumental in his conversion. Maternal images are continually evoked throughout the *Confessions*: for example, in God nurturing and carrying his children (7.24); in the human mother equated with Mother Church (1.17); and in the parable of the resurrected son restored to the widowed mother (6.1). To Augustine, conversion is imaged as both the spiritual reunion of mother and son and a return to the loving arms of Mother Church. "From the outset of his work Augustine intends that our 'conversion' and 'return' to God shall take the form of a suckling child returning to the maternal breast," Robert J. O'Connell states.[9] Thus the arrogant young man who scorns Monica's "womanish" advice, twists her words to belittle her, and gives her the slip as he sails for Rome finds himself running to her immediately after his garden conversion. In yet another garden, this time in Ostia, the two share a moment of deep harmony, a grace-filled wordless communion in God that unites them in spirit.

Throughout the *Confessions*, Augustine's insights into the twin mysteries of memory and time are profound. Memory, he believes, is a God-given faculty that has the power to resolve the problem of the fragmented self. Through memory, the soul turns inward, recalling events and searching for the truth behind them. Through memory, we can see

God's providence at work in our lives. Consequently, the right use of memory is essential to the Christian life for it provides the key to self-knowledge and knowledge of God. Moreover, through memory the problem of time itself is solved as past, present, and future unite: "Memory, with its capacity to make all things present, yields the clue to the idea of eternity."[10] Memory allows us to "collect" our scattered past and hold the pieces up to God for "reassembly" in the light of mercy and grace. "This power of memory is great, very great, my God," the bishop now exclaims (10.15). In fact, in the *Confessions*, Augustine even postulates a time prior to our birth when we preexisted in God (1.9). In our memory, he suggests, we retain an impression of God that directs our lifelong search for him. He sees a similar principle at work in the memory he retained from Monica of respect for the name of Jesus, a name he continued to search for in his reading long before he accepted Christianity.

Now, scrutinizing the past through memory, Augustine understands that divine providence has directed all things for good. In the hypocritical teachers who disciplined him, in Faustus whose pleasing style but ignorant answers swayed him from the heresy of Manichaeanism, in Monica's unceasing prayers and tears for him, in the books that seemingly fell by chance into his hands, even in his own casual remark that cured his friend Alypius from an obsession with the bloodthirsty gladiator games—in all these events, he now sees God operating. He likewise now comprehends that fornication—the turning away from God to self—necessarily results in blindness to the works of God in the world, producing restlessness, insecurity, worry, frustration, disorientation, and loss. The *Confessions*, then, is an exalted hymn of praise, a passionate expression of the profound joy of the lonely and lost searcher upon finding the lover so ardently desired but almost despaired of, the lover who fulfills all the yearnings of the human heart, provides the home the weary *peregrinato* seeks, and transfigures the disjointed past into one triumphant, seamless tale overflowing with meaning. It is a love song written for love of God's love (11.1). "Late have I loved you, beauty so old and so new: late have I loved you," the jubilant Augustine intones (10.38).

FOR FURTHER READING

Saint Augustine, *The City of God*. Written approximately between 413 and 427, this book by Augustine is a theological and philosophical study of all human history. It proposes a basic division in human beings between those who love God and those who love the world.

QUESTIONS FOR DISCUSSION

1. Augustine structures the *Confessions* around three garden scenes: the pear-stealing scene in book 2, the garden conversion in book 8, and the silent communion with Monica in Ostia in book 9. Compare these scenes and draw a conclusion as to their relationship and significance to the work.
2. How does Augustine strive throughout the *Confessions* to answer his own question, "Who then are you, my God?" (1.4) That is, what conception of God does the older, wiser man now have, and what mysteries remain?
3. Augustine models his story on the Prodigal Son, citing the parable explicitly in book 1.28. Read Luke 15:11–24 and discuss the elements of the story that Augustine applies to his own life. Consider how such statements as "Return to you is along the path of devout humility" (3.16) and "So from weariness our soul rises towards you, first supporting itself on the created order and then passing on to you yourself who wonderfully made it" (5.1) are central to what he wants to tell us about the journey of all humans.
4. List and discuss the major turning points on Augustine's road to conversion, including intellectual, emotional, and spiritual steps.
5. Consider Augustine's point about the right ordering of affections, especially as he discusses this issue in conjunction with his friend's death (book 4) but also applying your conclusions to the overall intent of the *Confessions*.

NOTES

Saint Augustine, *Confessions*, translated and introduced by Henry Chadwick (Oxford: Oxford University Press, 1998). All references are to this edition.

1. Peter Brown, *Augustine of Hippo* (Berkeley: University of California Press, 1969), 159.
2. Frederick J. Crosson, "Structure and Meaning in St. Augustine's *Confessions*," in *The Augustinian Tradition,* edited by Gareth B. Matthews (Berkeley: University of California Press, 1999), 31.

3. Karl Jaspers, *Plato and Augustine* (New York: Harcourt, Brace & World, 1962), 75.

4. Robert J. O'Connell, *Art and the Christian Intelligence in St. Augustine* (Cambridge, MA: Harvard University Press, 1978), 91.

5. Paul Rigby, *Original Sin in Augustine's Confessions* (Ottawa: University of Ottawa Press, 1987), 2.

6. Garry Wills, *Saint Augustine* (New York: Viking Penguin, 1999), 29.

7. Mary T. Clark, *Augustine: Philosopher of Freedom* (New York: Desclée Company, 1958), 3.

8. Margaret R. Miles, *Desire and Delight: A New Reading of Augustine's Confessions* (New York: Crossroad, 1992), 96.

9. Robert J. O'Connell, *St. Augustine's Confessions: The Odyssey of Soul* (Cambridge, MA: Harvard University Press, 1969), 43.

10. Genevieve Lloyd, "Augustine and the 'Problem' of Time," in *The Augustinian Tradition,* edited by Gareth B. Matthews (Berkeley: University of California Press, 1999), 44.

BIBLIOGRAPHY

Brown, Peter. *Augustine of Hippo.* Berkeley: University of California Press, 1969.

Dixon, Sandra Lee. *Augustine: The Scattered and Gathered Self.* St. Louis, MO: Chalice Press, 1999.

Mallard, William. *Language and Love: Introducing Augustine's Religious Thought through the Confessions Story.* University Park, PA: Pennsylvania State University Press, 1994.

O'Connell, Robert J. *Images of Conversion in St. Augustine's Confessions.* New York: Fordham University Press, 1996.

———. *St. Augustine's Confessions: The Odyssey of Soul.* Cambridge, MA: Harvard University Press, 1969.

Wills, Garry. *Saint Augustine.* New York: Viking Penguin, 1999.

ANONYMOUS
THE CLOUD OF UNKNOWING

BIOGRAPHY

Throughout Europe, the fourteenth century was an era of singular upheaval. Successive waves of the Black Plague decimated the population, the Hundred Years' War between France and England raged unabated, and the pope's defection from Rome to Avignon (1305–1378) followed by the Great Schism (1378–1417) substantially eroded Church authority. But despite such widespread social, political, and religious turmoil, an unprecedented wave of mystical spirituality arose during the period the intensity of which would not be seen again until the great Spanish mystics of the sixteenth century. While strong in Germany and Italy, this movement especially flourished in England where four influential mystics emerged who conventionally are grouped together: Richard Rolle, Walter Hilton, Julian of Norwich, and the anonymous author of *The Cloud of Unknowing*. This mystical upsurge across Europe is all the more remarkable because it followed closely upon the heels of the thirteenth century's emphasis on the synthesis of faith and reason into an orderly intellectual system, scholarship that reached its height with Thomas Aquinas's *Summa Theologiae*. Thus the great Catholic traditions of rational scholasticism and mystical spirituality—two distinct but complementary ways of understanding God—flourished nearly side by side during the late medieval era.

Despite much speculation over the years, the author of *The Cloud of Unknowing* remains unknown to us. Most likely he was a priest, perhaps a monk, living in the East Midlands area of England during the middle part of the century. It is surprising that he has never been identified by name, especially since ample evidence attests to the fact that his writings were highly popular and widely disseminated both during and after his lifetime. Many manuscripts of *The Cloud of Unknowing* exist, the earliest dating from the first part of the fifteenth century, and later spiritual writers were clearly familiar with his teachings. But the *Cloud* author may very well have chosen to remain anonymous. In fourteenth-century England, Church authorities were particularly zealous in their determination to root out heresy, especially condemning those persons or groups advocating unorthodox or individual religious experience. Since *The Cloud of Unknowing* emphasizes the legitimacy of a personal approach to God, its author may have felt it more prudent not to sign his work.

Six other texts or translations have come down to us that are attributed to the *Cloud* author: *The Book of Privy Counseling, The Epistle of Prayer, The Epistle of Discretion, The Discerning of Spirits, Denis' Hid Divinity,* and *The Study of Wisdom.* Of these, *The Cloud of Unknowing* and *The Book of Privy Counseling* contain the author's most salient teaching on the contemplative life. These two books, in fact, may be seen as companion texts, for *Privy Counseling* was written after the *Cloud* to further elaborate on some of its points.

While we know few facts about the *Cloud* author, it is possible to ascertain a great deal about his personality from his writing. We know, for example, that he was well educated and widely read in theology. He was also an orthodox believer in Catholic doctrine. A contemplative who knew firsthand the spiritual practices he taught, he was most likely an experienced spiritual director for he well understood human weaknesses. A skilled teacher, he impressed his readers at every turn with the tough-minded clarity of his thinking and anticipation of difficulties. Candid, down-to-earth, and wry, his striking style seems as fresh to us today as it must have to his original audience. In the following sketch, critic T. W. Coleman has cogently summarized the *Cloud* author's personality:

> He was a man of strong individuality. In disposition he was generous and genial. . . . His mind was acute and vigorous: his penetrative intellect could sound the depths of metaphysical speculation, and his keen imagination was undaunted before the loftiest ranges of spiritual adventure. His sure touch in dissecting mental processes and tracing them to their roots marks him an expert psychologist. His humor—quaint, subtle, shrewd—was delightful; as occasion arose he could exercise a playful fancy, or a mordant wit. Considering that he wrote when English was still passing through its infancy, his com-

mand over our mother tongue is astonishing: his force, fluency, and pungency of style are a constant surprise. Most of all, he had a distinctive religious experience—of the contemplative order—which gave color, tone, and strength to all his compositions. Gifts and qualities of this kind must have made our author not only a spiritual genius, but also a charming friend.[1]

CRITICAL OVERVIEW

The Cloud of Unknowing is a practical spiritual guide written by a person with clear literary talent. As the first such book of spiritual instruction written in the vernacular, it is a landmark of English literature and a masterpiece of medieval spirituality. The *Cloud* is designed to provide its readers with an understanding of the purpose, technique, and difficulties associated with striving for the state of soul known as the mystical contemplation of God. As such, its teaching is at once simple yet profound, for its purpose is to lead a person to fulfill perfectly the first and most important of all the commandments: to love God "with one's whole heart, whole soul, whole mind." Moreover, the central premise of the work is that God is ultimately incomprehensible to human reason, and that, therefore, if we want to know him, we must first learn to "unknow" him; that is, to leave behind all our preconceptions of what we *think* God is. The *Cloud* author writes to guide the reader to this stage of mystical "unknowing," and he does so in carefully ordered steps.

Although addressed specifically to a twenty-four-year-old man, *The Cloud of Unknowing* is really written for all Christians, both religious and lay persons, who want to grow in the love of God. The book's first chapter specifies four steps or degrees of the Christian life: ordinary, special, singular, and perfect. Those who practice Christianity to an "ordinary" degree are persons for whom religion is just a matter of rules and duties: avoiding mortal sin, saying a few prayers, and going to church on Sunday. Little or no effort is made to grow in intimacy with God. The next degree of Christian practice is "special"; this is when an individual, increasingly aware of God's presence, begins to serve him out of love and not just duty. As a person continues to respond to God, more grace is given to reach the third stage, "singular," where the person now dedicates his or her entire life to serving God, perhaps as a religious. The *Cloud* author assumes that the young man he is addressing has reached this "singular" degree of spirituality. Now, he seeks to lead his pupil to the fourth and final stage, the "perfect." But he's insistent in reminding us that achieving this stage is a work of grace alone. The Spirit blows where it will: God allows some to reach it relatively quickly and others only after years of disciplined prayer and meditation. Still, persons can learn about this stage and dispose themselves in such a way that they are ready to receive God's grace should it be given. Traditionally, the Catholic Church has viewed the mystical ascent to God as consisting of three stages: purgation, illumination, and union. The first stage, purgation, is the effort to do penance for sin and to detach oneself from earthly things. The second, illumination, is a movement by grace toward living in the love of God. The final stage, union, is complete self-giving and self-forgetfulness, when the will is brought into perfect harmony with the will of God. The saints and mystics often refer to this last stage as a "marriage," a union of love with God that is not a momentary feeling or single event, but a permanent, committed state. This final stage corresponds with the *Cloud* author's "perfect" degree of the Christian life. *The Cloud of Unknowing* tells us that perfect union with God may come about through the act of mystical contemplation.

Aware that some might misinterpret his teaching, the *Cloud* author at every point takes pains to explain himself fully. Our age, too, is prone to misunderstand his topic. Many equate "mysticism" with a type of vague, pleasurable feeling, a kind of self-induced dizziness far removed from daily reality. Some might think mystical contemplation is the effort to reach a vacuumlike state of "nothingness" or a nirvana. But the *Cloud* author understands, as indeed has always been Christian teaching, that mystical or spiritual contemplation has nothing to do with feeling, but is rather a work of the will and, in fact, constitutes the highest form of reality. Striving for this stage requires great care and discernment. Above all, as the author states in his Prologue, one who seeks this step must already have made progress in the spiritual life and now be "resolved with steadfast determination, truly and sincerely, to be a perfect follower of Christ" (101). The *Cloud* should *not* be read, therefore, by those who are merely intellectual or spiritual dilettantes.

While an original thinker in many ways, the author of *The Cloud of Unknowing* bases his work firmly on traditional Catholic teaching. His many influences attest to his keen absorption of most of the important theologians and spiritual writers of his day. The *Cloud* is grounded, first of all, in the Bible, both the Old and New Testaments. Its author also draws on, among others, the works of Origin, Clement of Alexandria, Augustine, Gregory the Great, Bernard of Clairvaux, Thomas Aquinas, and

Richard of St. Victor. But the *Cloud*'s most prominent source and the one our author credits explicitly in his text is the writing of the anonymous sixth-century Syrian monk, called Dionysius the Areopagite after St. Paul's first Greek disciple. The works of Pseudo-Dionysius, as he is commonly called, were first translated into Latin in the ninth century and subsequently exerted a powerful influence on medieval thinkers. In his *Mystical Theology*, a treatise on the spiritual life, Pseudo-Dionysius envisioned the ascent to God as climbing a type of ladder, with the final rungs entailing a suprarational experience. In this last stage, a person puts aside all intellectual activity and enters a "cloud of unknowing," a type of dark mist where God may be apprehended. As a foretaste of the Beatific Vision, this is the closest on earth we can hope to come to the divine presence.

Pseudo-Dionysius's suprarational approach to the mystical life is called "apophatic mysticism" or, more commonly, the "negative way" to God. It is "negative" in that such an approach acknowledges that God is so much greater than the human mind that, in truth, we really know nothing about him. In fact, we can better define God, perhaps, by what he is not than what he is. Influenced by Neoplatonic philosophy, which emphasized God's transcendence and unknowability, Pseudo-Dionysius also relied on the Old Testament story, in Exodus 19, of Moses climbing Mount Sinai to speak with God and entering a cloud that hid God's face in the darkness. The *Cloud* author, too, employs the image of Moses in the cloud, and he quotes his teacher in telling us that "The truly divine knowledge of God is that which is known by unknowing" (256). But while basing his work on the thought of Pseudo-Dionysius, the *Cloud* author differs from this spiritual master by characterizing the ascent to God through the cloud of unknowing as primarily an act of love. Both Thomas Aquinas and Bonaventure in the thirteenth century maintained that we can know God by love even though we cannot understand him with our minds. And the saints and mystics throughout the centuries have confirmed that love alone can penetrate God's deepest secrets. God "can be taken and held by love but not by thought," the *Cloud* states (130). In the act of contemplation, a person empties the self and yearns for God in blind love. It is then God's part to do the rest, to fill the longing soul with himself and to give illumination if and when he pleases. Thus this work is no more than "a simple and direct reaching out to God for himself," the *Cloud* explains (169).

As he develops his teaching, the *Cloud* author actually employs two separate cloud metaphors: the cloud of forgetting and the cloud of unknowing. The mystical state he is describing is one suspended, as it were, between these two clouds. In this state, a person must "forget" or blind himself to all of creation and to the desires of the self. All the natural human powers of reason, memory, and understanding are pushed down and covered over by the cloud of forgetting. The effects of original sin are so far-ranging, the *Cloud* author tells us, that they have radically disordered our love, resulting in our misplaced attachment to the things of this earth. Sin has "scattered" our focus, distracting us from God alone. Thus, with an effort of will, we must first strive to put a cloud of forgetting between us and created things, forgetting ourselves and pushing out all distracting thoughts. "Insofar as there is anything in your mind except God alone, in that far you are further from God," the *Cloud* insists (129). Then, with the cloud of forgetting underneath covering all sensory experience and intellectual thought in a misty fog, we enter the cloud of unknowing. While this cloud obscures the face of God, it is also where God may be directly encountered. In his *Spiritual Canticle,* the sixteenth-century contemplative John of the Cross, whose thinking on mysticism greatly resembles that of the *Cloud,* uses similar words to describe this experience. A soul must pass beyond everything to unknowing, he tells us: "The soul is moved in love, and thus the faculties have ceased to work, for when they reach their goal all medial operations come to an end. Thus that which the soul does at this time is to wait lovingly upon God, which is to love in continuation of unitive love."[2]

The aim of the Christian life is charity, attaining a perfect love of God and love of neighbor. The sacraments, pious practices, and theological teachings are but helps on the way to union with God in love: they are not the end in itself. Moreover, Christianity is concerned more with what one *is* rather than what one *does.* Following a long-standing tradition, *The Cloud of Unknowing* distinguishes between the active and contemplative modes of serving God. The author designates two levels in each of the modes, a lower and higher level. The first of the four levels, that of the lower part of the active life, consists of the practical works of mercy we carry out for our neighbor because of the love of God: feeding the hungry, clothing the naked, and so on. The second and third levels, the higher part of the active life and the lower part of the contemplative life, are combined: they represent the move from outward activity to a focus on the interior life through meditation on one's sins and on Jesus' sacrifice for us. The fourth and final level is the higher part of the contemplative life where the soul, in a state of passivity, achieves perfect union with the hidden God.

But what exactly is contemplation of this highest degree? First of all, it is a natural step in the Christian life and all are called to it although, because it is a work of grace in the soul, not all will attain it. Paradoxically, it is both very simple and extremely difficult, for while God cannot be grasped by the human mind, he is always immediately present to us in the secret center of our souls. In *The Interior Castle,* the sixteenth-century mystic Teresa of Avila envisions the human soul as a magnificent castle with numerous rooms and with Christ enthroned in its center. To reach him, one must steadfastly advance toward the goal and be prepared, especially in the early stages, to battle many obstacles. If we are ready to take the spiritual life seriously, the *Cloud* author maintains, we must be willing to forego our desires, detach ourselves from worldly things, and focus on God alone, waiting on him in love. "His will is that you should simply gaze at him, and leave him to act alone," the *Cloud* states (119). A modern contemplative, Thomas Merton, defines such mystical contemplation as "a supernatural love and knowledge of God, simple and obscure, infused by him into the summit of the soul. . . . It is a gift of God that absolutely transcends all the natural capacities of the soul and which no man can acquire by any effort of his own. But God gives it to the soul in proportion as it is clean and emptied of all affections for things outside of Himself."[3]

It is important to note that spiritual writers such as the *Cloud* author who advocate a negative approach to God are not anti-intellectual, nor do they deny the goodness of human reason. They maintain, however, that the intellect is limited in trying to apprehend the reality that is God. While good and useful in its own right, the mind is simply of no use for this work. Rational knowledge of God is ultimately inferior to knowledge gained through mystical contemplation. By striving to transcend reason, we thus acknowledge our inability to understand God with our minds and forego our tendency to anthropomorphize him: that is, to assume God is just like us. Mystical knowledge doesn't negate human reason, but builds on it. It is simply a different way of knowing.

In considering the value of the *Cloud*'s teaching for the Christian spiritual life, we recall that the Catholic Church traditionally teaches that all we can know about God comes from one of three sources. We can know something of God through his creation and through human reason: this is "natural theology." We can also know something of God through his own revelation to us; that is, through the teaching of his Son, Jesus, and through Scripture: this is "dogmatic theology." And finally, we can know something of God through direct, personal contact, through God's communicating of himself directly to our souls: this is "mystical theology." Those who have experienced this third type of knowledge, sometimes called "infused" knowledge, consistently relate that it greatly exceeds the other two types for it takes place at the core of one's being. Thus it is far richer and more transformative. A mystic may be defined as a person "for whom God and Christ are not merely objects of belief, but living facts experimentally known at first-hand."[4] Mystics don't just seek to know about God but to have intimate union with him. Moreover, as mystics attempt to describe their experience of God, they often find that words fail them. In his second letter to the Corinthians, for example, Paul describes in enigmatic terms the experience of being taken up into the "third heaven" and hearing there words so sublime they could not be repeated by human tongues. And after years of intense labor writing his massive compilation of all human knowledge about God, Thomas Aquinas had a direct vision of the Lord that made him consider all his vast learning as mere "straw" in comparison.

While mystical experience transforms a person's life, it doesn't annihilate individuality. Every mystic remains a product of his or her personality and environment. Some mystics experience such extraordinary spiritual phenomena as ecstasies, visions, or the stigmata; others do not. In the history of the Church, there are as many types of mystics as there are individuals: Paul, Augustine, Francis of Assisi, Ignatius of Loyola, Julian of Norwich, Catherine of Siena, John of the Cross, Thérèse of Lisieux, and Padre Pio, to name just a few. In all ages, God has given to his Church mystics whose intense love renews and revitalizes it. Evelyn Underhill has written about mystics,

> As artists and musicians, able to see and hear created beauty to which average eyes and ears are closed, interpret and express some of it for us in their works and so give us a new vision of the world; so the great mystics, who are geniuses in the sphere of religion, show to us the uncreated beauty of spiritual realities which we cannot find alone, and form a great body of witness to humanity's experience of God. In reading them, as in reading great poetry, we are taken out of ourselves, and become aware of deep regions of truth and beauty still beyond our reach.[5]

At first glance, it is perhaps natural to conceive of mystical contemplation—the soul lost in union with God—as a selfish act, a turning away from serving one's neighbor or combating evil in the world. But although frequently misunderstood, the lives of contemplatives are neither selfish nor useless. As the *Cloud* author explains, spiritual contemplation is, in fact, much more effective in destroying sin and helping others than active works of mercy, long prayers, or bodily penances. While the sacrament of penance is always a prerequisite to this work, contemplation has the unique ability to strike at the root of the seven capital sins—envy, anger, sloth, pride, covetousness, gluttony, and lust—that powerfully sway our sensual nature. Contemplation also obtains all the virtues, "for virtue is nothing else than an ordered and controlled affection which has God for its single object, himself alone" (147). Moreover, the act of contemplation not only purges the contemplative from sin and quickly raises him or her to a high degree of sanctity, but also has a social efficacy, for "charity covers a multitude of sins." Paradoxically, we only love and serve others well when we are focused solely on loving and serving God. The contemplative sacrifices his or her own desires for the love of God, offering up the self for all humanity as Christ did on Calvary. As John of the Cross states, "A very little of this pure love is more precious, in the sight of God and the soul, and of greater profit to the Church, even though the soul appear to be doing nothing, than are all these other [that is, active] works together."[6]

While in the cloud of unknowing, the contemplative finds that his prayer becomes much simpler and more immediate. All long, complicated prayers, whether oral or mental, are increasingly unnecessary as one gets closer and closer to God. Human language, in fact, soon becomes inadequate to express such intimate union. The *Cloud* author therefore recommends that any prayer uttered in this stage be reduced to just a single repeated word expressive of the soul's great longing, such as "God" or "love." He employs a vivid comparison for the type of brief but insistent prayer he prescribes. When a fire breaks out in a house, he tells us, a person screams "fire!" or "out!" or some such urgent, simple word indicating extreme need. A single word in a dire situation is much more effective in getting results than a long, eloquent discourse for "short prayer pierces heaven" (193).

All the mystics tell us that reaching the highest contemplative state of perfect union with God involves great suffering. In God's economy, there simply is no true holiness without suffering. The effect of sin on the human person has been so damaging that only by violence to the self, only by suffering, can a person turn back to God. What precisely is the suffering that a contemplative experiences? In a famous phrase, John of the Cross calls it the "dark night of the soul," and essentially, this is what the *Cloud* author means by his phrase, the "cloud of unknowing."

The contemplative suffers as he or she willfully lays aside all sensory and intellectual means of knowing and endures, in darkness, the intolerable emptiness of no longer being in command of his or her own life. Deep suffering also occurs at this stage precisely because a "cloud" of darkness covers the face of God whom the contemplative, in love, longs to see. Here is how Thomas Merton explains such pain:

> Contemplation is the light of God playing directly upon the soul. . . . [It] affects that soul the way the light of the sun affects a diseased eye. It causes *pain*. God's love is too pure. The soul, impure and diseased by its selfishness, is shocked and repelled by the very purity of God. . . . It has formed its own ideas of God: ideas that are based upon its natural knowledge and which unconsciously flatter its own self-love. But God contradicts those ideas. . . . The fire of His infused love launches a merciless attack upon the self-love of the soul attached to human consolations and to those lights and feelings which it required as a beginner, but which it falsely imagined to be the great graces of prayer.[7]

But while the dark night of the soul produces suffering, it is a superbly positive state for it leads to direct experience of God. In the darkness of the cloud of unknowing and in the midst of suffering, it may happen on occasion that God gives the contemplative the grace of illumination, a spiritual light that penetrates the darkness and fills the person with a deep, joyful assurance of God's love and truth. When and if this grace is given depends entirely on God. As the *Cloud* author explains, "Perhaps it will be his will to send out a ray of spiritual light, piercing this cloud of unknowing between you and him. . . . Then you shall feel your affection all aflame with the fire of his love, far more than I know how to tell you or may or wish to at this time" (174–75). As Thomas Merton describes this grace of illumination,

> Then suddenly comes the awakening. The soul one day begins to realize, in a manner completely unexpected and surprising, that in this darkness it has found the living God. It is overwhelmed with the sense that He is there and that His love is surrounding and absorbing it on all sides. At that instant, there is no other important reality but God, infinite Love. . . . The darkness remains as dark as ever and yet, somehow, it seems to have become brighter than the brightest day. The soul has entered a new world, a world of rich experience that transcends the level of all natural knowledge and all natural love.[8]

Those mystics who receive such illumination are completely transformed in being. One immediate effect is the increasingly urgent desire to participate in Christ's mission on earth to save souls through suffering love.

As did other early teachers of the Church such as Gregory of Nyssa and Augustine, the *Cloud* author evokes the Gospel story of Jesus in Bethany at the home of Mary and Martha to further elaborate on the superiority of the contemplative over the active mode of the Christian life. Martha serves our Lord actively by providing for his bodily needs and those of her guests: necessary and good, her work is one approach to God. Mary, however, seated at the feet of Jesus, is apparently "doing" nothing but listening to his preaching and contemplating his presence. When Martha tries to get Jesus to reprimand her sister, he refuses to intervene, replying to Martha that Mary has chosen the "best part, and it will not be taken from her" (Luke 10:38–42). In a creative interpretation of this reply, the *Cloud* author speculates on why Jesus used the superlative word "best" when the story actually involves only two characters, Martha and Mary, and portrays only two degrees of "goodness," that of Martha's activity and Mary's contemplation. That is, if Martha's work is "good" (note that Jesus does not condemn it) why doesn't Jesus call Mary's work, in contrast, "better"? In explaining this distinction, the *Cloud* author harkens back to the three ways of approaching God he has earlier outlined in his text: the lower active, the dual category of higher active and lower contemplative, and the high contemplative. Mary, sitting at the feet of Jesus, our author tells us, has attained the third stage, that of high contemplation. Jesus, therefore, rightfully tells Martha that Mary's is the "best" part and that—as a foretaste of the Beatific Vision, which lasts forever in heaven—it will not ever be taken from her.

We can understand this distinction more fully when we realize that the *Cloud* author views Mary of Bethany and Mary Magdalene as one and the same person, a common medieval interpretation. Mary Magdalene was the sinner who, when she anointed Jesus' feet with perfume and wiped them with her hair, was told by him that her many sins were forgiven because of her great love (Luke 7:36–50). Now at her home in Bethany she is, therefore, a changed person. The *Cloud* author thus views her as the ideal contemplative and the prime exemplar of all his teaching as she sits near Jesus lost in the pure love of spiritual contemplation. In this state of contemplation, our author maintains, Mary has not only "forgotten" the shameful memory of her sins but also "forgotten" the person of Christ as she looks beyond his human body to his divinity. As he explains, Mary

> hung up her love and her longing desire in this cloud of unknowing, and learned to love what she could not see clearly in this life by the light of understanding in her reason, or yet truly experience in sweetness of love in her affection; so much so that often enough she paid but little attention to whether she had been a sinner or not. . . . I expect that very often she was so deeply moved in her affection by the love of his godhead that she had no eyes for the beauty of his precious and blessed body as he sat in his loveliness, speaking and preaching to her; nor of anything else, corporal or spiritual. (155)

In the more active state of meditation, the *Cloud* author further explains, we rightfully recall our sins and weep over them, vowing to reform, but in this highest state of contemplation such as Mary has achieved, we cover even the memory of our sins with the cloud of forgetting and focus on God's overwhelming love and mercy alone. While God-become-Man in the Incarnation remains the foundation of Christian belief, *The Cloud of Unknowing* thus regards the state of mystical contemplation as going beyond this fact, or better said, through it, to God's divinity, just as Mary no longer meditates merely on Jesus' physical presence but looks beyond his humanity to his divine nature.

Toward the end of his book, the *Cloud* author warns his readers at length and in strong language against the inevitable spiritual charlatans, those neurotics, pretenders, or hypocrites who seek to deceive others into thinking they are close to God by having attained a state of mystical contemplation. Showing his wide experience as a spiritual counselor, the *Cloud* author carefully details the various delusions that can assail a person who sets out on the road to spiritual perfection. Thinking they can achieve it on their own, beginners often strain themselves in the effort and collapse in weariness or disappointment. Some persons desire intimacy with God only for the spiritual consolations or fulfillment they believe it will bring them and are equally soon discouraged. Others, in arrogance, dismiss the advice of their spiritual directors and try to advance to a high stage before they are ready, foregoing the more usual ways of attaining holiness such as prayer, meditation, and penance. With stern vehemence, the *Cloud* author rails against these false contemplatives: "mad," they merely succeed in demonstrating "signs of pride, of outlandishness, of exhibitionism and an inordinate desire for knowledge" (223). By contrast, the true contemplative can be recognized by pleasing and gentle behavior, a winning graciousness, honesty, and wisdom that proves attractive to all.

"From beginning to end, *The Cloud* is a treatise on divine love," writes William Johnston.[9] Because it discusses the summit of the spiritual life, the soul in perfect harmony with God through mystical contemplation, this book's teaching is difficult for most of us ordinary Christians to absorb. But our experienced, down-to-earth author, fully aware of our doubts and confusions, takes us by the hand and leads us gently into this unexplored region of the soul, the "best part" to which we are all invited.

FOR FURTHER READING

Pseudo-Dionysius, *Mystical Theology*
John of the Cross, *The Spiritual Canticle; The Dark Night of the Soul*
Teresa of Avila, *The Interior Castle*

QUESTIONS FOR DISCUSSION

1. God's very nature is love, and therefore the Church maintains that even the smallest act, performed out of love for God, is of far more value than many years' worth of "busy-ness" done for other reasons. Using the teaching of the *Cloud*, explain in your own words how apparently doing "nothing" but resting in God in contemplation can be far more effective for the Church, the Body of Christ, than even the most altruistic activity.

2. One modern mystic you may enjoy reading is St. Thérèse of Lisieux, the "Little Flower" who died in a French Carmelite monastery at the age of twenty-four. Although she was an "ordinary" Christian in that she lived a good but not unusual life, she clearly understood, especially in the last years of her life, that the summit of the Christian life was loving intimacy with God. In the final chapters of her autobiography, *The Story of a Soul*, she speaks of her "vocation" as that of love. She found that by attaining perfect love of God she fulfilled all her desires for other vocations as well, for love encompasses the roles of warrior, priest, apostle, doctor, and martyr. Read chapter 9, manuscript B, of *Story of a Soul* and comment on Thérèse's findings in light of the

teaching of *The Cloud of Unknowing* (*Story of a Soul,* translated by John Clarke [Washington, D.C.: I. C. S. Publications, 1996]).

3. What difficulties or questions occurred to you about mystical contemplation and the "negative way" to God as you read the *Cloud*? What questions were answered by the author, and which remain?

4. Are there any Catholic contemplative orders of men or women in your community? If so, try to learn more about their lives and the rule of life they follow. Visit the monastery, if possible.

5. In your own words, characterize the personality of the *Cloud* author as he comes across in his work.

NOTES

The Cloud of Unknowing, edited and introduced by James Walsh (New York: Paulist Press, 1981). All references are to this edition.

1. T. W. Coleman, *English Mystics of the Fourteenth Century* (Westport, CT: Greenwood Press, 1971), 85.

2. John of the Cross, *The Spiritual Canticle,* in *The Complete Works of Saint John of the Cross,* vol. 2, edited and translated by E. Allison Peers (Westminster, MD: Newman Press, 1953), 267.

3. Thomas Merton, *What Is Contemplation?* (Springfield, IL: Templegate, 1981), 36.

4. Evelyn Underhill, *The Mystics of the Church* (Greenwood, SC: Attic Press, 1975), 10.

5. Underhill, *The Mystics of the Church,* 13–14.

6. John of the Cross, *The Spiritual Canticle,* 328.

7. Merton, *What Is Contemplation?* 41–42.

8. Merton, *What Is Contemplation?* 52–53.

9. William Johnston, *The Mysticism of The Cloud of Unknowing* (St. Meinrad, IN: Abbey Press, 1975), 109.

BIBLIOGRAPHY

Dupré, Louis. *The Deeper Life: An Introduction to Christian Mysticism.* New York: Crossroad, 1981.

Johnston, William. *The Mysticism of The Cloud of Unknowing.* St. Meinrad, IN: Abbey Press, 1975.

Knowles, David. *The English Mystical Tradition*. New York: Harper and Brothers, 1961.

Merton, Thomas. *What Is Contemplation?* Springfield, IL: Templegate, 1981.

Szarmach, Paul E., ed. *An Introduction to the Medieval Mystics of Europe*. Albany: State University of New York Press, 1984.

Underhill, Evelyn. *The Mystics of the Church*. Greenwood, SC: Attic Press, 1975.

JULIAN OF NORWICH
REVELATIONS OF DIVINE LOVE

BIOGRAPHY

We know little of Julian of Norwich besides what she tells us in her book. Even her real name is unknown. An English woman born in 1342 and living in Norwich, England, Julian fell ill at the age of thirty in May 1373, and received the last rites of the Church. On the eighth day, her condition had so worsened that those attending her, including her mother, expected her to die. A priest directed her to gaze at the crucifix held before her eyes. As she obeyed, she saw a light shine from it while all else in the room grew dark. Suddenly, the crucifix came alive, vividly reenacting Christ's suffering from the crown of thorns. Over the next five hours, Julian received fifteen revelations, or "showings," from God while still beholding various scenes of the Passion. As she explains, those revelations came to her in three ways—bodily (or physical) sight, words formed in her understanding, and spiritual sight—and each revelation contained multiple spiritual lessons. When Julian awoke, she at first thought the visions stemmed from her delirium until a religious man in whom she confided took them seriously. When she fell asleep several hours later, the sixteenth and final revelation ensued. Once again, Julian woke up, this time completely healed.

Julian recorded two versions of her revelations. Soon after her mystical experience, she wrote down a brief account, the so-called "Short Text" that consists of twenty-five chapters. Twenty years later, she penned a second version, this time augmenting the account based on nearly two decades of what must have been continual reflection on their meaning. This "Long Text" of eighty-five chapters is especially rich in spiritual insight and is the text we will examine here. Scholars conclude that Julian's work was most likely not widely disseminated in her day, for only four manuscripts survive, the earliest dating to the mid-fifteenth century. First published in 1670, *Revelations of Divine Love* has the distinction of being the first existing book written by a woman in the English language.

In Julian's time, Norwich was, next to London, England's largest city and a thriving East Anglian center of trade and religious life. All the important religious orders of the day—including the Franciscans, Dominicans, Carmelites, Benedictines, and Augustinians—had monasteries in the town. While Julian refers to herself as unlearned, this probably just meant that she was not fluent in Latin. In fact, her writing suggests that she was quite well educated for a woman of her time. As a girl, she may have even boarded at the famous Benedictine convent close to Norwich, Carrow Abbey, where the nuns were dedicated to educating young women. Perceptive and intelligent, she no doubt also absorbed a great deal from the lively intellectual and religious atmosphere of the city.

At some point, Julian became an anchorite at St. Julian's Church in Conisford, just outside of Norwich, the church from which she derives her name. Although we don't know for sure, it seems probable that she embraced this form of religious life as a result of her extraordinary mystical experiences. The word *anchorite* derives from a Greek word meaning "to retire." Neither a nun nor a hermit, an anchorite withdrew from the world to draw closer to God in solitude while still performing an important role in civic life. We can gain an idea of what the vocation entailed from an existing thirteenth-century handbook for anchorites, the *Ancrene Riwle*. After being examined by the local bishop to ensure that the call to such a life was authentic, the anchorite, who could be either male or female, proclaimed vows of celibacy, obedience, and stability. A solemn procession brought the anchorite to a small cell attached to a church. Once established in the anchorhold, the anchorite lived a disciplined life devoted to prayer, meditation, intercession for the town, and spiritual counseling of others. A typical cell had three windows, one that opened into the church so that the anchorite could hear Mass, one for supplies to be handed in, and one covered by a curtain through which the anchorite could converse with those townsfolk seeking prayers or advice. It has been estimated that there were over two hundred anchorites throughout England during the fourteenth and fifteenth centuries.

As an anchorite, Julian gained renown for her holiness and good sense. The eccentric English mystic Margery Kempe sought Julian's counsel about the authenticity of her own visions around 1415, when

Julian was seventy-three, and recorded their meeting in her *Book of Margery Kempe*, concluding that "the anchoress was expert in such things and could give good advice."[1] Besides this famous meeting, historical evidence of Julian's repute can be found in a number of extant wills from the period. Local folk who had received counsel or prayers from Julian would often bequeath her token sums of money. In 1393 or 1394, for example, a Roger Reed left two shillings to "Julian anakorite." And we know that Julian was still alive in 1416 because yet another will cites "Julian, recluz a Norwich."

Although Julian's original cell was destroyed during the Reformation, a modern reconstruction and chapel at the site continues to draw thousands of pilgrims each year.

CRITICAL OVERVIEW

While *Revelations of Divine Love* is a complex work containing profound insights on sin, prayer, the nature of God, and eschatology (that is, a consideration of the Last Things), its overall intent is summed up well by its title. More than fifteen years after the revelations, Julian still struggled with their meaning until she one day received a succinct answer: "'Do you want to know what your Lord meant? Know well that love was what he meant'" (179). All of her visions tell of God's unfathomable love for humankind, a love supremely evident in Jesus' Crucifixion. Julian's messages reveal the astonishing humility of God and his longing for an intimate relationship with us. Since we are created in the image of God who is love, love, Julian tells us, is inherent in our very being. While Julian writes to all people, she specifically addresses those who truly want to serve God but who may have little sense of the depths of God's love for them. Writing for our comfort, she bids us be at peace, for God is holding us very securely.

Thomas Merton called Julian "the greatest of the English mystics."[2] In fact, Julian's revelations are at the heart of the rich tradition of Catholic mysticism. During the Middle Ages, an extraordinary outpouring of such mysticism occurred throughout Europe, with many devout persons—women greatly predominated—claiming to have received visions or messages from God. Some of these mystics, who around Julian's era included Hildegard of Bingen, Angela of Foligno, Catherine of Siena, and Bridget of Sweden, also experienced other supernatural phenomenon such as the stigmata or the mystical marriage. Julian may have been familiar with some of the widely circulated writings of these visionaries. She may also have read two other mystical texts that were well known in her day, Walter Hilton's *Scale of Perfection*, a book of advice addressed to anchorites, and *The Cloud of Unknowing*. Yet while Julian's book falls well within the mystical tradition of the Church, her content and expression are original.

Julian's work is best approached by placing it in the context of her times. Across Europe, the fourteenth century was a time of tremendous unrest, producing in many an anxiety bordering on despair. The Black Plague struck England in waves throughout the century, the first occurring in 1348 when Julian was just six years old. Nearly a third of the population perished. It is impossible to overestimate the psychological toll of such widespread disaster on the survivors: no aspect of social, political, economic, and cultural life was left untouched. Throughout both Britain and the continent, hopelessness even bred a type of mass hysteria, a combination of licentiousness and guilt that resulted in such odd behavior as that of the Flagellants, who undertook public penance, or a reversion back to pagan practices. In addition, throughout the century England was engaged with France in a bitter and futile struggle, the Hundred Years' War. And finally, conflict even wracked the Catholic Church when, in 1305, Pope Clement V moved the seat of the papacy from Rome to Avignon. This situation lasted until 1378 when an even greater catastrophe, the Great Schism, resulted in two and then three contenders vying for the Throne of Peter. Not until 1417 was the predicament fully resolved. In Julian's time, then, all of these events combined to create a sense of general doom and overwhelming fear of God's anger for the sin presumed to be the cause of such manifold troubles. Julian's message of love, trust, and confidence, therefore, is remarkable in such a pessimistic atmosphere. At every point, her unwavering theological optimism counters the dread, cynicism, and hopelessness of her day.

We can also consider Julian's writing in the context of the new, affective form of spirituality that was prevalent during the late medieval era. Between approximately 1000 and 1200, religious expression in the West gradually moved toward an increased emphasis on personal and emotional experience. This new way of thinking about the spiritual life permeated both popular piety and art. In pious practice, this meant a concentration on Christ's suffering humanity rather than on his glorified divinity. The goal of meditation became an entering imaginatively into Christ's redemptive act so as to evoke compassion for his suffering, love of God, and remorse for sin, a form of *imitatio Christi* promulgated by such influential spiritual teachers as Bernard of Clairvaux and William of St. Thierry. In art, such affective spirituality manifested itself in a gradual change from the Romanesque conception of a glorified, austere Christ on the cross to the Gothic view of the dreadful suffering of Christ's sacred humanity. In their naturalistic depictions of a bruised and bloody crucified Christ together with the sorrows of Mary, Mary Magdalene, and John as they stood under the cross, artists of the Gothic school were intent on evoking great pathos. In fact, during the fourteenth century the East Anglian school of art, located in Norwich, was well known for producing such scenes. As she describes with vivid, pictorial detail the bleeding and dying Jesus, Julian recalls seeing, as she tells us in the "Short Text," local paintings of such crucifixion scenes.

Like her contemporary Geoffrey Chaucer, Julian is also a master of English prose. Although her work suffers in translation due to the fact that some key words of Middle English have changed in today's usage, most translations still manage to capture her lyrical and memorable style replete with literary devices such as alliteration, metaphor, turns of phrase, rhyme, and rhythm. Unlike that of most theologians or preachers of her time, Julian's writing is refreshingly lively, concrete, and immediate. Her style is recursive and incremental: she introduces her themes, returns to augment them, and then works to unify them into a carefully wrought whole. Moreover, while Julian's content and expression is singular, her teaching fully conforms to Catholic doctrine. In fact, some of the most provocative passages in the *Revelations* occur when Julian's visions seem, to her, to contradict what she has been taught by the Church. In these moments, Julian demonstrates a mature intellectual integrity: she embraces the tensions of the paradox while waiting for resolution. Refusing to abandon the Church's doctrine in favor of her visions, she also will not deny the truth of what is being shown her.

It is clear that, by the time of the revelations, Julian was already well advanced in spiritual practice. As she tells us, at some point earlier in her life she had petitioned God for three gifts, or graces: a "vivid perception of his Passion," "bodily sickness in youth at thirty years of age," and the "three wounds" of contrition, compassion, and sincere longing for God (42–43). She asks for the first two petitions, an experience of spiritual and physical suffering, in order to imitate Christ more fully. At a time when the plague killed its victims so swiftly, receiving time to prepare for death by a grave illness would be a great grace indeed. Julian asked for these first two gifts only if God wished her to have them. But she placed no reservation on her request for the three wounds for she understands that these virtues are necessary to spiritual growth. As she explains in the "Short Text," Julian refers here to the three wounds of St. Cecilia, a martyr of ancient Rome killed for professing her faith by being struck three times on the neck by an executioner's sword. Popular in Julian's day, the legend of St. Cecilia appears in Jacobus de Voragine's *The Golden Legend* and is also retold in Chaucer's *Canterbury Tales*. What is interesting to note is that Julian interprets St. Cecilia's three wounds metaphorically: to Julian, the graces of contrition, compassion, and desire for God serve to "wound" one's self-love and thereby engender greater humility, charity, and singleness of heart. Even before her revelations, then, Julian's understanding of the spiritual struggle marks her as deeply devout woman.

While the *Revelations* contains numerous theological and spiritual insights, its major themes convey lessons about God's nature, our relationship to God, and the role of sin. From the first, God reveals himself to Julian as profoundly friendly, compassionate, and loving. In Julian's dialect, God is, above all, "homely," a word related to "humble" and best translated as "down-to-earth" or "unpretentious." Using the language of the chivalric or courtly love tradition, Julian also tells us God is "courteous," a refined and gentle being. God never changes: he is always loving, humble, and kind, and his perfect plan for salvation is not altered by human sin. Moreover, God's great humility is best seen in Jesus' salvific Redemption, an act that irrevocably tied God (in Julian's language, "knit" him) to all of humankind. While witnessing scenes of the Passion, Julian is told that God's love for us is so great he would have taken on even more suffering for us had it been possible. In the eighth vision, Julian is so troubled by viewing the torments of the suffering Christ that she is tempted to look away from the cross, up to the Father in heaven. She refuses, however, and is rewarded with the understanding that, while in exile on earth, we must keep our focus on this the preeminent evidence of God's love for us, his Son's Crucifixion: "thus was I taught to choose Jesus as my heaven, though at that time I saw him only in pain" (69).

Besides being Christocentric, Julian's revelations are also deeply Trinitarian in their emphasis on the reciprocal charity and self-giving of the three Persons of the Trinity: the Father, Son, and Holy Spirit. In the first revelation, Julian senses the Trinity as she contemplates the crucifix: the Godhead in its totality is revealed in the Son's Atonement. As Grace M. Jantzen states, "This throws another light on [Julian's] comment that the whole of the Trinity is comprehended in Christ. He, after all, is the one who makes incarnate this love of God, the one who brings the love of the divine Trinity into the experience of humankind."[3] And similar to the thought of the Church Fathers who described the separate but related functions of the Persons of the Trinity in creation and salvation, Julian often refers to God the Father as maker or nature; God the Son as wisdom or mercy; and God the Holy Spirit as keeper or grace. In the thirteenth revelation, she applies the verbs "may," "can," and "will" to the Persons of the Trinity who together bring about the great and perfect plan for salvation. "May," indicating omnipotence, is applied to the Father; "can," indicating the wisdom needed to carry out the work, is the quality of the Son; and "will," indicating the motivation that impels the act, is proper to the Holy Spirit. Together, the three Persons of the Trinity "shall" bring about our redemption.

Julian's well-known teaching on Christ as Mother culminates all her revelations concerning God's nature. Her thought here is by no means new, for conceiving of God in feminine terms is common in the work of early theologians. The idea of the Church as Mother, *Mater Ecclesia*, has existed since the early Christian era. Both Isaiah in the Old Testament and Jesus in the New evoke maternal images for God's love: in Luke 13:34, Jesus speaks of himself in the image of a sheltering mother hen. In the second century, Clement of Alexandria stated, "God himself is love; and out of love to us became feminine. . . . In his compassion to us He became Mother."[4] In the fourth century Ambrose of Milan, the bishop who so influenced Augustine's conversion, wrote that "Christ is the virgin who entered into marriage, carried us in her womb, gave birth to us, and fed us with her own milk."[5] Augustine, too, as we have seen, viewed his return to the faith in terms of female images: the wayward son returning to the Mother. And in a prayer Julian may have known, the eleventh-century Benedictine Anselm of Canterbury beautifully evokes the motherhood of Christ:

> And you, Jesus, are you not also a mother?
> Are you not the mother who, like a hen,
> gathers her chickens under her wings?
> Truly, Lord, you are a mother;
> for both they who are in labor
> and they who are brought forth
> are accepted by you.[6]

Julian's unique contribution to such thought is to elaborate on the metaphor of the motherlike qualities of God and employ it as the summation of all her teaching on the Trinity, Incarnation, Eucharist, and

Redemption. Extending her triad metaphors, she tells us that the Persons of the Trinity work for us as Father, Mother, and Lord. The second Person of the Trinity, Jesus, is similar to a human mother in nurturing, loving, guiding, and forgiving us. Jesus gives us both physical birth and spiritual rebirth, feeds us with his own body, allows us to fall as a lesson but never to be in true danger, and tenderly nurtures us into maturity. And because God is the best of mothers, it is simply impossible to think of him as a cold, angry, or impartial judge, for we are his dearly beloved children. Thus, our response to him should be that of the trusting child who, "when it is hurt or frightened . . . runs to its mother for help as fast as it can" (144). More than five centuries later, this same attitude of "spiritual childhood" is given its fullest expression in the theology of St. Thérèse of Lisieux.

Finally, in the revelations concerning God's nature, Julian also learns of God's absolute and loving control over all creation. In the first vision, Christ places a hazelnut in the palm of her hand. In this tiny nut (a word linguistically related to *nucleus* and *nuclear*), God explains to Julian, is contained all that exists. Were it not for God's love, all creation would fall instantly into nothingness. But it exists and endures because of God's faithful love and care. The lesson, therefore, is one of perspective: all created things are miniscule in comparison to God. Julian understands that we must try to dwell on the long view, God's perspective, for otherwise we easily get entangled in things that are relatively inconsequential and which can never bring us peace. Echoing Augustine, Julian concludes that rest can only be found in God, for "he is rest itself" (47). In the third vision, God reveals himself to Julian in an "instant" (or, in some translations, in a "point"). Both Dante in *The Divine Comedy* and T. S. Eliot in *Four Quartets*, a poem based on the *Revelations*, use a similar image: God is the point or fixed center of all creation's movement. "See that I am in everything," God tells Julian. "See that I lead everything on to the conclusion I ordained for it before time began, by the same power, wisdom and love with which I made it. How can anything be amiss?" (59).

In the *Revelations*, Julian repeatedly confronts the problem of sin and questions God over and over about it. While adhering to Church teaching as she understands it, she formulates from her visions a singular theology about the existence of evil. To Julian, sin is a terrible "scourge" and a deadly serious matter (95). All the pain and suffering on earth, Julian understands, stem from sin. But unlike Augustine who emphasizes the choice of the free will in sinning and God's righteous punishment, Julian focuses on those who sin primarily through blindness and weakness and on the overwhelming mercy of God. In order to understand Julian's thoughts on sin, it is important to remember that, repeatedly, she insists that her revelations concern only those who will be saved; that is, those of upright will who strive to love God but who often find themselves falling into sin. She is *not* addressing those who willfully turn from God to embrace sin. In fact, in persons who desire to serve God, Julian even posits two selves or "natures," a higher nature permanently united to God, which never consents to sin and a lower nature, or sensual self that may succumb to temptation. And, Julian maintains, God fully understands the weakness and ignorance of our lower or "animal" nature; he does not blame us for such sin. No matter how hard she looked, she insists, she could discover no anger in God. In addition, corresponding with the two "natures," Julian also understands that there are two judgments for sin. The "lower" judgment of the Church rightly takes human sin seriously, requires sacramental confession of the sinner, and imposes penance, for humans need such awareness and discipline to help them gain heaven. But the "higher" judgment of God does not condemn right-minded persons who fall into sin, for God judges us as the *imago Dei*, his beloved creatures made in his image and inextricably united to Jesus through the Atonement. Thus sin, Julian tells us, must always be viewed in the context of God's love and Christ's Redemption. "We should cling reverently to God, trusting in him alone; for man and God regard things in two quite different ways; it is proper for man humbly to accuse himself, and it is proper for God in his natural goodness kindly to excuse man," Julian states (127).

Moreover, Julian proposes that individual sin recapitulates the *felix culpa*, or "happy fault." It was St. Anselm who stated that Jesus' redemptive act turned Adam's sin into a fortunate fall because in God's supreme generosity we as humans actually benefited much more from this act than if we had never fallen in the first place. "O necessary sin of Adam, which gained us such and so great a redeemer," the Exultet sung at the Easter Vigil joyously proclaims. Julian called sin "behovely," a word whose usage is now lost to us but can yet be observed in such phrases as "It would behoove you to do your homework now." "Behovely" in Julian's Middle English means "profitable," "beneficial," even "necessary." Astonishingly, then, Julian tells us that sin can be "profitable" or "necessary" to us! By the process of sinning, repenting, confessing, and performing penance, she states, we gain vital knowledge of our need of grace and of God's love and mercy. By falling we become more humble and thus gain greater compassion for others. And in those who shall be saved, the pain caused by sin—the sadness and guilt we feel in knowing we have offended God and harmed others—begins already on earth our purgation. As we suffer from the consequences of our own or of another's sin, we become more like Jesus: "The struggle against sin, in which we, too, may feel forsaken, is our equivalent of the passion," states Frances Beer.[7] Thus, to Julian, sin is both useful and necessary to spiritual growth. But she is quick to answer the objection Paul also addresses in Romans 6:1–2, "'If this is true, then it would be a good idea to sin in order to have a greater reward'" by a resounding "no." "Any such impulse," she declares, ". . . is false and comes from the Enemy" (97–98).

God reminds Julian that while she will inevitably sin she should never succumb to fear because he is "keeping [her] very safe" (93). Like a wise mother, God sometimes allows us to fall for our own good, but we can never fall out of his constant compassion, love, and mercy. In revelation seven, God shows Julian just how unsteady she really is: nearly twenty times he allows her mood to alternate sharply between confidence and despair. Julian thus learns not to depend on her emotions but to trust in God who promises to turn all things into good for those who love him. Every experience of sin, suffering, and fear endured meekly can work for the greater good of the soul. In God's eyes, a person's "scars of healed wounds . . . do not deface but ennoble him" (96). Julian cites the cases of famous sinners, such as Peter, Paul, and Mary Magdalene (we can add Augustine to the list) whose repentance led to far greater humility, love, and faith. And as Robert Llewelyn sensitively notes, such an idea is really not alien to us:

> As I look back on my life with its sins and failures I can say with some confidence that they were necessary, that without them God could not have broken through the hard shell of pride which resisted mercy and grace. I needed my sins, not for their sake, but for the sake of the self-knowledge in which I must be grounded if the work of grace is to be made complete. I need them for the better understanding of the depth of the love which receives me again, and will never cast me off. So I see that my sins were necessary, and although as actions they are frozen hard in history, in value they for ever remain fluid to become the instrument of a deeper penitence and love. But they have, too, damaged others, and what then can I say? I must believe that they were foreseen and permitted from the beginning of time, and I must hand over their consequences to the mercy and wisdom of God, who can yet bring good out of evil and use suffering for the ultimate purpose of love.[8]

But, Julian asks, how can God possibly turn all things into good when the effects of evil on earth are so devastating? And what about those who deliberately choose sin over evil and remain unrepentant? Will they be damned, or not? Julian receives no specific answers to her questions, but is told only of a mysterious deed to be performed by God at the end of time that will, finally, make all things "well." The consoling words "All shall be well, and all manner of things shall be well" confirm the ultimate triumph of God's love and power even if evil, suffering, and fear seem at times overwhelming (79). Julian understands that while we will experience sin, pain, loss, and confusion on earth, God will resolve all matters perfectly in the end, with all wrongs made right and no detail forgotten. In fact, when we meet God, we will have no cause whatsoever to complain to him, "'Lord, it would have been very good if it had been like this'" (178). Rather, we will rejoice in astonishment at God's triumph and praise him for doing all things wonderfully. At work in creation, God is constantly turning evil into good, although in our limited perspective we are often blind to his actions. Flannery O'Connor once stated that in her view the devil "accomplishes a good deal of groundwork that seems to be necessary before grace is effective," a statement Julian would assent to.[9] In revelation thirteen, she bursts out laughing at the hapless Satan who loses far more by our repentance after sin than he accomplishes in getting us to sin in the first place and who will be—already is—completely defeated in God's plan.

In proposing that everything will be well in the end, Julian has sometimes been accused of adhering to the notion of universal salvation; that is, at the end of time, all humans will be saved. But the charge is unfounded for such a stance would deny the existence of free will, a belief Julian clearly accepts. "This is why it is impossible for Julian to be a universalist," Grace M. Jantzen comments. "It would trivialize the freedom which God has given us, and the courtesy and humility by which he allows us not to be in his presence—though we thereby create our own hell." But, Jantzen continues, "Julian may hope, as indeed all Christians may hope, that the compassionate love of God which reaches even into hell to woo all men and women will eventually triumph, so that all will finally turn to him."[10] While the Church teaches that the existence of hell can be deduced logically from the doctrine of free will, Christian charity makes us pray for all people to reach heaven in the end. Since Julian's revelations concern the astonishing love and generosity of God, we may hope that God will secure the salvation of even the worst of sinners.

But can God really love us *so* much? Julian understands how, in our guilt and misery, we find it difficult to believe that God really loves us so utterly. "Some of us believe that God is all mighty and has power to do everything, and that he is all wisdom and knows how to do everything, but that he is all love and is willing to do everything—there we stop," she states (162). We don't really believe he can bring good out of evil, and we too easily become bogged down in anxiety over our failures and life's sufferings. But, Julian tells us, this "doubtful fear" of God's mercy and love is what chiefly hinders our spiritual progress. Since fear indicates a lack of trust in God, we must strive to accept ourselves as limited creatures and abandon ourselves to his love and care. Such abandonment to God brings deep peace, security, and joy. Thus Julian writes her book to transform our perspective of both God's nature and sin: God is tremendously compassionate, not wrathful, and sin, if repented, actually becomes an opportunity for us to achieve greater humility and charity. Moreover, in the fourteenth and fifteenth revelations, Julian learns that God is the foundation of all prayer, both its impetus and destination. By prayer, the soul becomes more fully conformed to God's will. Since God impels us to pray for the things we need and takes joy in giving them, how, then, can he refuse to give us what we pray for? But we must cast aside the doubts that hold us back and petition God in a way that shows we really trust him to hear us and answer us.

Throughout the *Revelations*, Julian demonstrates a refreshingly positive, balanced, and wholesome view of human nature, a view that understands that the body as well as the soul is good. This position counters much of the thinking of her time that considered the body corrupt. But in Julian's profoundly incarnational thinking, the *imago Dei* is stamped on the whole person, both the physical and spiritual sides of our nature. Along with the Church, Julian thus sees grace as perfecting and not destroying human nature. Essential to our whole being, the image of God in us cannot be eradicated. Created in that image, our dignity is immense. While sin has distorted the divine image by taking away part of our essential goodness, God promises to return us to wholeness. The Christ who constantly mothers his beloved children has—and is now—restoring us through his Redemption.

Julian found all her revelations summarized in the parable of the lord and servant, a vision that makes up the long chapter 51 in her book. Acted out like a medieval "morality" play, the vision presents a type of parable rich in biblical associations. Eager to perform his lord's will and setting off at a run, a servant tumbles into a pit. Injured and alone, he suffers there miserably, unaware that his lord, whom he cannot see, is already advancing to rescue him. In fact, the lord is "rejoicing greatly" as he observes the scene for he is planning to reward his faithful servant with honors that far exceed those he would merit if he had not fallen (116). Julian understands immediately that the servant stands for Adam; that is, all human beings. Desiring to serve God, Adam nevertheless falls inadvertently and, in his weak condition, struggles in pain, anxiety, and helplessness. But at the end, the lord lifts the servant from the hole and restores him to an even greater dignity in compensation for his troubles. Julian realizes that this interpretation of the parable confirms her understanding that individual sin effects a type of *felix culpa*. Still, elements of the vision confuse her, for in the servant she also observes other qualities that don't correspond with Adam. But then, after nearly twenty years of meditating on this vision, Julian received an answer that finally resolved her confusion. The servant, she suddenly realized, not only signifies Adam but also Christ, the second Adam. Like the servant, Christ "fell" into the womb of Mary in the Incarnation as he hastened to do the Father's will, and likewise "fell" into the suffering of his Passion. And since through his Incarnation and Passion Jesus has become united with humankind, when the Father judges us he imputes no more guilt to us than he does to his Son. Thus when the Father looks on Adam, he sees only Jesus. All the major themes of Julian's revelations culminate in this parable of the extreme worth of human nature achieved through the wondrous love of God in the Redemption. In addition, the parable skillfully rounds out Julian's narrative as Ritamary Bradley points out: "The *Showings* had begun with the crowning of thorns, a mockery of one who claimed to be a king. The chapter which recounts the lord and servant parable ends with a reversal and consummation of that crowning: we who caused the bloody, painful crowning are in the end his garland of glory."[11]

Julian of Norwich's optimistic theology, so beautifully and memorably expressed, has influenced numerous writers in recent times. Some view her message of hope as particularly relevant in today's world. With admirable honesty, Julian confronted the paradox that God promises to make all things well yet evil and sin abound in the world. She tenaciously adheres to the belief that despite our failings and the sufferings all around us, God is perfectly accomplishing his divine plan and will, in a marvelous manner, make all things work together for good in the end. Julian's work has influenced Annie Dillard's *Holy the Firm*, especially in its struggle with the reality of suffering in the world. Denise Levertov based several poems, collected in her last volume, *The Stream and the Sapphire*, on Julian's themes. But it is perhaps T. S. Eliot who did more in the twentieth century to bring Julian's message to a modern audience than any other author. In "Little Gidding," the last section of *Four Quartets*, Eliot meditates on Julian's words of comfort and hope in a fearful and chaotic world:

> And all shall be well and
> All manner of thing shall be well
> When the tongues of flame are in-folded
> Into the crowned knot of fire
> And the fire and the rose are one.[12]

FOR FURTHER READING

T. S. Eliot, *Four Quartets*

Annie Dillard, *Holy the Firm*

Denise Levertov, "On a Theme from Julian's Chapter XX" and "The Showings: Lady Julian of Norwich" (both in *The Stream and the Sapphire*)

QUESTIONS FOR DISCUSSION

1. In Revelation 2, Julian is led by God under the sea. What is the significance of this vision in light of the vision of the hazelnut and Julian's frequent theme of spiritual safety in God?

2. Explain in detail what Julian means when she states that sin can be "behovely" (in this translation, "befitting"). Cite examples from your own life or that of others to illustrate what Julian is trying to express.

3. Find several passages where Julian's revelations seem, to her, to contradict Church teaching. How does Julian describe the paradox, and how is it resolved?

4. In the course of her revelations, Julian has three visions of the Virgin Mary: one at the Annunciation, one as she stood under the Cross, and one in glory in heaven. How do these visions complement or augment the spiritual lessons of the revelations?

5. In the sixth revelation, Julian sees Jesus presiding over a banquet in his house. Explain how this vision adds to Julian's understanding of God's "homely" nature.

6. Discuss in detail Julian's teaching on (1) the motherhood of God; (2) the value of prayer; (3) God's judgment and the "Great

Deed" to be performed at the end of time; (4) the "proper" type of fear.

NOTES

Julian of Norwich, *Revelations of Divine Love*, translated by Elizabeth Spearing, introduced by A. C. Spearing (London: Penguin Books, 1998). All references are to this edition.

1. Margery Kempe, *The Book of Margery Kempe,* translated by B. A. Windeatt. (London and New York: Penguin, 1994), 77.
2. Thomas Merton, "The English Mystics," in *Mystics and Zen Masters* (New York: Farrar, Straus & Giroux, 1967), 140.
3. Grace M. Jantzen, *Julian of Norwich: Mystic and Theologian* (New York: Paulist Press, 1988), 114.
4. Clement of Alexandria, quoted in Frances Beer, *Women and Mystical Experience in the Middle Ages* (Suffolk, Eng.: Boydell Press, 1992), 152.
5. Ambrose of Milan, quoted in Beer, *Women and Mystical Experience in the Middle Ages*, 152.
6. Anselm, "Prayer to St. Paul," in *The Prayers and Meditations of St. Anselm,* translated by Sister Benedicta Ward (New York: Penguin, 1973), 153.
7. Beer, *Women and Mystical Experience in the Middle Ages*, 144–45.
8. Robert Llewelyn, *All Shall Be Well: The Spirituality of Julian of Norwich for Today* (New York: Paulist Press, 1982), 131.
9. Flannery O'Connor, "On Her Own Work," in *Mystery and Manners,* edited by Sally and Robert Fitzgerald (New York: Farrar, Straus & Giroux, 1961), 117.
10. Jantzen, *Julian of Norwich*, 179.
11. Ritamary Bradley, *Julian's Way: A Practical Commentary on Julian of Norwich* (London: HarperCollins, 1992), 131.
12. T. S. Eliot, "Little Gidding," in *Four Quartets* (New York: Harvest/Harcourt, Brace & Co., 1971), 59.

BIBLIOGRAPHY

Baker, Denise Nowakowski. *Julian of Norwich's "Showings": From Vision to Book.* Princeton, NJ: Princeton University Press, 1994.

Bradley, Ritamary. *Julian's Way: A Practical Commentary on Julian of Norwich.* London: HarperCollins, 1992.

Jantzen, Grace M. *Julian of Norwich: Mystic and Theologian.* New York: Paulist Press, 1988.

Llewelyn, Robert. *All Shall Be Well: The Spirituality of Julian of Norwich for Today.* New York: Paulist Press, 1982.

Molinari, Paul, S. J. *Julian of Norwich: The Teaching of a 14th Century English Mystic.* London: Longmans, Green, and Co., 1958.

Pelphrey, Brant. *Christ Our Mother: Julian of Norwich.* Wilmington, DE: Michael Glazier, 1989.

DANTE ALIGHIERI
THE DIVINE COMEDY

BIOGRAPHY

One of the world's greatest poets, Dante Alighieri was born in Florence, Italy, in May 1265, to a family that stemmed from the nobility but was no longer well-to-do. His mother died when he was seven, and his father, who most likely supported the family by rental income, married again to a woman with whom he had several more children. The young Dante was probably schooled in the usual *trivium* (grammar, logic, rhetoric) and *quadrivium* (arithmetic, music, geometry, astrology), but his encyclopedic knowledge came mostly from self-study.

Dante's life revolved around Florence, then one of the most cultured and wealthy cities in Europe. Architecture, music, and sculpture flourished, and painting achieved new heights under such masters as Giotto and Cimabue. Florence's economy was prospering due to its manufacture of woolen goods, furs, and leather, and its currency unit, the *florin,* was the most stable coin in Europe. But Florence was also a volatile place, engaged as was all of northern Italy in the constant political and social agitation resulting from the struggle for temporal power waged between the emperor and the pope. Dante's fate would eventually be determined by this warfare.

At the age of nine, Dante encountered the woman who was to become his lifelong muse, Beatrice Portinari. Although at the time she too was only a child, Dante's senses were strongly and irrevocably aroused, and this surge of emotion was powerfully renewed upon their second meeting nine years later. The teenager was soon channeling his feelings into amatory verses that he boldly sent to some of the best-known poets in Florence. When Beatrice died at the age of twenty-five, Dante was inconsolable. To relieve his grief, he collected thirty-one of the poems he had written about his beloved into his first book, *La Vita Nuova* ("The New Life"). Around this time, Dante married Gemma Donati, to whom he had been betrothed since the age of twelve. The couple had three (possibly four) children.

In 1295, Dante commenced what had all indications of a brilliant political career. But he entered politics just at the time when tensions were rising between two long-standing political groups, the Guelfs, who supported the pope, and the Ghibellines, who supported the emperor. In Florence, the Guelfs split into two rival factions, the Whites and Blacks, each led by a powerful family clan. Dante's relative by marriage, Corso Donati, headed the Black Guelfs, the group favored by Pope Boniface VIII who eagerly sought to bring Florence under his control. Dismayed by the pope's meddling, Dante sympathized with the Whites. But in 1300, he and the other city priors voted to expel from Florence the most troublesome leaders of both factions. While Dante was in Rome consulting with Boniface, the Blacks seized power in Florence and Dante along with others was tried in absentia. When he refused to return to defend himself, he was sentenced in 1302 to death by burning should he ever again set foot in the city.

No one is certain where exactly Dante spent his nineteen years of exile although it is known that he lived from time to time under the patronage of noblemen in such cities as Verona, Ravenna, and Lucca. While bitter, his exile paradoxically fostered his creativity. James Collins suggests that the experience, in fact, was central to the writing of the *Divine Comedy*: it "proved to be the occasion, if not one of the principal causes, for Dante's perception of the Christian's life as a kind of exile and pilgrimage toward his true home."[1] Dante most likely began his masterpiece around 1307 and finished it shortly before his death. He circulated portions of the work among the literati as he completed them with the result that, by about 1315, he was already recognized as a great poet. Dante died of malaria at the age of fifty-seven on September 13, 1321, and is buried in Ravenna's Church of San Francisco. Besides the *Comedy*, his other major works include an unfinished, didactic piece on knowledge, *Il Convivio* ("The Banquet"); a study of language, *De Vulgari Eloquentia* ("On Vernacular Eloquence"); and a philosophical and political treatise advocating monarchy, *De Monarchia* ("Concerning Monarchy").

The sheer number of critical commentaries on the *Comedy*, beginning in the fourteenth century, attests to its astonishing intellectual and popular appeal. In 1373, fifty years after his death, Dante's genius was finally recognized in his hometown with the establishment of a chair in Dante studies at the University of Florence. While the *Comedy* has gone in and out of literary fashion over the years, it enjoyed a strong revival during the eighteenth and nineteenth centuries due to the Romantics' keen interest in all things medieval. Closer to our own time, the great modernist poet T. S. Eliot called Dante "the most persistent and deepest influence upon my own verse."[2]

CRITICAL OVERVIEW

Dante's *Comedy* ("divine" was added to the title after Dante's time) is a long poem consisting of 14,233 verses arranged in one hundred cantos. These cantos, in turn, are divided into three sections of thirty-three cantos each, corresponding to the three divisions of the afterlife, *Inferno* (Hell), *Purgatorio* (Purgatory), and *Paradiso* (Heaven). The first canto serves as a general prologue to the whole work. Dante composed his poem in *terza rima*, a rhyme scheme he invented and one well-suited to the poem's quick-paced, almost marchlike movement. Evoking the mystic number three, a symbol of the Trinity, Dante employs three-line groupings, each of which forms a closed unit but is also linked to the next grouping by the rhyme. The pattern—*aba, bcb, cdc,* and so forth—allows the unrhymed middle line of each tercet to prepare us for next one to follow. A skilled poet, Dante also fills his work with an entire range of rhetorical devices, including coined words, repetition, alliteration, invocations, and more. His signature device, however, is the simile, a word picture that makes an unfamiliar thing understandable by comparing it to something already known. By one count, there are an astonishing 676 similes in the poem.[3]

An epic of the Middle Ages in its wealth of philosophical, theological, social, and scientific thought, the *Comedy* is the work of a man blessed with remarkable intellectual and literary skills. Dante does here what few have dared to do, so thoroughly ground his work in historical reality that his pages team with the stories of actual friends, enemies, acquaintances, politicians, religious leaders, and events of his day. But it is the *Comedy*'s lofty religious theme that will most appeal to the Catholic reader. Dante's work has attracted readers for over six hundred years because it deals directly with the most fundamental metaphysical and moral questions: why God created us, the consequences of choosing evil over good, and what happens to the human soul after death.

Dante's first literary work, *Vita Nuova*, anticipates the *Comedy* in important ways. In its sensitive analysis of feeling, this collection of poems with prose commentaries relies heavily on the courtly love tradition popular in Dante's day. Derived from French troubadours, courtly love exalts a particular, usually unattainable woman to an imaginative ideal. Sighs, tears, and the heart's longing for the beloved are hallmarks of these expressive lyrics, which are the forerunners of our own conception of romantic love. Following the convention, Dante minutely records in *Vita Nuova* each of his memories of Beatrice—his first meeting with her, his first poem to her, her death—and all the exquisite emotions associated with these events. But he also does something new in this work by elevating the courtly love tradition to a higher, spiritual level. Envisioning Beatrice in heaven, his new hope is to be reunited with her there. Beatrice thus becomes for him a source of grace, her sensual beauty on earth a means of attraction to the beauty and goodness of God. Dante leaves us in *Vita Nuova* "resolve[d] to say no more about this blessèd one until I would be capable of writing about her in a nobler way," a clear indication of a sequel yet to come.[4]

The *Comedy*'s opening canto provides the reason for the protagonist's fantastic journey into the afterlife. Dante has lost his way in the dark woods. Although he sees a light at the top of a mountain, his efforts to climb toward it are thwarted by three beasts that block his way. A guide, Virgil, suddenly appears and proposes to the desperate man that they reach the light by taking a different road. Afraid at first to trust him, Dante relents when Virgil explains that he's been sent from heaven to help Dante by a chain of command originating with the Virgin Mary and proceeding through Beatrice. With this, the journey begins.

Before trying to make sense of this deceptively simple scene, we must realize that the *Comedy* is an extended allegory from its first to its last page. Evoking medieval scripture scholarship, Dante, in fact, identified four levels of interpretation in his poem, literal, allegorical, moral, and anagogical, but we can simplify matters by thinking in terms of just two levels, the literal and the figurative. "Literal" by no means implies that the *Comedy* is true to fact in all its aspects. It is, rather, a work of imaginative fiction, requiring us, like all fiction, to "suspend our disbelief" in order to enjoy the good story. The figurative or allegorical level demands more effort: employing a type of double vision, we must raise our minds to see that the story, operating on a spiritual plane, concerns *every* person's journey to God over difficult paths. Dante employs allegory in a far different, more complex way than is generally understood by this term. In writing his classic allegory, *Pilgrim's Progress*, for example, John Bunyon began with abstract concepts, such as Mercy or Despair, and then created fictional characters to embody those concepts, resulting in a simple, one-to-one correspondence between abstract idea and character. Dante, however, reverses this method. He starts with a real, historical person or event and then uses that real thing to illustrate a higher quality or idea. Beatrice, for example, is an actual person, but in the *Comedy* she also stands for divine wisdom or Christian revelation. The *Comedy* appeals precisely because its characters are far more psychologically complex and true-to-life than Bunyon's relatively flat characters. Dante's genius resulted from his ability to depict vividly the particular and definite while constantly evoking the ineffable and universal. In only one scene of the poem, in fact, does he employ straightforward, simple allegory: that of the great pageant of the Church Militant that Dante witnesses just before he enters paradise.

Dante's use of allegory illuminates his purpose in composing the *Comedy*. As a literary artist, he hoped his work would entertain but he also had a serious didactic intent. As he stated to his friend Can Grande, he wanted the poem to lead the unhappy on earth to a state of happiness.[5] Throughout the *Comedy*, we receive along with the protagonist a great deal of theological and moral instruction, so much so that the poem may be read as a kind of spiritual guidebook designed to lead us to live lives worthy of salvation. Within the work itself Dante reminds us frequently of its purpose to instruct and edify. In *Purgatorio*, for example, Beatrice insists that he relate what he has learned back on earth (33:76–78), and in *Paradiso*, his great-great-grandfather Cacciaguida states that the poem "once well-digested / . . . will become a vital nutriment" for its audience (17:131–32). "I put the food out; now you feed yourself," Dante curtly informs us at one point, reminding us that as we read we must strive to reflect on the spiritual import of the content (*Paradiso*, 10:25).

We return, then, to the figurative significance of the initial canto. Dante represents himself here as being lost in the wood at midlife, a usual time for many people to reassess the direction of their lives. While we aren't told exactly what his error or failing was, what is most important is that his conscience is suddenly awakened and he realizes he is in spiritual trouble. Although he knows which way to turn—he sees the light—he is unable to reach it by his own effort. The three beasts that block his path, taken from Jeremiah 5:6, are the forces of sin that keep us down: the power of lust (the leopard), of pride (the lion), and of greed (the wolf). Realizing that he can't reform his life on his own—for conversion is ultimately a work of God's grace—he humbly accepts the offer of his heaven-sent guide to set out along a path he'd rather not traverse but one that is necessary to achieve salvation.

This difficult path not only informs the overall structure of the *Comedy* but also reflects a Christian pattern of conversion. St. Paul describes conversion as "a natural body is put down and a spiritual body comes up" (1 Corinthians 15:44). This pattern of falling in order to rise is modeled in Jesus' life on earth. In order to save us, God descended in humility to be born a human being, fell even further into horrific suffering and death by crucifixion, and while yet in the tomb "descended into hell" to rescue those good persons who had died before the Resurrection opened the gates to heaven. As Beatrice explains to Dante in the seventh canto of *Paradiso*, the enormous consequences of Adam and Eve's sin, a pride that desired to exalt the self rather than to serve God, meant that only a supreme countering act of humility could rectify it. By analogy, therefore, in order for us to conquer sin, we must follow the same pattern of falling to rise: we must understand fully the horror of sin so as to freely embrace the good. "By [Christ's] descent to humility He atoned for man's ascent in pride, thus opening the way for man himself to ascend," states Charles Singleton. "Our Redemption through Christ rests, therefore, upon a fundamental pattern of *descent-ascent*."[6] Led by Virgil, Dante descends first into hell to witness the end result of choosing evil, climbs with great difficulty the cleansing mountain of purgatory, and then free of sin's weight soars up to heaven and to God. While conversion is expressed in the *Comedy* symbolically in outward terms of physical movement, it is in reality an inward struggle, a "journey of self-knowledge into the possibilities of depravity," which results in a complete reorienting of one's life.[7]

The pagan poet Virgil seems at first glance a curious choice of a guide to lead Dante along the road of Christian conversion. Dante the writer, however, clearly admired this poet whose tragic epic on the founding of Rome, the *Aeneid*, influenced his own work. Moreover, Virgil was regarded as a prophet of the coming of Christ because in one of his *Eclogues*, poems written about 40 B.C., he predicts the birth of a child who will usher in a new era of justice and peace. For Dante, Virgil represents both poetic inspiration and the light of natural human reason: he is the voice of conscience, which stirs Dante to turn back to God. But Virgil can only guide Dante through hell and purgatory, for as a nonbeliever he is barred from heaven. Therefore a second guide, Beatrice, representing Christian wisdom, takes over at this point and leads Dante much of the way throughout paradise. As Dante reaches the highest realm of heaven, yet a third guide is needed, the mystic St. Bernard of Clairvaux, who shepherds Dante the rest of the way into the most sublime of God's mysteries. The movement of conversion by grace, then, begins through natural reason, moves to supernatural wisdom, and culminates in mystical knowledge. This tripartite way is the classic expression of the Christian path to God.

We return to the *Comedy*. Having begun in medias res with no elaborate introduction, the poem now moves swiftly as we find ourselves along with Dante and Virgil almost propelled downward into the Inferno. As Dante the writer imagined it, hell is a funnel-like pit at the center of the earth created when Lucifer fell after refusing to serve God. The soil heaped up as a result of his fall formed the mountain of purgatory, and thus—in poetic justice—Satan not only dug his own grave in rebelling but also created the means by which fallen humans can once again attain salvation. Dante's cosmology is based on love, the foundation and ordering of all of the universe, "the seed of every virtue growing in you, / and every deed that merits punishment," as Virgil informs him (*Purgatorio*, 17:104–5). If, in free will, humans persistently choose to love a lesser good than God, and if they refuse God's loving mercy at the moment of death, they merit hell. Dante's hell is divided into nine concentric circles (nine being the square of the mystic number three) arranged in descending order from the least to the gravest of sins. Because the sins of incontinence or sensuality offend God the least (lust, gluttony, avarice and prodigality, wrath) they are punished in the highest rounds. Sins of bestiality or violence, whether against God, neighbor, or oneself, are punished in the middle rounds. Sins of fraud, including flatterers, hypocrites, and thieves, follow. Dante reserves the pit of hell for the worst of sinners, the traitors. Because they have willfully violated bonds of trust and love between human beings, they have earned the perpetual sight of Satan himself.

Strongly visual and dramatic, Dante's *Inferno* is a veritable whirlwind of activity as, on each level, souls are punished for their sins against God and man. Living in a time and place when physical torture was the usual penalty for crime, Dante envisions the punishment of hell as the infliction of bodily pain. He employs the principle of *contrapasso*: the punishment fits the crime. Thus, for example, the gluttons in the third circle who have stuffed their mouths with too much rich food on earth are punished by having to gorge perpetually on filth, and the soothsayers in the eighth circle, who tried to foretell the future that only God can know, are punished by having their heads twisted backwards on their bodies. Popular culture depicts hell as a grisly, Halloweenish place of fire, screams, and devils with pitchforks, and in large measure Dante's *Inferno* has contributed to this childlike view. But Dante is simply giving us an imaginative metaphor, presenting the agony of the physical torture we can understand as a graphic representation of the utterly unglamorous and horrific end result of sin. For her part, the Church confirms only that hell is the absence of the Beatific Vision, which, because we are made for God, is its own torment. Whatever the punishments endured by souls in hell (and in purgatory too, as we shall see), they aren't imposed by a vengeful or sadistic God, but are, rather, the direct effect of the choice of sin. God, in short, damns no one to hell: those in this place of misery have freely chosen to be there. Although modern people are often uncomfortable with the idea of hell, Jesus spoke of it in urgent terms, and the Church has always confirmed its existence. Free will, in fact, would be a mockery if God could force us to love him. As Dorothy Sayers cogently put it,

> We cannot repudiate Hell without altogether repudiating Christ. . . . It is quite fatal to come to the study of the *Divine Comedy* with our minds irrevocably set in a frivolous, or superior, or righteously indignant attitude to the very idea of hell. . . . If we are ever to make head or tail of the greatest of Christian poems, we must at least be ready to understand what is meant by damnation, and why every believing Christian recognizes it as a terrible possibility for and within himself, and why it matters to our comprehension of God and Heaven and Man.[8]

As they enter hell through its gate with the despairing inscription, "Abandon every hope, all you who enter," the first area Dante and Virgil arrive at is antehell, a kind of vestibule to hell proper. Here are confined those persons in life who "rode the fence" in apathy or indecision, never fully committing themselves to either good or evil, God or the devil. They are, therefore, rejected by both heaven and hell, scorned or forgotten by all. Their fitting punishment is to be goaded by swarms of stinging wasps into endlessly running behind a blank banner. Dante reminds us sharply here of the harsh warning by God in Revelations 3:16: "Because you are lukewarm, neither hot nor cold, I will spew you out of my mouth." Virgil appropriately hurries Dante along: "Let's not discuss them; look and pass them by" (*Inferno*, 3:51).

Ferried across the river Acheron, Dante and his guide now enter the first circle of hell, a shadowy place of sighs and sadness but no physical pain. Relying on the notion of limbo, a popularly held concept at the time but never formal Church doctrine, Dante here places unbaptized children and virtuous pagans, those who are blameless of sin but who in life did not know Christ and salvation by grace. Dwelling in a separate castle within this realm are many of the great poets and thinkers of antiquity, Homer, Horace, Ovid, and Lucan, whom Dante is eager to meet. But when he sees Virgil pale at the sight, he realizes that to this place of a certain quietude, but no light or joy, his beloved guide, too, is confined for all eternity.

Leaving limbo, Dante now descends into the four circles that make up the first major division of hell, that of incontinence. Here he finds the lustful, perpetually ravaged by fierce winds; the gluttons, forced to lie on their bellies in pelting, cold rain while eating mud; the prodigal and avaricious, eternally clashing at each other with enormous weights; and the wrathful and slothful, the former naked and clawing each other in the muddy River Styx and the latter mired up to their mouths in the dirty swamp. Always sympathetic toward lovers, Dante indicates by this hierarchy that lust, which imitates love but perverts it, is the least offensive sin meriting hell. As he passes through this circle, Dante pauses to speak, in one of the *Comedy*'s best known scenes, with Francesca da Rimini who relates her mournful tale to him. The daughter of a nobleman (and a relative of Dante's patron in Ravenna), Francesca was wed by her family for political reasons to a deformed man named Gianciotto. Gianciotto's brother Paolo, however, was good-looking and charming. As Francesca tells it, she and Paolo were moved to commit adultery while alone together in the house and reading the Arthurian tale in which the married Queen Guinevere, to reward the handsome young knight Lancelot, kisses him on the mouth. Caught by Gianciotto in the act, Francesca and Paolo were murdered by the enraged husband. While Dante, the naïve pilgrim, nearly faints with pity upon hearing this melancholy story, Dante the author subtly indicates, in a scene replete with moral irony, that Francesca's seductive words merely veneer her selfishness and self-pity. Like all those in hell, she expresses no regret or repentance for her actions.

Dante now enters the gates of lower hell, the city of Dis, located across the Styx. In the sixth circle, he meets the heretics, lying in open tombs of fire. Next he arrives at the circle of the violent with its three distinct divisions. Souls who committed violence against persons or property are punished by being immersed in a boiling river of blood; those who committed violence against their own natures, the suicides, are turned into strange, misshapen trees; and those who committed violence against God, the blasphemers, usurers, and homosexuals, are condemned to a vast desertlike area continually rained on by flames of fire. In the eighth circle, Dante finds ten separate trenches, the *malebolge* or "evil pockets," each of which contains a group of sinners punished in various ways for fraud: seducers, flatterers, simonists, soothsayers, grafters, hypocrites, thieves, deceivers, sowers of scandal and schism, and falsifiers. In the trench of the simonists, those who sold church favors, such as indulgences, for money, Dante meets Pope Nicholas III, punished by lying face down in a pit with fire licking his heels. At first, he mistakes Dante for his successor, Pope Boniface VIII, whom he predicts will also merit hell for the same crime (Boniface died in 1303). Dante was indeed outraged by Boniface's corruption and believed his greed and power mongering responsible for much of the violence perpetrated between Florence's political factions. While he takes aim at many corrupt political and religious leaders in his poem, his invective is especially reserved for this figure who is excoriated numerous times in the work. "[He] has turned my sepulchre into a sewer / of blood and filth," states St. Peter of Boniface in the *Paradiso*, causing all of heaven to blush with shame (27:25–26). In the trench of the deceivers, Dante comes across another well-known figure, the mythic Greek adventurer Ulysses, confined to this region of hell because of his invention of the Trojan horse, the enormous statue that allowed the Greeks to conquer the Trojans, the ancient ancestors of the Italians. Dante's story of Ulysses's last voyage here is his own. Always restless for adventure, Ulysses leaves his family and urges his men to undertake yet another voyage into the unknown from which they all perish. "The burning wish / to know the world and have experience / of all man's vices, of all human worth," a type of selfishness that results in injury to others, has multiplied Ulysses's sins (*Inferno*, 26:97–99).

Finally, Dante and Virgil reach the lowest circle of hell where those who maliciously betrayed country, friends, or family dwell. And here they find not fire but ice, the frozen lake of Cocytus with souls submerged to various degrees within it. As the opposite of the warmth and light of God, ice reflects the utter lack of love these persons exhibited on earth. Here, too, frozen at the pit of hell, is the grotesque figure of Lucifer himself, a gigantic parody of the Trinity with his three mouths each chewing on one of the great traitors of history, Brutus and Cassius, who betrayed Julius Ceasar (and hence the Roman Empire), and Judas, who betrayed Jesus. In this region of horror, Dante discovers a former nobleman from Pisa, Ugolino della Gherardesca, who served as a traitor in

Italy's political struggles and was, in turn, betrayed by his supposed friend Archbishop Ruggieri degli Ubaldini. Along with his sons and grandsons, Ugolino starved to death in prison in 1288. Now, eternally frozen in Cocytus, he gnaws on the head of Ruggieri, a grotesque sight that starkly portrays the result of the treachery and violence that marked the enmity between church and empire in Dante's era. Dante fittingly chose cannibalism—the act of feeding off each other—to express the worst of human hate and exploitation.

To leave hell, the pilgrims must literally climb Satan's body—grapple with the origin of sin itself. At a certain point, they find themselves reversed and begin to climb upwards, a complete turning of position that is the very essence of conversion. The trip through hell began on Good Friday. Now, they arrive at purgatory on Easter morning, a time of hope and resurrection. Dante's purgatory is a steep mountain girded round by seven ledges, or terraces, corresponding to the seven capital sins. These sins, in turn, are arranged in three major divisions, that of perverted love, insufficient love, and excessive love. The regions of antepurgatory and the Earthly Paradise, or Eden, at the top of purgatory, bring us to the mystical number nine. As the pilgrims emerge from hell, at once the atmosphere is completely changed. Souls here are humble, glad, and hopeful. Whereas in hell there was no time and therefore no progress, in purgatory time is crucial as souls hurry about their penances so as to hasten their ascent to God. While they suffer as intensely as those in hell, their suffering is not useless but purging and, unlike the pains of hell, it will at some point come to an end. In addition, the atmosphere of purgatory is far more inward and meditative than that of hell as souls reflect on their sins in the light of God's mercy and spur themselves on to the practice of virtue.

The Catholic Church teaches that purgatory exists to cleanse the soul before it is fit to come into the pure presence of God. While sincere repentance reunites a sinner with God, it doesn't eliminate the residue of sin, the deeply ingrained tendency to do wrong. Acts of penance can remove this stain, but most people don't do enough penance on earth. Thus, purgatory exists as a necessary vestibule to heaven, a kind of hospital where the wounds of sin are healed. Here too, as in hell, the suffering experienced by souls is not inflicted by God but is the natural effect of sin. But unlike the resentful and self-pitying souls in hell, in this realm suffering is willingly and joyfully welcomed as a sign of God's mercy and love. In fact, according to Dante, souls are not detained by God in purgatory, but keep themselves at each level until they know they are purged of a particular sin and free to rise up to the next. And in the economy of the Body of Christ, based on the bonds of charity, one's sojourn in purgatory can be shortened by the prayers and penances of those on earth. Repeatedly as he walks about this realm, Dante is beseeched by souls for prayers.

Along with newly arrived souls, Dante and Virgil approach the base of the mountain, wondering how to set about the steep climb. Here they discover the region of antepurgatory where souls that were slow to repent on earth, died without the sacrament of penance, or were excommunicated by the Church must wait, sometimes hundreds of years or more, to even start their purgation. Among the crowd, Dante encounters an old acquaintance from Florence, Belacqua, famous for his laziness. He also meets Manfred, the illegitimate son of Frederick II of Swabia, who was killed in battle in 1266 after having been excommunicated by the pope. Manfred recounts to Dante how he repented at the last moment and thus was saved. In Manfred's story as elsewhere in the *Comedy,* Dante's liberality of mind is evident: God's mercy is greater than ecclesiastical judgment. "The church's curse is not the final word, / for Everlasting Love may still return, / if hope reveals the slightest hint of green," Manfred states (*Purgatorio,* 3:133–35).

Finally, after much delay, Dante is transported to the entrance of purgatory proper. There, an angel inscribes seven "p's" standing for *peccatum,* the Latin word for sin, on his forehead. While Dante was merely an observer in hell, in purgatory he too undergoes purgation: as he passes through each level a "p" will be wiped from his forehead. Now, to begin the arduous climb, he first mounts three stairs colored white, black, and red, symbols of the three conditions necessary before one can be absolved of sin: self-examination, sorrow for sin, and satisfaction made through penance.

On the first of the seven terraces, Dante and Virgil encounter the proud whose penance consists of bearing on their backs tremendous weights of stone, their once-haughty gazes now bent in humility and tears toward the ground. Here, as on each terrace, souls are urged on by spurs and checks, some heard, some spoken, and some written. Spurs are edifying examples of the virtue being sought, and each spur begins with an example from the life of the Virgin Mary, the most virtuous of all humans. On the terrace of pride, for example, Mary's humility in the Annunciation, her declaration of complete servitude to God in her words *Ecce ancilla Dei,* is held up as the antidote to pride. Checks, by contrast, are displays of the ugliness of the particular vice punished, a means of engendering loathing for sin. On this first ledge, the checks are stone carvings of classic examples of the downfall of the proud—Nimrod, Saul, the cities of Troy and Illium—which the penitential souls observe as they go about their painful rounds. When Dante leaves this terrace and the first "p" is removed from his forehead, he discovers to his surprise that he is much, much lighter and the climb correspondingly much, much easier. Pride, Dante suggests, is a heavy weight to carry and keeps our spirits from rising to the light.

On the second terrace, Dante and Virgil find the envious, their once-covetous eyes now pitifully sewn shut; and on the third, the wrathful, purged by being enveloped in a thick, foul-smelling fog. These first three "deadly" faults of pride, envy, and anger are the worst sins of purgatory and comprise the category of perverted love, that which has chosen the wrong goal. Next comes a single terrace of too little, or insufficient love: here the slothful, too lazy to move in life, rush about doing good works so as to lose no time in serving God. On the final three terraces the sins of excessive love are purged, that love which was directed too much toward the good things of earth. On the fifth round are the avaricious, forced now to lie facedown in the dust and contemplate poverty and generosity. Here, Dante and Virgil are joined by the Roman poet Statius, who, having just been freed from this level, accompanies the pilgrims on the rest of their journey through purgatory. Statius, who died in A.D. 96, credits Virgil's fourth *Eclogue* with his conversion to Christianity. As a convert, he marks the transition in Dante's path from the natural human reason symbolized by Virgil to Christian belief. On the sixth terrace, that of the gluttonous, Dante sees starving souls who must contemplate a fruit-laden tree but cannot eat of it. He pauses to converse with an old friend from Florence, Forsee Donati, who relates that he's been able to gain this high level of purgatory quickly through the prayers of his wife, Nella. Interestingly, Dante positions members of the Donati family, his relatives by marriage, in all three realms of the afterlife. Corso Donati, a ruthless man responsible for the outbreak of violence in Florence, is in hell; Forsee Donati, a good man but lacking in temperance, is in purgatory; and Piccarda Donati, sister to these two, Dante will later find in heaven.

On the seventh and final ledge of purgatory, an extremely slippery slope, the lustful are punished by fire, a symbol of their excessive passion but now turned into a means of their cleansing. Dante, too, must be purged of this fault along with any remaining tendency to sin by walking through a wall of fire in order to enter purgatory's final area, the

Earthly Paradise. Empty since Adam's fall, the Earthly Paradise, the original starting point of all humans, must once again be traversed before reaching heaven. As Dante hesitates to plunge himself into the flames, Virgil urges him on by reminding him that Beatrice waits on the other side. But before the longed-for moment of reunion takes place, Dante witnesses a spectacular pageant parade before his eyes, an allegory of the Church Militant similar to the medieval processions Dante the writer was familiar with. Heavy in symbolism based on the Book of Revelations, the grand affair recounts salvation history: a magnificent chariot (the Church) is bound to a tree (both Eden's tree of Good and Evil and the Cross) by a griffon (Christ) and then beset by various enemies (the Church's persecutions). The whole ritual, played out in two scenes, frames Beatrice's arrival in the manner of a "grand entrance rite."[9] And now Dante finally comes face to face with his beloved, she who has helped orchestrate the entire journey. But the meeting is not at all what he (or we) had expected. Far from a romantic or even a warm reunion, it is, rather, Dante's final judgment. Beatrice berates the hapless man and exacts from him a confession for his misdeeds. Overcome by remorse, Dante faints whereupon he is plunged by Beatrice's handmaid, Matelda, into the two blessed rivers that flow nearby, Lethe, which brings forgetfulness of sin, and Eunoë, which revives memories of good works. With this, Dante is now fully cleansed and ready to approach God's throne.

Dante's paradise is structured on the cosmology of Ptolemy, the Greek astronomer who placed Earth at the center of the universe with nine heavenly bodies revolving around it. As Dante the pilgrim learns, for his sake heaven displays itself as a hierarchy corresponding to these heavenly bodies, but in reality all souls in paradise are in Empyrean, the realm above the spheres where God resides. If the atmosphere of *Inferno* is one of frenetic activity, and that of *Purgatorio* one of inward meditation, *Paradiso* imparts a mystical, visionary mood. Drama now turns into poetry, and it is increasingly difficult for Dante to describe what he sees. Paradise is love, beauty, and song, but especially bright light, light that grows ever more blinding and splendid as he moves upward. Beatrice's beauty, too, grows so astonishingly radiant that Dante's eyes can hardly bear it.

Indeed, Dante's problem in depicting paradise was how to render ever-increasing shades of spiritual light, beauty, and joy. It seems an impossible task. Most of us, after all, can't really picture heaven except in childish terms of harps, angels, white robes, and clouds. Someone once quipped that our only conception of heaven is that of "a choir practice in a jeweler's shop." Dante the writer further complicates the matter by indicating that heaven is for his pilgrim only a mystical vision: Dante never fully sees a person here but just vague images or gleams of light. But despite such difficulties, Dante succeeds in once again doing what few have attempted: describe the indescribable. Like his hell and purgatory, paradise is full of vivid, sensuous detail and memorable personalities. T. S. Eliot put it best: "Never dry, [*Paradiso*] is either incomprehensible or intensely exciting. . . . Nowhere in poetry has experience so remote from ordinary experience been expressed so concretely."[10]

On the first three levels of heaven are souls who, in some way, fell a bit short on earth in their commitment to God. Each of heaven's levels is associated with a particular virtue. The first sphere, that of the Moon, is associated with the first of the three theological virtues, faith—albeit imperfect faith. It is home to those who in some way reneged on their religious vows. Here Dante encounters a third member of the Donati family, Piccarda, who had been forced from the convent by her brother Corso and married for political reasons. As Beatrice explains, she has merited this lower area of heaven because her will at least partially consented to the act. Dante is curious about whether souls in these lower realms envy those above, but Piccarda assures him that all souls in paradise are absolutely content with their assigned lot. "In His will is our peace," she tells him (*Paradiso* 3:85). The second heavenly sphere, Mercury, associated with imperfect hope, consists of souls who were a bit too eager in life for fame and glory, and the third, Venus, associated with imperfect love, of souls who loved earthly things or other humans a little too strongly.

The next four spheres correspond to the four cardinal virtues, prudence, fortitude, justice, and temperance. In the sphere of the Sun, Dante comes upon theologians and others famed for their wisdom and prudence. Here, singing and dancing in garlandlike circles, he meets members of the two great religious orders founded in the thirteenth century, the Franciscans and Dominicans. Thomas Aquinas, a Dominican, steps forward to praise the Franciscans, and then Bonaventure, a Franciscan, returns the favor. King Solomon of old, too, is here. Next, Dante soars upward to Mars, associated with fortitude. On this level abide those souls who in life fought bravely for the faith: Joshua, Maccabees, Roland, Charlemagne, and many others. And here a surprise meeting takes place between Dante and his great-great-grandfather, Cacciaguida, who died fighting in the second crusade. With affection and joy at having met his offspring, Cacciaguida recounts to the younger man their family history and foretells both Dante's exile and the eventual fame of the *Comedy*. "You will have a future that endures," he tells him. "Do not resort to lies, / let what you write reveal all you have seen" (*Paradiso*, 17:98, 127–28). Jupiter, the next and sixth sphere, is associated with justice: here Dante sees souls soaring above arranged in the form of an eagle, symbol of justice. In the realm of Saturn, associated with temperance, Dante comes across some well-known contemplatives, such as the saints Peter Damian and Benedict.

As Dante continues to soar upward, he now arrives at the realm of the Fixed Stars, a place above the heavenly spheres. Dante's language grows more and more obscure as he struggles to put what he experiences here into words. "Now bear in mind the weight of my poem's theme, / think of the mortal shoulders it rests on, / and do not blame me if I stagger here," he implores (23:64–66). In a blinding flash of light, he sees a triumphant Christ and his glorious mother Mary ascending with all the blessed into the Empyrean. Beatrice requests that Dante be allowed to participate in some measure in the knowledge of God experienced by the elect. In response, as a test before such honor can be granted, saints Peter, James, and John come forward to quiz Dante on faith, hope, and charity, an exam he passes with flying colors. Then suddenly, he finds himself transported upward to the ninth realm of heaven, the Primum Mobile, the sphere that God, the unmoved mover of all, moves directly and which, in turn, moves all other spheres in the universe. In yet another instant he has gained the Empyrean, a word that means "flaming with fire." Through the glare of intense light, he sees a marvelous vision unfold before him: all the souls in paradise arranged in the form of an immense white rose, with angels buzzing like bees between them and God. As Beatrice departs to assume her seat in the rose's third tier, a third and final guide, St. Bernard of Clairvaux, appears at Dante's side. A great mystic who was devoted to the Virgin Mary, Bernard shepherds Dante into the advanced stage of mystical knowledge that alone can reach God. With a prayer, Bernard invokes Mary's help, and she who has initiated Dante's journey now requests of her Son that he grant Dante a glimpse of the Beatific Vision, God himself. Straining his sight upward, Dante makes out the three circles of the Trinity with the image of a man superimposed on one. In a flash he comprehends the great mystery—but "at this point power failed high fantasy," and the final vision itself is left to our imaginations (*Paradiso*, 33:142).

Helen Luke captures the remarkable accomplishment of the *Divine Comedy* in these words:

> There are poets who bring alive for us the beauty and ugliness of this world, and there are those who penetrate the heights and depths of

the emotions; in others clarity of intellect and penetrating thought shine through their verse into our minds; and yet others open to us through their intuitive vision the elusive country of the Spirit. But only the greatest of the great do all four of these things. Dante's journey is the bringing to consciousness of them all into one great patterned whole.[11]

FOR FURTHER READING

Dante, Alighieri, *La Vita Nuova*

QUESTIONS FOR DISCUSSION

1. Mark Musa's translation (the one recommended in this essay) does not attempt to preserve the rhyme scheme of Dante's original Italian. This is a good thing, since trying to do so in an English translation generally distorts the meaning of a passage so it becomes almost unreadable. However, all students of Dante should have a sense of his considerable skill as a poet. Find an original, Italian version of the work and read through at least the first five tercets of *Inferno*. Mark the *terza rima* scheme with *a*'s, *b*'s, *c*'s, and so forth, and also mark the hendecasyllabic meter: that is, eleven syllables per line. Then, locate several other translations of the text in English—for example, those by Henry Wadsworth Longfellow, Dorothy L. Sayers, Charles S. Singleton, or John Ciardi—and compare the same five tercets to Musa's translation. Which translation do you like best? (You may also wish to read Musa's very enlightening comments on the choices he made in translating the work, located in *The Portable Dante*.)

2. Discuss the Christian pattern of conversion—falling to rise—as it informs both the overall structure of the *Comedy* and Dante the pilgrim's journey through the depths of sin to the heights of paradise. What other biblical or literary sources come to mind as following this same pattern? You might, for example, compare the *Comedy* to the pattern of conversion in Augustine's *Confessions*.

3. Consider Dante's imaginative use of *contrapasso*: the punishment is suited to the crime. Choose at least four levels of *Inferno* and

four levels of *Purgatorio* and discuss exactly how this principle is applied.

4. Do you agree with Dante's arrangement of sins and sinners in hell? If not, what kind of hierarchy of evil would you create in the modern world?

5. As we have noted, one of the major intents of the *Comedy* was to instruct. As Dante moves through hell, purgatory, and heaven, he becomes more and more the listener as his guides and the conversations he holds with various persons impart theological and philosophical teachings. Find and examine at least five of these incidents and consider why Dante might have positioned a particular lesson in a particular place.

6. Locate and read the passages on hell, purgatory, and heaven in the *Catechism of the Catholic Church*. Is Dante always orthodox—true to Church teaching—in his imaginative version of the afterlife?

NOTES

Dante Alighieri, *The Divine Comedy*, in *The Portable Dante*, translated, edited, and introduced by Mark Musa (New York: Penguin Books, 1995). All references are to this edition.

1. James Collins, *Pilgrim in Love: An Introduction to Dante and His Spirituality* (Chicago: Loyola University Press, 1984), 2.

2. T. S. Eliot, "What Dante Means to Me," July 1950 address to Italian Society of London, quoted in R. W. B. Lewis, *Dante* (New York: Viking Penguin, 2001), 195.

3. Thomas G. Bergin, *Dante* (Boston: Houghton Mifflin, 1965), 285.

4. *La Vita Nuova XLII*, in *The Portable Dante*, edited and translated by Mark Musa (New York: Penguin, 1995), 649.

5. Letter to Can Grande, in Jefferson Butler Fletcher, *Dante* (New York: Henry Holt, 1916), 199–200.

6. Charles S. Singleton, "'In Exitu Israel de Aegypto,'" in *Dante: A Collection of Critical Essays,* edited by John Freccero (Englewood Cliffs, NJ: Prentice, Hall, 1965), 110.

7. Dorothy L. Sayers, *Introductory Papers on Dante* (New York: Barnes and Noble, 1969), 132.

8. Sayers, *Introductory Papers on Dante,* 45.

9. Collins, *Pilgrim in Love,* 176.

10. T. S. Eliot, *Dante* (London: Faber and Faber, 1929), 50, 54.

11. Helen M. Luke, *Dark Wood to White Rose: Journey and Transformation in Dante's "Divine Comedy"* (New York: Parabola, 1989), xvii–xviii.

BIBLIOGRAPHY

Collins, James. *Pilgrim in Love: An Introduction to Dante and His Spirituality.* Chicago: Loyola University Press, 1984.

Lewis, R. W. B. *Dante.* New York: Viking Penguin, 2001.

Luke, Helen M. *Dark Wood to White Rose: Journey and Transformation in Dante's "Divine Comedy."* New York: Parabola, 1989.

Royal, Robert. *Dante Alighieri: Divine Comedy, Divine Spirituality.* New York: Crossroad, 1999.

Sayers, Dorothy L. *Introductory Papers on Dante.* New York: Barnes and Noble, 1969.

GERARD MANLEY HOPKINS
SELECTED POETRY

BIOGRAPHY

Born in 1844 at Stratford in Essex, Gerard Manley Hopkins, the eldest of Manley and Kate Smith Hopkins's eight children, inherited a rich cultural, artistic, and religious family background. Both parents were devout members of the High Anglican Church and nurtured their children in the faith. In addition, both parents as well as other members of the extended family passed on to the Hopkins children a love of music, art, and literature. Manley Hopkins, who ran a prosperous marine insurance firm, was a published poet, author, and occasional literary critic whose artistic endeavors highly influenced young Gerard. Gerard's maternal aunt, Maria, instructed the boy in drawing. Other aunts and uncles were accomplished painters or musicians.

After attending boarding school, Hopkins entered Balliol College of Oxford University where he studied for a degree in Classics. A brilliant scholar, he quickly rose to the top of his class. In his spare time, he continued to pursue his artistic and literary interests, creating detailed and realistic nature sketches and writing verses influenced, in particular, by John Keats and Christina Rossetti. At Oxford, Hopkins forged a lifelong friendship with fellow student Robert Bridges who is credited with preserving and publishing Hopkins's poetry after the author's death. His years at Oxford were also instrumental in bringing about profound changes in Hopkins's religious sensibility. Although the height of the Oxford movement had passed some twenty years before, the university continued to be deeply embroiled in religious controversy. The High Anglican Church, to which Hopkins belonged and which Oxford

professed, was a kind of "middle ground" between the increasingly liberal reforms of Protestantism and the ancient heritage of Roman
Catholicism. Like Roman Catholics, Anglo-Catholics affirmed the value
of tradition as well as Scripture in interpreting the faith and believed in
Apostolic succession, but they did not accept the authority of the pope.
But when prominent Anglican churchman John Henry Newman, concluding that such a halfway position was intellectually untenable, converted to the Roman faith in 1845 and brought many disciples with
him, Oxford reeled from the upheaval in a manner that still reverberated
in Hopkins's day. Adding new fuel to the fire, Newman's precise account
of the steps leading to his conversion, *Apologia Pro Vita Sua*, was published in 1864 when Hopkins was a sophomore. With his deeply religious temperament and keen intellect, Hopkins found himself, as Newman had before him, growing increasingly convinced of the truth of
Roman Catholic doctrine. He sought out the older man for instruction,
and, in 1866 at the age of twenty-two, was received by Newman into the
Catholic Church. Hopkins's conversion exacted a high personal toll, for
it irrevocably estranged him from some members of his family.

Two years later, heeding a call to the priesthood, Hopkins entered
the Jesuit order. Over the next decade, he was moved frequently to serve
in various parishes and among the poor throughout Britain. By far his
happiest period proved to be the three years spent at St. Beuno's parish in
North Wales. It was in this place of great natural beauty and serenity that
Hopkins, who had previously burned his poetry believing such work incompatible with his vocation, broke his long poetic silence in 1875 with
The Wreck of the Deutschland, a masterful and innovative poem commem-
orating a tragic shipwreck that had occurred earlier that year. When it
and a second poem, *The Loss of the Eurydice*, were rejected by a Jesuit magazine as too unconventional to print, Hopkins never again sought to publish his work. But he continued to write as much as time allowed, and
while at St. Beuno's composed many of his best nature sonnets.

In 1884, Hopkins moved to Dublin to assume a position as Professor of Greek at University College, which Newman had founded. By
now in poor health and uncomfortable as an Englishman in Ireland during the period of Irish agitation for "Home Rule," Hopkins found his
duties in that city stressful. His depression apparently grew into deep spiritual and emotional agony, feelings recorded in a group of poems known
as the "Terrible Sonnets" for their wrenching expression of inner anguish. In 1888, he fell seriously ill with what was only belatedly diagnosed
as typhoid fever. He died on June 8 of that year, at the age of forty-four.

In 1918, thirty years after the poet's death, his college friend Robert Bridges, to whom he had sent much of his writing over the years, released a slender collection of Hopkins's poems. It was not until the 1930s, however, that through the promotion of the New Critics Hopkins became recognized as a major poet. A prodigious writer in many other genres as well, his collected prose works, including literary criticism, letters, notebooks, sermons, and theological and devotional writings, fill five volumes.

In 1976, Hopkins was assigned a place in Poet's Corner in Westminster Abbey. His stone's epitaph there contains a single phrase from one of his poems: "Immortal Diamond."

CRITICAL OVERVIEW

When first published in 1918, Gerard Manley Hopkins's poetry was nothing short of revolutionary. While leaning toward romanticism in its focus on nature and exploration of the subjective states of the individual consciousness, it also anticipated modernism in its compression, ambiguity, and experimental form and style. Added to this is Hopkins's religious subject matter and deeply Catholic sense of incarnationalism and sacramentality. The combination of all these elements makes his work utterly unique and sometimes difficult to read, much less interpret.

A perceptive and articulate analyst of his own work, Hopkins was fully conscious of his technical innovations and of the particular spiritual vision he wished to convey. In fact, in an attempt to explain the latter, he invented two words, *inscape* and *instress*. While the terms are slippery to define (even Hopkins was inconsistent in the way he used them), *inscape* may be described as the essence of a thing or person that makes it a unique entity in creation. To Hopkins, every animate and inanimate thing in the world not only possesses a particular individuality but also "selves," or reveals it at certain times. And to Hopkins, this core essence derives from Christ, "for whom and through whom all things were made." All creation radiates the Son of God, and perceptive persons can intuit, through grace, the God at the center of all that exists. *Instress*, on the other hand, may be defined as the dynamic power or divine energy within created things that impels them to "selve," to make their unique beings known. This stress or primal force comes from God's power to manifest his glory in his works. Because of their essential inscape and by means of their instress, all things in the natural world can serve to raise our minds and hearts to the Creator God constantly at work among us. Hopkins's beautiful sonnets celebrating nature provide us with his clearest statements of inscape and instress.

Hopkins's poems constantly return to a sense of the unity and wholeness of all things incorporated into the Body of Christ. Although all created things are unique, their common origin in Christ means that everything is connected to everything else. A major influence on Hopkins's thinking in this regard was the writing of the thirteenth-century British theologian, Duns Scotus. In Scotus, Hopkins found not only corroboration for his idea that all things contained an individual "self" derived from the Incarnation but also that humans could grasp by intuition a sense of the one unchanging God behind the diversity of the natural world. Poetry thus became for the author a vehicle for expressing God's presence in the world. As Philip Ballinger explains, "In the perception of something's self-expressiveness, its beauty, its inscape, Hopkins believed one perceives the unique 'Christic stem or selving' given in an individual reality. Furthermore, Hopkins held that this unique revelation given in each individual thing or experience could be conveyed to others through language, or more precisely, through poetic language. Therefore, for Hopkins, poetry had a truly sacramental function."[1]

Hopkins viewed the fact of Christ's Incarnation in the world as inseparable from the truth of the Real Presence of the Eucharist. To Catholics, the bread and wine consecrated at the Mass become Jesus himself, Body, Blood, Soul, and Divinity: they are not merely symbols of him or a type of memorial offering. Each time the priest pronounces the words of consecration over the gifts of the altar, Jesus' Incarnation, Passion, and death are reenacted, and this reenactment is taking place constantly throughout the world. Hopkins converted to the Roman Catholic faith partly because of his strong belief in the Real Presence, for he understood that without this belief Protestantism had become increasingly devoid of vitality and meaning. Moreover, for Hopkins, the sacrament of the Eucharist went beyond the altar to give energy to all of creation. Hopkins saw this constant reenactment, this continual self-giving of Christ, as the primal life force animating all things, the "spark" that ignites and sustains all that exists. Focused on the dynamic energy of Christ whose force quickens the universe, Hopkins frequently employs the language of physics in his poetry in his use of such words as "charged," "heat," "stress," "pitch," "fire," and the like. Even the hard stressed rhythm he favored, called Sprung Rhythm, was selected to express the energy pulsating throughout creation. "All things . . . are charged with love, are charged with God and if we know how to touch them give off sparks and take fire, yield drops and flow, ring and tell of him," he once wrote.[2]

The fact that Hopkins did not write to publish gave him the freedom to experiment boldly. His eccentric style has at times both baffled and delighted readers. He favored, for example, the sonnet, a traditional form of prosody consisting of fourteen lines and written in iambic pentameter. The Petrarchan version, which Hopkins primarily used, is divided into two main parts, an octave and a sestet, with each part employing two major end rhymes. In Hopkins's sonnets, the octave typically describes a concrete scene or experience, and the sestet broadens the perspective by meditating on its significance in universal and spiritual terms. But while adhering to sonnet form, Hopkins also bent the rules considerably at times. For example, some of his sonnets are more than fourteen lines long and some less, and his meter is usually irregular. Hopkins generally composed in the irregularly stressed rhythm called Sprung Rhythm because of its closeness to the cadence of natural speech and its ability to express strong emotions. In Sprung Rhythm, each line of the poem has a specific number of stresses, but the number of unstressed syllables can vary widely.

Hopkins's style is characterized by compression, ambiguity, paradox, and dramatic metaphors. Above all, he loved words and gave great attention to both their sound and meaning. His poems are stripped of all nonessential words, and every word used was carefully chosen and positioned by the poet to do the maximum amount of work. He especially favored archaic, monosyllabic words with Anglo-Saxon roots over Latinate-derived words because of the former's strong, powerful stress. His use of heavy-stressed single syllable words lends particular force to his writing, and, as noted, imitates the divine energy he saw as animating all of nature. Exercising considerable poetic license, Hopkins delighted in breaking syntactical rules and even created new words, such as "unleaving," "wanwood," and "leafmeal" (all of which appear in the poem, "Spring and Fall"). In his notebooks, he frequently jotted down strings of related words whose sound or etymology intrigued him.

Hopkins's best known and most characteristic poems, at once highly dramatic and profoundly spiritual, may be conveniently divided into two broad types: those praising the wonders and beauty of nature and nature's God, and those expressing intense spiritual and emotional pain. While representing radically different moods, both types complement each other and form a unity in the author's canon. They find precedent, for example, in the Psalms of David, which similarly reveal the intense emotional highs and lows of a sensitive life lived in the presence of God.

Poems Celebrating Nature and Nature's God

In a remarkable few months' time in 1877, while serving at St. Beuno's in North Wales, Hopkins composed ten nature sonnets expressing his strong sense of the sacramentality of the natural world through which God communicates his power and glory. Sustaining all creation, the energy of Christ cannot be contained but, as he puts it in "God's Grandeur," "will flame out, like shining from shook foil." Constantly being renewed in Christ, nature is always fresh and vibrant, always "telling" of the Godhead. Yet most adults lose a sense of wonder at the radiance of nature as they become consumed by toil for material gain and the routine cares of life. By close and prayerful observation of nature, however, the human spirit can be renewed and a sense of joy regained as the interconnectedness of all things in God is experienced. Hopkins's nature poetry provides us with a means to this renewal and deepening of the spiritual life through its call to contemplation. In fact, these sonnets are modeled on the structure of St. Ignatius of Loyola's *Spiritual Exercises* with which Hopkins, as a Jesuit, was quite familiar. Designed to lead the participant from the concrete to the spiritual realm, Ignatian meditation consists of three parts each of which engages one of the three aspects of the intellect. First, through the use of memory, the participant envisions or "composes" in the mind's eye a specific, detailed scene (for example, that of the Annunciation or Nativity); next, through the use of the understanding, the participant analyzes the scene's moral and spiritual meaning; finally, through the use of the will, the participant dialogues with God in prayer, recommitting him- or herself to God's will. The aim of such meditation is to imaginatively "enter into" certain aspects of the life of Christ and thus come to imitate him more fully. Each of Hopkins's nature poems follows the same pattern, from close observation of a particular natural object or scene, to meditation on its significance, to prayer and praise for its Creator. Such careful observation and contemplation—his encountering of God in the natural world—was at the heart of Hopkins's spiritual life.

Hopkins's sensitivity to the loveliness and intricacy of the natural world was strong. Beauty, he found, opens the heart to goodness and truth, and therefore to God. Each individual thing in creation and especially each human person reveals a part of God's astonishing fullness and magnificence. As Hopkins put it in one of his sermons, the world "is a book [God] has written, of the riches of his knowledge, teaching endless truths, full lessons of wisdom, a poem of beauty: what is it about? His praise, the reverence due to him, the way to serve him; it tells him of his glory."[3] Throughout his life, he was preoccupied with seeking beauty in nature, admiring for a certain period of time, for example, the shape, color, and form of a particular flower or tree and storing its impression carefully in his memory before moving his attention to another object. Thus he had at hand a bank or treasury of beautiful things to draw on as he composed his poetry.

While Hopkins shares the Romantics' delight in nature and expression of its sensuous beauty, he never merely celebrates the natural world for itself alone nor does he depict it as only a subjective projection of the mind. To him, nature is primarily an objective fact, created by and constantly pointing toward God who alone holds the key to its meaning.

"THE WINDHOVER"

This remarkable poem is among Hopkins's best known and certainly the most analyzed of his nature sonnets. "There is no other poem of comparable length in English, or perhaps in any language, which surpasses its richness and intensity or realized artistic organization," one critic has enthused.[4] Characteristic of the poet's original style and bursting with vivid imagery, "The Windhover" also expresses in full Hopkins's deeply sacramental view of nature. In the poem's octave, the narrator, speaking in first-person, observes ("catches") one morning a windhover—a falcon, or kestrel—as it soars and dips in controlled but graceful flight, presumably from the hand of its trainer. His enthusiasm mounting, the speaker finds himself deeply affected by the magnificent display: "My heart in hiding / Stirred for a bird,—the achieve of, the mastery of the thing!" But as the octave continues, we become aware that something more is occurring here. Our attention drawn back to the poem's dedication—"To Christ our Lord"—we begin to see that the poet is using the scene of the falcon in flight as an extended metaphor for Christ. Several clues in the octave, such as the word "Falcon" being capitalized, prompt the comparison.

These associations become clearer in the sestet, which is divided into two parts. In the first, still describing the bird's flight in breathless terms (note the buildup here of short, strong stressed words), the speaker tells us that all of the windhover's remarkable powers suddenly "Buckle!" resulting in even greater beauty now emanating from it. The poem's key word and one much discussed by critics, "buckle" is purposely ambiguous. On the one hand, it can mean "come together" or "merge," and thus the speaker, contemplating the scene, is able to grasp for a moment all the masterful attributes of the falcon in their totality. On the other hand, "buckle" can mean "to collapse" or "give way under pressure." This latter sense furthers the poem's metaphoric interpretation by suggesting Christ's twofold "fall": both the "fall" of his self-emptying *kenosis* in putting aside his Godhead in the Incarnation, and the "fall" of his ignominious Passion and death. Yet it is precisely through these sacrifices, the poet suggests, that "fire" "a billion / Times told lovelier, more dangerous" bursts forth from Christ. Returning to the several chivalric words of the octave, Jesus can be viewed, therefore, as both "dauphin" (a king's son) and "minion" (a servant), just as the falcon is both a proud and regal animal by nature but performs even more beautifully when tamed by submission to the falconer.

Finally, in the second part of the sestet, the poet meditates more fully on the fact that a certain energy or "shine" often comes through things that are "buckled." He gives us two examples: first, the slippery shine that appears when a piece of earth is trampled down by many feet; and, second, the bursting of embers into color when they fall in a fireplace. "No wonder of it," he concludes: such phenomenon seen in the natural world are readily applicable to the spiritual life. As Christ himself modeled for us, the dedicated life of sacrifice and service will result, in time, in true heroism and glory.

"PIED BEAUTY"

This beautiful poem, a shortened version of a sonnet, announces its theme in the first line: it praises God for "dappled things"—that is, for things in nature that are variously colored, irregularly shaped, or otherwise imperfect. Very often, we consider pleasing to the eye only those objects that are symmetrical or unblemished, but here the poet singles out for celebration those quirky and mottled items that lend rich diversity and delight to creation. In the initial sestet, the speaker provides numerous examples: a spotted cow, a rainbow-hued trout, autumn colored chestnut leaves, multicolored finches' wings, plots of farmland in various stages of cultivation, and, memorably, the panoply of human sporting activities, each of which comes with its own interesting array of "gear and tackle and trim."

In the work's second part, consisting of four and a half lines, the poet moves from a description of concrete particulars to a meditation on their significance in the spiritual realm. In doing so, he makes an important theological point. All that is "counter, original, spare" in creation, all the endless variety of the changing world, emanates from Christ who, paradoxically, does not change. The sheer wealth and diversity of nature should constantly prompt us to wonder at and glorify God's incredible creativity and bounty, the endless expansiveness and infinite multitude of his works. In God, all opposites and differences are reconciled: he is their source and sustainer. While such diversity-within-unity remains a mystery to us ("who knows how?"), the poet bids us, at the conclusion, simply to "Praise him."

"GOD'S GRANDEUR"

In this sonnet's octave, the speaker is awestruck while contemplating God's magnificent power and energy—his "grandeur"—which not only animates the world but gives off vibrant sparks of light like electricity or like "shining from shook foil." And for the poet, this divine energy pulsating through creation is not merely a pious speculation but an observable fact: God's glory within his works is palpable. Consequently, in line four, the speaker wonders why, given God's obvious power and presence in the world, many refuse to acknowledge his supremacy and submit to his rule ("reck his rod"). His answer to the rhetorical question he poses comes in the following quatrain when he postulates that, over the generations, humans have become so separated from nature they have grown insensitive to its wonders. Note how the threefold repetition of the word "trod" echoes the weariness and drudgery of human toil and evokes images of dirty, smoke-filled nineteenth-century industrial cities (such as Liverpool and Manchester where Hopkins worked for a time). Here, nature is denuded, covered over, and "shod" feet have lost primary contact with the earth. Yet despite this grim reality, the sestet concludes, the world is continually renewed and refreshed by the faithfulness of the Holy Spirit. Each morning brings with it a new invitation to experience God's marvels through the beauty of creation, if only we pause long enough to regain a childlike sense of wonder. The poem itself is a call to heed this invitation.

"AS KINGFISHERS CATCH FIRE"

This sonnet conveys explicitly Hopkins's theory of instress, the idea that all created things possess a unique essence, or "self," derived from Christ that on occasion makes itself known. In the first quatrain of the octave, the speaker gives us four examples of beings or things "selving" in the natural world, two visual and two auditory. Kingfishers and dragonflies catch light and flash as they fly through the air; stones thrown into a well ring out as they bounce off the sides; a bell tolls. After this accumulation of specific instances, the poet states his point directly: every living thing naturally produces an outward effect from the wellspring of that which is within; that is, each being reveals a unique self and has, according to God's ineffable plan, a particular purpose in the world. Each being, in effect, cries out to all who listen, *"What I do is me: for that I came."*

In the sestet, the poet deepens his argument to arrive at a profoundly spiritual and theological conclusion. After giving both inanimate and animate examples (stones, dragonflies), then generalizing about all living things, he now focuses specifically on human beings whose "selvings" are far more complex than all lower forms of nature because they are made in God's image. Following his theory, all people, the speaker suggests, manifest or demonstrate outwardly—that is, look, think, speak, or act—the depth of their interior life, what is going on in their hearts. Thus, a person who is "just," that is who keeps God's law and remains in a state of grace, will not only act justly but also spread justice at home, in the workplace—everywhere he or she goes in life. And when God sees the just person, he sees his own Son, Jesus, for it is only through the indwelling of God himself, through supernatural grace, that a person can be just. The person in a state of grace, therefore, while never losing his or her unique individuality and mission, is another Christ, for "Christ plays in ten thousand places, / Lovely in limbs, and lovely in eyes not his / To the Father through the features of men's faces."

Poems of Pain and Desolation: The Terrible Sonnets

Approximately eight years after the burst of creativity that produced his joyful nature sonnets, Hopkins penned a series of poems while working as a professor in Dublin that reflect a much altered mood. The Terrible Sonnets express great agony of heart, loneliness, spiritual dryness, disgust with the self, and, at times, a feeling of being trapped or imprisoned. Hopkins's sensitive nature was subject to bouts of *acedia*, or spiritual dryness, and the difficult years in Ireland seem to have augmented his emotional turmoil. Especially trying was the fact that during this time he felt he had lost poetic inspiration. Such spiritual and artistic aridity was not new; as early as 1879, he wrote to Robert Bridges that all feeling seemed gone, leaving him bereft both in his religious devotions and in his attempts to write poetry.[5] But unlike his Romantic predecessors who often cultivated what was then a "fashionable" sense of melancholy, Hopkins did not wallow in his increasing depression as much as strive to convert it through poetry into prayer.

St. Ignatius describes two common ways that God leads a person to himself, the way of consolation, when God draws the soul by beauty, joy, and light, and the way of desolation, characterized by "darkness of soul, turmoil of spirit, inclination to what is low and earthly, restlessness rising from many disturbances and temptations which lead to want of faith, want of hope, want of love. The soul is wholly slothful, tepid, sad, and separated, as it were, from its Creator and Lord."[6] The way of desolation or *via negativa* is a well-described step in the spiritual life, one that saints and spiritual writers such as John of the Cross, Teresa of Avila, and Thomas à Kempis have considered necessary in the ascent to God. In this stage, the anguish of interior pain, the disgust at one's self because of sin, and the sense of abandonment by God are purgative and lead the soul through interior darkness to a deeper, purer faith. In his agony on the cross, Jesus himself experienced some mysterious type of spiritual desolation, the "dark night of the soul," as he cried out to the Father, "My God, my God, why have you abandoned me?" Thus the Terrible Sonnets, which Hopkins said came to him against his will, express profound pain but never doubt God's existence or resort to despair. On the contrary, they acknowledge the "tormenting pangs of rebirth," crying out to God for relief and expressing trust in God's ways even in the midst of suffering and blindness.[7] In short, as a priest and a Jesuit, Hopkins well knew how to interpret his interior affliction in a Catholic context, as a means of purgation permitted by God to bring about spiritual growth. Certainly, the mystery of suffering is central to the Christian life and must be embraced as such. As Walter Ong explains, "Any suffering, accepted with love, has positive value; this conviction marks Christian belief from its beginnings. . . . In so far as we are aware of ourselves standing destitute before God, we are close to him, and he is close to us. This is hard, it is frightening, it is tough, and it is at the heart of Christian faith. It is also a declaration of total love. It is the cross on which Jesus died, stripped naked."[8] It is with this firm belief that Hopkins composed these poignant works. As Norman MacKenzie correctly states about the Terrible Sonnets, "What emerges in poem after poem is [Hopkins's] refusal to give way to his depression, or to believe that God is dead; just as in letter after letter during the

same period we find his astonishing mind busying itself with some rec-
ondite enquiry or exhilarated by some new insight. Even in the dark-
est hour he orientates himself towards the dawn."[9]

"I WAKE AND FEEL THE FELL OF DARK, NOT DAY"

This sonnet has been called the poet's *de profundis*, a cry of the heart
from the very depths of interior agony. As such, it echoes David's plea
in Psalm 130: "Out of the depths I cry to you, O Lord; Lord, here my
voice!" Anyone who has ever awakened in the middle of the night
alone and full of inner pain can comprehend the speaker's distress.
Awakening suddenly, the poet tells us he feels the "fell" of darkness, a
well-chosen word not only for its alliterative value in the line but also
because of its rich connotations. Related linguistically to the Old English word *pellis*, "fell" evokes the image of a smothering animal pelt
weighing the speaker down. But it also reminds us of the Fall itself, the
condition of original sin from which all human sorrow springs. The
speaker shudders as he recalls the horrible movements of his heart during the past long hours of spiritual darkness. Indeed, it is far more accurate, he realizes, to say that he has experienced such anguish not
merely for a matter of hours but for years. His whole life, in fact, has
been a failure; his agony of soul unrelieved. And his prayerful supplica-
tions for help seem to go unheeded: like dead letters, they appear to go
astray and don't even reach God.

In the sestet, the poet's descriptive words for himself, "I am gall, I
am heartburn," well express the depths of his misery. "Gall" recalls the
bitter herb offered to Jesus on the cross and thus ties the poet's suffering
to Christ's suffering. Moreover, the poet's heart "burns" with longing
not only for respite from his pain but also for Jesus, the "dearest him,"
who seems to have abandoned him. In all ways, Job-like, the speaker feels
chastised by God: bones, flesh, and blood are cursed. The "yeast" of his
spirit, too, is no longer able to raise the "dull dough" of his self. But the
poem ends on a note that, however tepid it may sound, confirms the
speaker's steadfast faith. He compares his own suffering, which he knows
imitates that of Christ and is thus potentially redemptive, to the suffering of unrepentant sinners ("the lost") and realizes that they are far
worse off that he. Not only does their earthly pain have no positive value
because of their lack of faith, but it will continue forever in hell whereas
his is only temporary.

"THOU ART INDEED JUST, LORD, IF I CONTEND"

This sonnet is prefaced by an epigraph in Latin, from Jeremiah 12, in which the prophet inquires of God why he allows wickedness to flourish on the earth. In the initial quatrain, the poet, addressing God directly but formally as "sir," echoes Jeremiah's lament by first asking generally, "why do sinners' ways prosper?" and then wondering why his own efforts, in contrast to the undertakings of those who don't serve God, constantly end in failure and disappointment.

In the poem's ten-line second paragraph, the poet acknowledges God as his "friend," but speculates that if God were actually his enemy he couldn't treat the speaker any worse than he is treating him now. This recalls Teresa of Avila's famous complaint to God, "If this is the way you treat your friends, no wonder you have so few!" The poet further notes how even the "sots and thralls of lust," that is, the drunkards and the lustful, appear to be rewarded in life whereas he, who has been faithful in God's work, is cursed. Then, turning his gaze from himself to the world around him, he points out to God how, now that it is spring, long-dormant nature has once again regained its vibrancy as leaves and flowers break out anew, a fresh wind blows, and birds prepare for their young by building nests. Signs of fertility and growth are everywhere. But there is no such similar renewal in the poet's spirit. Straining toward his goal, he feels merely powerless and unproductive in the face of passing time: he is "Time's eunuch." Thus the sonnet ends with a heartfelt prayer, a poignant request of God to refresh the poet's spirit even as he has so favored nature: "Mine, O thou lord of life, send my roots rain."

"MY OWN HEART LET ME MORE HAVE PITY ON"

This poem's structure involves a reversal, a sudden change in the poet's tone from the octave to the sestet. In the first four lines of the octave, the speaker, exhausted from intense self-criticism, resolves that hereafter he must try to have more pity on himself, to be more gentle and forgiving. In short, he knows he must do all he can to attempt to relieve his tormented mind and leave off such destructive overscrupulousness (note the powerful effect in these lines of the threefold repetition of "torment"). After all, God's command is that we love not only our neighbors but ourselves as well. In the next part of the octave, the speaker realizes that comfort is not to be found within himself, just as a blind man cannot find daylight in his darkness or a thirsty man at sea quench his thirst in the waters that surround him. The metaphors of blindness and thirst are powerful ones here, indicating the poet's extreme need and longing.

In the sestet, cajoling himself in mocking terms—"come, poor Jackself"—the speaker again advises himself to "let be; call off thoughts awhile." While he can't grasp at comfort or command it to come to him, he can make space for it within himself, anticipating that in time it will be given. And now comes the change in attitude as the poet, drawing on his faith, acknowledges that the possibility of joy is real and that God in his graciousness may bestow it on his creatures at any time. God's "smile" cannot be forced ("wrung") but comes in unexpected ways, just as light suddenly breaks from the sky between mountains to illuminate the darkness. (Note Hopkins's neologism here, "betweenpie," which means, roughly, "variously hued in lights and darks.") In faith and hope, the poet rests in the assurance that God will eventually open a path for him, easing his troubled heart.

"No Worst, There is None"

Perhaps the most terrible of the Terrible Sonnets, this poem expresses wrenching interior agony. "Pitched past pitch of grief," the poet has reached the far-flung regions of sorrow, and he anticipates that any future pain will be even worse than what he is now enduring. In anguish, he cries out to the Holy Spirit, the Comforter, and to Mary, the Mother of God, begging for the help they have promised. In the second quatrain, the speaker tells us that his greatest "woe" is less a specific pain than "world-sorrow." Thus he reminds us of original sin, the origin of all human suffering. Like the force of a hammer on an anvil, the first sin struck a brief but severe blow to all humankind, the effects of which he is now experiencing personally. As in the poem "I wake and feel the fell of dark, not day," described above, the word "fell" here is used intentionally to evoke the Fall.

The poem's sestet begins with the vivid image of steep "mountains" of the mind, treacherous cliffs where one may easily slip and fall at any moment. "Hold them cheap / May who ne'er hung there," the speaker warns: that is, only those who have never experienced such torture of the mind will take the poet's pain and fright lightly. And the only relief the speaker can muster from his inner torment is a mitigated one. "Here!" the poet tells himself: take comfort in the only comfort to be had: the thought that such agony *will* end at death, and that the torture of day *will* eventually be put to rest with sleep.

FOR FURTHER READING

St. Ignatius Loyola, *The Spiritual Exercises*
The Book of Psalms in the Old Testament

QUESTIONS FOR DISCUSSION

1. Pick two of Hopkins's sonnets described above and scan them for rhyme scheme and meter (that is, identify the pattern of the end rhymes by marking them with *a*'s, *b*'s, *c*'s, and so forth; and mark the stressed and unstressed syllables in each line). In what ways do these sonnets adhere to or deviate from traditional sonnet form? In the poems you choose, also discuss Hopkins's use of the following: alliteration, assonance, wordplay, metaphors or similies. If you are unfamiliar with these terms, look them up in a handbook on literature.
2. Discuss in detail Hopkins's theory of instress and inscape as it applies to the four nature sonnets discussed above.
3. In what ways might Hopkins's Terrible Sonnets be viewed as complementary to his nature sonnets?
4. Read through the Old Testament Psalms and comment on how David's understanding of himself before God may be likened to Hopkins's sense of self before God as revealed in his poetry. What other similarities exist between the Psalms and Hopkins's poetry?
5. Compare and contrast Hopkins with Annie Dillard in terms of both artists' view of the sacramentality of the natural world.
6. Choose two additional Hopkins's poems from the following to explicate: "The Starlight Night," "Spring," "Hurrahing in Harvest," "Spring and Fall," "Carrion Comfort," "Patience, hard thing!"

NOTES

Gerard Manley Hopkins, *"God's Grandeur" and Other Poems* (New York: Dover Publications, 1995). All references are to this edition.

1. Philip A. Ballinger, *The Poem as Sacrament: The Theological Aesthetic of Gerard Manley Hopkins* (Louvain, Belgium: Peeters Press, 2000), 20.
2. Christopher Devlin, ed., *The Sermons and Devotional Writings of Gerard Manley Hopkins* (London: Oxford University Press, 1959), 195.

3. Devlin, *The Sermons and Devotional Writings,* 239.

4. Herbert Marshall McLuhan, "The Analogical Mirrors," in *Gerard Manley Hopkins: The Windhover,* edited by John Pick (Columbus, OH: Charles E. Merrill, 1969), 24.

5. Claude Colleer Abbott, ed., *The Letters of Gerard Manley Hopkins,* 2nd edition (London: Oxford University Press, 1955), 66.

6. Louis J. Puhl, *The Spiritual Exercises of St. Ignatius* (Chicago: Loyola University Press, 1951), 142.

7. Jeffrey B. Loomis, *Dayspring in Darkness: Sacrament in Hopkins* (London: Associated University Presses, 1988), 142.

8. Walter J. Ong, *Hopkins, the Self, and God* (Toronto: University of Toronto Press, 1986), 147–48.

9. Norman H. MacKenzie, *A Reader's Guide to Gerard Manley Hopkins* (Ithaca, NY: Cornell University Press, 1981), 173.

BIBLIOGRAPHY

Bergonzi, Bernard. *Gerard Manley Hopkins.* New York: Macmillan, 1977.

Bump, Jerome. *Gerard Manley Hopkins.* Boston: Twayne, 1982.

Ellsberg, Margaret R. *Created to Praise: The Language of Gerard Manley Hopkins.* New York: Oxford University Press, 1987.

Loomis, Jeffrey B. *Dayspring in Darkness: Sacrament in Hopkins.* London: Associated University Presses, 1988.

MacKenzie, Norman H. *A Reader's Guide to Gerard Manley Hopkins.* Ithaca, NY: Cornell University Press, 1981.

Ong, Walter J. *Hopkins, the Self, and God.* Toronto: University of Toronto Press, 1986.

Walhout, Donald. *Send My Roots Rain: A Study of Religious Experience in the Poetry of Gerard Manley Hopkins.* Athens: Ohio University Press, 1981.

SIGRID UNDSET
KRISTIN LAVRANSDATTER

BIOGRAPHY

One of Norway's most renowned authors, Sigrid Undset was born in her mother's ancestral village of Kalundborg, Denmark, on May 20, 1882. When she was two, the family relocated to Oslo (then Kristiania), Norway. Sigrid's father, Ingvald Undset, was an internationally famous archeologist and author who passed on to his daughter a passion for Scandinavian history, mythology, and literature. Undset recalled her childhood as a happy one, with idyllic summers spent at her paternal grandparents' home in the Trondheim area of northern Norway. Ingvald was sickly, however, and when he died in 1893, Sigrid's mother, Charlotte Gyth Undset, was left in straitened circumstances with three young daughters to raise. At sixteen, Undset left school to work as a secretary for a German company in Oslo, a position she held for ten years although she found it tedious. To exercise both mind and body, she took long walks around the city with the intent of observing each neighborhood and the lives of ordinary working people. She also read broadly and deeply, especially in literature and history, and soon was trying her hand at writing fiction. When a publisher rejected her first attempt at a historical novel, she focused her next work on the life of a contemporary Oslo woman. *Mrs. Marta Oulie,* a realistic novel about infidelity in marriage told in the first person, was published in 1907 when Undset was twenty-five. Two other books soon followed, both of which sold modestly: *The Happy Age* (1908), a collection of short stories, and *Gunnar's Daughter* (1909), a short novel. The latter, set in early medieval Scandinavia and based on Old Icelandic sagas, is significant because it heralded

Undset's return to historical fiction, the genre that most interested her and for which she was particularly gifted.

In 1909, Undset received a writer's grant from the Norwegian government that allowed her to quit her office job and travel outside of the country. In Rome, she became acquainted with a group of expatriated Scandinavian writers and artists among whom she met the painter, Anders Castus Svarstad. Thirteen years older than Undset, Svarstad was married at the time, but he obtained a divorce and the couple wed in 1912. After a brief hiatus in London, they returned to Norway where, over the next few years, Undset bore three children while also caring for Svarstad's three children from his previous marriage. Their marriage, however, did not last, and upon their separation in 1919, Undset moved with her children to a house she had built on fifteenth-century foundations near Lillehamer, called Bjerkebaek. To support her family, she wrote continuously, often late at night once her household chores were done.

Such steady, disciplined writing resulted over the course of Undset's career in eleven novels, several collections of short stories, three autobiographical works, and many translations and essays. The 1911 *Jenny*, a frank story of a woman artist who, after a series of love affairs, commits suicide, shocked the public with its graphic realism but also served to make Undset known as an important author. Today, Undset is best known for her two epic masterpieces of historical fiction, the trilogy *Kristin Lavransdatter* (1920–1922) and the tetrology *The Master of Hestviken* (1925–1927). Both works were translated into numerous languages and made Undset famous around the world. In 1928, she was awarded the Nobel Prize in literature "for her powerful pictures of Norwegian life in medieval times."

Raised an agnostic, Undset converted to Roman Catholicism through her research in medieval Catholic Norway while writing *Kristin Lavransdatter*. Increasingly, she found herself attracted to the Church's central authority, consistent moral teaching, and incarnational emphasis. She was also drawn to the Catholic saints, whom she referred to as "God's friends." Because of her status as a prominent author, her conversion caused a sensation in staunchly Protestant Norway. Perhaps understandably, then, her later work tended toward didacticism as she sought to explain and defend Catholic teaching both in her essays and in such novels as *The Wild Orchid* (1929) and its sequel *The Burning Bush* (1930). Undset also penned a number of books with explicitly Catholic content, such as *Saga of Saints* (1934), which explores Norway's legendary saints such as St. Sunniva, St. Halvard, and St. Olav, and *Catherine of Siena* (1951), a posthumously published biography of the fourteenth-century Italian saint and Church reformer.

As Hitler's threat spread throughout Europe, Undset publicly denounced Nazism and took an active role in aiding refugees from Central Europe. As a result, the Nazis banned her books, and she was forced to flee Norway in 1940. After stops in Sweden, Russia, and Japan, she settled in the United States where her celebrity status enabled her to continue to speak out against Nazism and promote Scandinavian literature and culture in frequent speeches and articles. Undset returned to Norway at the end of the war, and in 1947 was awarded that country's highest honor, the Grand Cross of the Order of St. Olav, for her distinguished writing. Her last years spent in seclusion, she died at her home in Lillehamer in 1949.

CRITICAL OVERVIEW

Kristin Lavransdatter is a work so rich and intricate that it is all but impossible to discuss its many facets in a brief space. It is nothing less than an epic, a narrative intent on capturing the history, ideas, politics, customs, and religious practices of an entire culture, in this case fourteenth-century Norway. Like all superb works of literature, the trilogy of books that comprise *Kristin* are multilayered and can be approached by readers in various ways. As a meticulously researched historical document, the novel provides both a panoramic and intimate view of late medieval Scandinavian life. As a powerful love story, it relates a compelling tale of a passionate, tragic love affair with all its intrigues and complications. And as an outstanding work of Christian vision, the book immerses readers in a culture in which all aspects of daily life, both the mundane and transcendent, are permeated by faith. In each human heart, Undset tells us, lies the choice between hedonism and Christianity, between choosing to serve the self and choosing to serve God. The narrative illustrates this grand theme by focusing on one woman's life, that of Kristin, a strong willed and passionate child, wife, mother, and widow, who, like most of us, wants both choices at once and consequently struggles throughout life with the insecurity and lack of peace that result from a divided heart. Only toward the end of her difficult and lifelong spiritual journey does she surrender herself fully to God. As Erasmo Leiva-Merikakis has correctly noted, *Kristin Lavransdatter*'s overarching theme is "how the Beatitudes—thirst for justice, purity of heart, poverty of spirit, joy in suffering persecution for Christ's sake—gradually come to be *the* operative principles in a human heart, dramatically replacing ambition, lust, arrogance, and the spirit of self-promotion."[1] According to Undset, it often takes one's entire life and the hard lessons of experience to understand God's perspective and learn to trust his ways.

Kristin is grounded in history. By the time she began writing the novel, Undset had already spent years pouring over old Norse and Icelandic manuscripts, maps, laws, sagas, ballads, and other ancient texts. Thus, while *Kristin* is fiction, Undset set her work in such a real context that its content is almost entirely plausible. In fact, a number of characters were real persons: the several kings mentioned such as King Magnus, King Sverre, and King Haakon; the nobleman Erling Vidkunssön who figures prominently in the trilogy's second book; Munan Baardsön, Erlend Nikolaussön's friend and cousin; and Lady Groa, the stately abbess of the Nonneseter convent. Even Erlend's manor house, Husaby, was an actual estate located near Nidaros (current day Trondheim), the foundations of which are still visible. Undset's realism also extends to the geography of the country as well as its flora and fauna. But in recreating the medieval past so closely, the author was not merely indulging in sentimental or nostalgic longing for an ideal culture. Rather, writing about the past lent her the perspective she needed to explore her themes of the troubled human heart, the mystery of life, and the ability of the Catholic faith to answer the deepest needs of our being. To Undset, human nature, with its wayward desires and great potential for good or evil, essentially remains the same across times and cultures. Thus, while *Kristin Lavransdatter* is firmly situated in a particular historical moment, its themes are universal and timeless.

Undset also chose to set *Kristin Lavransdatter* in fourteenth-century Norway because she found this era to be an especially interesting period of transition. By the time the novel opens, Christianity, which in comparison to the rest of Europe had come late to Scandinavia, had been practiced in Norway for only three hundred years. Condemning the worship of the Viking pagan gods such as Thor, Woden, and their underworld entourage of elves, gnomes, and trolls, King Olav Haraldssön, who reigned from 1016 to 1030, established Christianity in Norway and was later proclaimed a saint by the people although he was never officially canonized by the Catholic Church. The Christian-based laws he introduced with the document known as "St. Olav's Code of Laws" countered in almost every way the Viking notion of virtue, replacing, for example, the Viking right to allow the weak and elderly to die by exposure with a new concept of human dignity that gave preference to the poor, suffering, and sick. But such a radically new set of beliefs did not simply supplant long-entrenched habits overnight. For several hundred years at least after Olav's time, pagan customs and superstitions vied with new Christian ways, with the older practices tending to surface, as Undset demonstrates throughout the novel, in times of stress. In *Kristin*, moreover, Undset raises the historical and literal alteration between paganism and Christianity in medieval Norwegian culture to a figurative level as she develops her point that all human beings are inwardly torn between such "pagan" desires as selfishness, anger, envy, ambition, lust, and pride, and the Christian virtues of self-sacrifice, humility, generosity, patience, fidelity, and forgiveness. An inner struggle—the constant downward pull of unredeemed human nature versus the upward movement of the Christian spirit—thus underscores Undset's view of the human condition. In fact, Undset was convinced that the arrival of the Catholic Church in Norway served to counteract the natural downward spiral of unchecked human passions exemplified by Viking hedonism and thus enabled Norwegian civilization to rise to new heights, a subject she discusses at length in the opening essay to her volume, *Saga of Saints.*[2]

Kristin Lavransdatter provides us with an intricate portrait of a society in which lives are fully lived in a Catholic context. Undset's God is omnipresent, all powerful and all knowing, secretly guiding humans with a firm yet loving hand. While Jesus' sacrifice atoned for sin, humans have free will and can choose in pride, passion, or selfishness to turn away from the good and thus determine their own fate. Although moments of joy do occur, life on this earth is more often a "vale of tears" where humans must work out their salvation in fear and trembling. Even small actions have wide-ranging consequences and help to forge the course of an individual's path either to or away from God. In this culture, life is viewed as a pilgrimage, a journey aided at every step by the many helps the Church provides for the wayfarer, such as the sacraments, the examples of the saints, devotional practices, and the disciplines of fasting, almsgiving, and prayer. Here, time is marked in the Catholic way by reference to the liturgical calendar of feast days, fast days, and saints' days. The village church plays a central role in the people's spiritual and civic lives, and the parish priest, as teacher, doctor, counselor, and bringer of the sacraments, is an all important figure.

The trilogy, therefore, provides us with a thorough education in the inculturation of faith; that is, how religious belief is lived and expressed in a particular time and place. It is interesting to contrast the norms of

Undset's Norwegian medieval Catholic culture with, for example, American Protestant–based culture. Immediately striking is the fact that the existence of an objectively acknowledged common faith in Undset's Norway means that familial and community bonds take on far more significance than American individualism allows for. Undset's narrative repeatedly suggests that human actions should be centered on objective reason, not subjective emotion, and must also take into account their effect on others. The good of the group is always to be preferred over the fulfillment of an individual's desire. By portraying in fascinating detail the ripple effect that selfish decisions and individual sins produce in a close-knit community, Undset succeeds in conveying a vital sense of the universal brotherhood of all humans within the Body of Christ. In acting on passion alone, the teenaged Kristin makes rash choices in a streak of independence that flies in the face of her careful upbringing under the tutelage of her devout father and mother. In their far-reaching consequences, her actions not only shape the course of her own mental, emotional, and spiritual health and her relationships, but also deeply mark the lives of others. In the Augustinian-like struggle between head and heart, flesh and spirit, that Kristin experiences as a result of her sin, Undset's point is clear although guaranteed to be an unpopular one today: "doing one's own thing" does not bring true freedom or inner peace, but rather can irrevocably harm the self and others.

Kristin Lavransdatter has rightly been called one of the most fully realized characters in all of literature. In Kristin, Undset presents a vivid and complete portrait of a remarkably strong and complex woman, a character who, as Maura Boland notes, is one of very few romantic heroines who are allowed to grow old.[3] Book 1 of the trilogy, *The Bridal Wreath*, focuses on her girlhood and marriage; book 2, *The Mistress of Husaby*, her middle years as wife and mother; and book 3, *The Cross*, her old age and widowhood. The beautiful daughter of Lavrans Björgulfsön and his wife Ragnfrid, Kristin grows up on the family's farm of Jörundgaard in the Sil valley. Throughout the novel, Undset develops her themes through numerous comparisons and contrasts. Early in *The Bridal Wreath*, therefore, two contrasting scenes, that of the lure of the elf-maiden and that of Kristin's first meeting with the saintly monk, Brother Edvin, establish the trilogy's major theme. Camping overnight with her father in a wooded area, seven-year-old Kristin is enticed by the elf-maiden who extends to her a golden garland, a symbol of the choice of selfish desires and worldly delights. Note especially the striking Narcissus image here as Kristin, just prior to the sprite's appearance, studies her own face approvingly in the stream. We will be reminded of this image at the end of the book. Later, we will learn that the supposed witch-woman, Lady Aashild, reminds Kristin of the elf-maiden, and Lady Aashild's nephew Erlend is, by extension, continually equated with the hedonistic pleasures of the mountain king's domain. It is Lady Aashild, moreover, who sows in Kristin's mind the seeds of discontent for the fat and jovial Simon Darre, Kristin's father's choice of a suitor, in favor of the dark-haired, lean, sorrowful-eyed Erlend. But for now the child Kristin pulls back from the elf-maiden in fright, rejecting what she offers. Lavrans throws his great cross around her neck for protection, a relic she will wear on her breast throughout her life.

Yet, significantly, while later walking with Brother Edvin through Hamar Cathedral, Kristin also turns down his suggestion that she give herself totally to God as a nun, for she had no desire to relinquish her "heritage of health and beauty and love" (*Bridal Wreath*, 62). Edvin invites her to climb up the scaffolding in order to view the magnificent colored light streaming into the dark, cold cathedral through a stained glass window of Christ, an image of God's transforming grace poured out on the world. But he also tells her soberly in words she cannot yet fully comprehend of the fate awaiting those persons who both covet all the world offers yet wish to live in God's joy and peace. A heart divided in this way only produces unhappiness and dissatisfaction, he explains. Thus are we provided with the key to Kristin's lifelong inner turmoil.

At the age of fifteen, Kristin is betrothed by mutual consent of their fathers to Simon Darre, a worthy young man and a fitting husband for her in terms of social rank. As the wedding draws near, she secretly parts from her childhood friend, Arne, and on her way back from their clandestine meeting, is attacked and nearly raped by the drunken man, Bentein. Here again Undset proceeds by way of contrasts, with the two encounters representing the opposition between an innocent yet immature love and the negative force of unrestrained human passions. Her young mind confused, Kristin begs her father to allow her to spend a year with the sisters at Oslo before she is wed to Simon. Although in the convent she is expected to learn to obey, ironically Kristin does just the opposite. Now discontent with her betrothed, Simon, she easily falls under the spell of the charming Erlend Nikolaussön, an older man with a checkered past that includes a longtime mistress, Eline, two children born out of wedlock, and a ban by the Church. Erlend seduces Kristin, but she is not unwilling. Stirred by passion, Kristin is soon deceiving her way out the convent to meet Erlend at a brothel in town. Here we see, then, the alteration between convent and brothel, the spiritual love of *agape* and the passionate love of *eros*, made manifest in Kristin who, with her well-formed conscience, is aware of her transgressions against both God and family yet cannot halt her wayward actions. Only now does she understand the words Brother Edvin spoke to her years before of the struggles of the divided heart, and she also realizes the need for a Redeemer to heal such division. "When I was a girl at home," she tells Edvin when she seeks him out for counsel, "'twas past my understanding how aught could win such power over the souls of men that they could forget the fear of sin; but so much have I learnt now: if the wrongs men do through lust and anger cannot be atoned for, then must heaven be an empty place" (142).

Although Lavrans strongly opposes the union between Erlend and Kristin, Kristin holds out against her father until, broken down by her resistance, he consents. But the wedding day, achieved with much scheming and deceit, is not the joyous occasion it should be. By now, Kristin has soberly realized that sin's results are far-reaching. In disobeying her parents, hurting her relationship with her family, deceiving the nuns at the convent, engaging in sexual relations with Erlend while yet betrothed to another man, and even being implicated in Eline's death by suicide, Kristin's transgressions have harmed not only herself but many others as well. As she stands before the altar offering up the customary golden garland, emblem of virginal purity, she is nearly overcome with guilt and sorrow—as well as the secret fear of her pregnancy, hidden even from Erlend. She feels utterly alone, cut off from all that had previously tied her to family and community. This is Undset's point. Flouting God's law and pursuing selfish ends with little or no consideration of others has not brought Kristin self-fulfillment or peace but rather self-doubt, guilt, and a trail of harmed or broken relationships.

But does it follow, then, that Kristin is wrong to choose Erlend as her husband rather than merely submit as a dutiful daughter to her father's desire that she marry Simon? The answer is no. Kristin clearly loves Erlend over Simon, and although he has many faults, Erlend's love for Kristin is unquestioned. For his part, Simon, it can be argued, doesn't really love Kristin: when Lavrans puts the question to him directly, he only answers that he "know[s] her worth" (86). Still, Simon is a good, simple man, a "family boy" as Andrew Lytle aptly calls him, and throughout the trilogy he is contrasted with the dashing but heedless Erlend.[4] When Simon bursts in on Kristin and Erlend in the brothel and insists that she accompany him back to the convent, Kristin to her shame recognizes his superiority over Erlend. But the novel is not as concerned with weighing the relative merits of one man against the other as it is with depicting the choice presented to Kristin of a predictable, conventional marriage on the one hand and a passionate, adventurous one on the other: the choice between head and heart, reason and passion. Kristin pays dearly for choosing Erlend, but one can't disapprove of her choice. As such, the novel comments on the inscrutable complexity of the human heart. At one point in the last book of the trilogy, *The Cross*, Kristin muses on the fact that although Simon had proven to be all Erlend was not in terms of courage, generosity, and service, she had never once been able to love him. Thus does Kristin's saga echo the wondering cry of the prophet Jeremiah: "More tortuous than all else is the human heart, beyond remedy; who can understand it?"[5]

If Undset had ended *The Bridal Wreath* with a happy wedding scene, readers would have a satisfying, utterly conventional romantic tale: after much struggle, the beautiful girl finally wins her handsome knight and they ride off into the sunset to live happily ever after. But Undset is a realist, and a Christian realist at that. At the end of *The Bridal Wreath*, the novel has actually just begun: Undset has much more to tell us about the consequences of sin and the slow, often painful process of growth toward spiritual maturity. *The Mistress of Husaby* focuses on Kristin's marriage to Erlend. The time frame of this dramatic book extends from about 1319 to 1335. Initially dismayed at how Erlend's wasteful ways have deteriorated the once-grand estate of Husaby, the young wife works tirelessly to restore the large property to its former glory although at times her longing for her mother and father and for the order and peace of Jörundgaard almost overwhelms her. When Erlend finds out that Kristin is pregnant and, indeed, had been so at their wedding, his desire to redeem his good name in the community with an honorable marriage is bitterly shattered. On Kristin's part, the nagging resentment she began to feel for Erlend even before they were wed now increases with each slight. Although great moments of joy and forgiveness occur between the couple over the course of their relationship, far more common are tensions and misunderstandings. "When Erlend was in question," Undset tells us, "[Kristin] could forget nothing, and every least scratch on her soul went on smarting and bleeding" (*Mistress of Husaby*, 307). "You are slow to forgive," Erlend admonishes his wife at one point, a judgment that is correctly levied against the stubborn and brooding Kristin (52).

In the early months at Husaby, Kristin has reason to brood, for she is in tremendous dread for the child she is carrying. An Old Norse superstition maintained that a pregnant woman who gazed at a burning building, as Kristin had when the church caught fire, would give birth to a monster. This superstition mingles in her worried mind with the fear that a vengeful God seeks to punish her for her sins. Thus at her wedding she vows a pilgrimage to the tomb of St. Olav if her child is born healthy. Undset's depiction of the birth of Kristin's first son is one of the most harrowing scenes in all of literature. But little Nicholas, nicknamed Naakkve, arrives healthy, and Kristin fulfills her promise by walking the twenty-mile pilgrim's route to the great cathedral at Nidaros, alone, barefoot, and carrying her baby. Looking down from the Feginsbrekka, the Hill of Joy above the city, she experiences an overwhelming sense of God's love and forgiveness. In fact, throughout the novel Undset intersperses such "high" moments of life, those fleeting times when we grasp the "larger" picture of our lives in divine perspective, with our more usual view of ourselves as enmeshed in daily cares and responsibilities. This high moment on the mountain top echoes that on the scaffolding in Hamar Cathedral when the young Kristin saw the world and herself bathed in the light of Christ.

But the peace and comfort Kristin finds during her pilgrimage of atonement to Nidaros Cathedral does not last. Responsible for all the work of running Husaby, and bearing child after child—eight sons in all—she is consumed with cares and worries as the years fly by. Although Kristin and Erlend love each other deeply, their intense emotional love does not easily weather the continual demands of daily life and child raising. Although courageous in war and adventure, Erlend is restless at home, dislikes husbandry, and is often untrustworthy and unwise in small matters. With a house full of small children and a peevish, often sickly wife, he increasingly prefers to be away from home. Impatient and restless herself, the quick-tempered Kristin above all can never relax her need to exercise control: an exalted sense of responsibility enslaves her to constant anxiety. In fact, one of Undset's superb skills in this novel is her close analysis of the nuances of human relationships. An extraordinarily sensitive observer, she illustrates how the smallest of things—a cold or unthinking word, a sudden urge to be mean spirited, a betrayal—can undermine the relationship between husband and wife. In a telling scene in *The Mistress of Husaby*, Erlend's brother, Gunnulf, a priest, reminds Kristin in her anguish of the consequences of the Fall: when sin entered the world, the flesh rebelled against the spirit and strife and misunderstanding between persons spread. All human love, Gunnulf points out, is but a shadow of divine love and more often than not produces greater sorrow than joy. Yet through and even because of such struggles, love can be purified and elevated to the level of true charity. We see this occur, for example, in the relationship between Lavrans and Ragnfrid, who despite pain and misunderstandings in their marriage succeed in achieving a deep and true love for each other, an *agape* love. Their marriage serves as a contrast to that of Erlend and Kristin.

Part two of *The Mistress of Husaby* introduces a new and dramatic plot involving political intrigue. And here once again Undset demonstrates her historical acumen, for while Erlend's scheme to depose the king and set up a rival in Norway is fictional, its context is factual and, in fact, the plot very well could have occurred exactly as planned.[6] In 1319, three-year-old Magnus Eirikssön rose as heir to the throne of both of the kingdoms of Norway and Sweden. But as Magnus came of age, he took far more interest in Sweden, a fact that caused dissatisfaction with his rule among Norway's citizens. In Undset's narrative, Erlend spearheads a plot to regain Norway's independence by setting up Magnus's half brother, Haakon Knutssön, as king of that country. Had the plan succeeded, Erlend would certainly have been regarded as a national hero and given a high-ranking leadership position. It is thus no small irony that his plans are thwarted by his own foolish indiscretion: he accidentally drops an incriminating letter in the bedroom of Lady Sunniva, with whom he has had a brief affair. Arrested for treason and tortured on the rack, Erlend refuses to reveal the names of those who collaborated with him. In yet another ironic twist, Simon, now kin to Kristin and Erlend through his marriage to Kristin's sister, Ramborg, helps Kristin work to free his longtime rival from prison. While Erlend manages to escape with his life, he is forced to forfeit all of his wealth. In this second book of the trilogy, the depiction of a society rocked by political agitation serves to mirror the inner turmoil of Kristin as, throughout her years as wife and mother, her heart swings repeatedly between worries and cares and all-too-fleeting moments of happiness and peace.

In *The Cross*, which covers the period from about 1335 to 1349, Kristin's growth to both physical and spiritual maturity reaches completion. With their property confiscated, Erlend, Kristin, and their sons retreat back to Kristin's inherited childhood farm of Jörundgaard where they live uneasily among neighbors who scorn Erlend for his treason and still regard Kristin as Lavrans Bjorgulfssön's undutiful daughter. Although she has promised herself that she will not blame Erlend for their misfortune, Kristin cannot contain her resentment over all they have lost. She agonizes continuously about her growing sons' future and, finally, her frustration reaches its peak when she one day accuses Erlend of not being as worthy a man as Lavrans. At this point, Erlend has had enough. He leaves her and moves, ironically, to the "haunted" croft of Haugen, the former home of the ill-fated couple, Lady Aashild and Bjorn. When Kristin gives birth to her eighth and last son, she is accused of committing adultery with her house servant, Ulf. Returning to Jörundgaard to defend his wife's name, Erlend is slain in a fight and dies like a pagan hero, "unshriven and un-houseled" (*Cross*, 298).

"All fires burn out at last," the narrator tells us (269). After Erlend's death, each of Kristin's grown sons, except one, leaves home to seek his fortune. Gaute, the only son interested in running the farm, brings home a wife, Jofrid, and Kristin soon has her first grandchild. But as Gaute and Jofrid assume the management of Jörundgaard, Kristin begins to feel pushed aside and useless. Thus, she sets out upon her final journey, walking once again the pilgrim's road to Nidaros to seek entrance to the convent at Rein. Now that she has been forced to let go of all her authority and possessions, a transformation takes place: her lifelong impatience, anxiety, and bitterness give way to a new spiritual calm and acceptance. As she mounts the Feginsbrekka for the last time, she achieves the grace of Christian perspective, the ability to see her life through the work of Christ's Incarnation and Redemption. She now understands that at the end of her journey

> there waited for her one who had ever beheld the life of mankind as men's parishes look, seen from the mountain brow. He had seen the sin and sorrow, the love and hate, in the hearts of men, as one sees the rich manors and the humble cots, the teeming cornfields and the aban-doned wastes, all borne on the bosom of the same countryside. And he had descended; his feet had trodden the peopled lands, and stood in palaces and in huts; he had gathered up the sorrows and the sins of rich and poor, and lifted them aloft with him upon a cross. (362–63)

On this earth, Undset reminds us, we can only achieve glimpses of God's ways and only partially comprehend the relative insignificance of all earthly strivings in the overarching plan of salvation.

Kristin spends just a short time in the Rein convent when the Black Plague erupts. As the horror of the disease spreads, eventually killing nearly half of Norway's population, desperation seizes the people. While helping the sisters nurse the sick and dying, Kristin takes the lead in rescuing a young boy, Tore, who is about to be sacrificed to the pest-goddess Hel by a group of men who, in terror, have resorted to pagan practices. In response to the men's challenge, she also recovers and buries the body of the boy's prostitute mother, Steinum, already dead several days in her isolated hut by the sea. Kissing the dead woman's foot, Kristin realizes that, before God, she who now aspires to become a nun is no better than the prostitute, for all are sinners equally in need of salvation. Thus the trilogy returns once more to the opposition of brothel and convent, the image of the divided self now seen as healed by the grace of God. In Christ, head and heart, flesh and spirit, are reconciled. As she herself succumbs to the plague, Kristin offers up her only remaining possessions, Lavran's relic cross and her wedding ring, to have masses said for the dead woman. As she removes the ring from her finger and sees that the mark left behind looks like an "M" for the Virgin Mary, she understands clearly that, despite all the troubles in her life and her own sins and failings, "God had held her fast in a covenant made for her without her knowledge by a love poured out upon her richly. . . . A handmaiden of God had she been—a wayward, unruly servant . . . yet had he held her fast in his service" (*Cross*, 401).

Kristin's brave act of rescuing Tore from the open pit where he is about to be buried alive culminates the book's theme of the alteration in this late medieval society between pagan and Christian values. Likewise, her act signals the completion of Kristin's inner transformation. Erasmo Leiva-Merikakas interprets this dramatic event on three levels. Kristin's act of charity is courageous and selfless, showing her inner change: "The 'new-kindled fire' within her, fueling her boldness, is now no longer the burning of self-will and lust, but the thirst for divine charity and justice." Secondly, the scene illustrates the transforming power of the Catholic Church "in the midst of a ruthless society, nominally Christianized some three hundred years before yet still in the throes of the struggle between Christianity and paganism." And finally, the scene strongly conveys the "good news" of Christ's Redemption: "When Kristin raises Tore out of the open grave, we are witnessing the power of the Resurrection entering the world. . . . [W]e see the Church bringing the light of Resurrection-faith to the older Nordic grimness."[7]

Undset's careful structure thus brings this last volume of the trilogy, *The Cross*, full circle from the first volume, *The Bridal Wreath*. The cross Lavrans has placed for protection against pagan evil around the child Kristin's neck when she took fright upon seeing the elf-maiden and which she wears throughout her life becomes a symbol of the crosses Kristin and all Christians must bear throughout life: the cross of circumstances, the cross of the consequences of our own choices, the cross of bearing with others' faults, the cross of our own wayward temperaments, sins, and failings. Carrying the cross means accepting what is counter to human desires and thus always entails an inner struggle. And everywhere we turn in life we meet the cross. "The preachers of God's word were right," Kristin now realizes through her own experience. "The life of the body was tainted with unrest beyond all cure; in the world where men mixed, begot new generations, were driven together by fleshy love, and loved their own flesh, there came heart-ache and broken hopes, as surely as rime comes in autumn" (338). Yet God's mercy and love can use our sufferings, trials, and temptations, for our salvation. Thus astonishingly "in her final moment, Kristin realizes that the marriage she had chosen was not her lifelong torment but God's instrument of her salvation."[8]

Perhaps the greatest strength of Undset's epic tale is that through it we can observe what we often cannot see in our own lives: the divine plan at work in the world despite our choices and failings. Undset succeeds in portraying the great dignity of each human being, the consequences of free will, and God's loving and providential action in the lives of those he leads by winding paths. In *Kristin Lavransdatter*, God is "omnipresent, and men are part of him, never outside his knowledge or attention, never in any real sense, in this life, separated from him. . . . God is the still center of change, the calm at the heart of the universe, the silence at the center of our fretful lives."[9] Despite the suffering of life and the agony of our own deeply divided spirits, Undset's vision of human nature is, in the end, a profoundly hopeful one, for God uses and restores to us what we have lost or squandered by sin or foolishness. The novel thus invites us to renew our trust in God, for trust is needed to have faith that God is caring for us despite our wavering spirits, in mysterious and unfathomable ways.

A superb storyteller with a profoundly Catholic sensibility, Sigrid Undset refused to shy away from the hard truths of life. She once advised Catholic writers:

> Tell the truths you have to. Even if they are grim, preposterous, shocking. After all, we Catholics ought to acknowledge what a shocking business human life is. Our race has been revolting against its Creator since the beginning of time. Revolt, betrayal, denial, or indifference, sloth, laziness—which of us has not been guilty in one or more or all of these sins some time or other? But remember, you have to tell other and more cheering truths, too: of the Grace of God and the endeavor of strong and loyal, or weak but trusting souls, and

also of the natural virtues of man created in the Image of God, an image it is very hard to efface entirely.[10]

"A monument of the human imagination," *Kristin Lavransdatter* embraces all of life deeply lived in the presence of God and in doing so indeed confirms the dignity of human nature made in God's image.[11]

FOR FURTHER READING

Sigrid Undset, *Catherine of Siena*
————, *The Master of Hestviken*
————, *Saga of Saints*
Jacobus de Voragine, *The Golden Legend*. This compilation of saints' legends was extremely popular throughout the Middle Ages. Often more imaginative than factual, it makes for fascinating reading and provides helpful background information for medieval pious beliefs and practices.

QUESTIONS FOR DISCUSSION

1. As Gunnulf suggests to Kristin when he counsels her, her story—and all our stories—replicate Redemption history: Innocence, Fall, and Restoration (*Mistress of Husaby*, 139). In what ways does Undset pattern the entire work on this theme?
2. At the end of *The Bridal Wreath*, we learn why Ragnfrid's mood is often "heavy" or dark. How is Kristin both like and unlike her mother? How does the marriage of Lavrans and Ragnfrid serve as a contrast to that of Erlend and Kristin?
3. Chapter 1 of *The Mistress of Husaby* is entitled "The Fruit of Sin." Although Kristin thinks that God's anger at her sins will result in a deformed child, she comes to learn that God does not operate in this manner. To Undset, sin's consequences are seen primarily in the sadness and confusion of broken relationships, broken families, and personal guilt and anguish. Discuss in detail how "the fruit of sin" can be seen throughout the novel.
4. Describe Erlend in detail. What kind of a man is he; what are his faults and his virtues? What do we discover throughout the novel about his own self-knowledge and spiritual growth? Also,

consider his similarity to, or contrast with, his priest-brother Gunnulf.

5. At various times in the novel, we enter Simon Darre's point of view. What are his faults and virtues? What are his lifelong struggles as a result of losing Kristin, and how does he react to them? Especially consider the scene of his death where he is intent on telling Kristin one thing but finds himself saying another (*Cross*, 196).

6. What other "high" scenes or "mountain top views" occur in the novel, and what perspective on her life does Kristin gain from them?

NOTES

Sigrid Undset, *The Bridal Wreath*, vol. 1 of *Kristin Lavransdatter*, translated by Charles Archer and J. S. Scott (1923; New York: Vintage/Random House, 1987); *The Mistress of Husaby*, vol. 2 of *Kristin Lavransdatter*, translated by Charles Archer (1925; New York: Vintage/Random House, 1987); *The Cross*, vol. 3 of *Kristin Lavransdatter*, translated by Charles Archer (1927; New York: Vintage/Random House, 1987). All references are to these editions.

1. Erasmo Leiva-Merikakis, "Sigrid Undset: Holiness and Culture," in *Sigrid Undset: On Saints and Sinners*, edited by Deal W. Hudson (San Francisco, CA: Ignatius Press, 1993), 70.

2. Sigrid Undset, "The Coming of Christianity to Norway," in *Saga of Saints* (New York: Longmans, Green, and Co., 1934).

3. Maura Boland, "Rediscovering Sigrid Undset," *Commonweal* 107 (November 7, 1980): 622.

4. Andrew Lytle, *Kristin* (Columbia: University of Missouri Press, 1992), 32.

5. Jeremiah 17:9, *New American Bible*.

6. A thorough summary of the political situation that forms the context of *The Mistress of Husaby* can be found in Sherrill Harbison's introduction to the Penguin edition of the novel (1999).

7. Leiva-Merikakis, "Sigrid Undset," 65, 66.

8. Mitzi M. Brunsdale, "A Lifetime of Penance for an Hour of Happiness: The Life and Fiction of Sigrid Undset," in *Sigrid Undset: On Saints and Sinners*, edited by Deal W. Hudson (San Francisco, CA: Ignatius Press, 1993), 136.

9. J. C. Whitehouse, "Religion as Fulfillment in the Novels of Sigrid Undset," *Renascence* 38, no. 1 (1985): 10–11.

10. Sigrid Undset, "Truth and Fiction," *America* 67 (June 13, 1942): 270.

11. David A. Bovenizer, "Mr. Lytle's 'Kristin,'" in *Sigrid Undset: On Saints and Sinners*, 154.

BIBLIOGRAPHY

Bayerschmidt, Carl F. *Sigrid Undset*. New York: Twayne, 1970.

Boland, Maura. "Rediscovering Sigrid Undset." *Commonweal* 107 (November 7, 1980): 620–23.

Brunsdale, Mitzi M. "Stages on Her Road: Sigrid Undset's Spiritual Journey," *Religion and Literature* 23, no. 3 (Fall 1991): 83–96.

Hudson, Deal W., ed. *Sigrid Undset: On Saints and Sinners*. San Francisco, CA: Ignatius Press, 1993.

Lytle, Andrew. *Kristin*. Columbia: University of Missouri Press, 1992.

McCarthy, Colman. "Sigrid Undset," *Critic* 32 (January–February 1974): 59–64.

Whitehouse, J. C. "Religion as Fulfillment in the Novels of Sigrid Undset." *Renascence* 38, no. 1 (1985): 2–12.

Winsnes, A. H. *Sigrid Undset: A Study in Christian Realism*. Translated by P. G. Foote. New York: Sheed & Ward, 1953.

GRAHAM GREENE
THE POWER AND THE GLORY

BIOGRAPHY

Born on October 2, 1904, at Berkhamsted in Hertfordshire, England, Graham Greene was the fourth of the six children of Charles Henry Greene and Marion Raymond Greene. As a youth, he boarded at an Anglican school where his father was headmaster, an experience that proved traumatic for the sensitive young man who found his classmates cruel and who was painfully aware that only a single door separated him—literally—from his comfortable family home. The feeling of straddling the border between two existences, of living a type of double life, haunted him for years and emerges repeatedly in his writing. Greene's emotional upheaval during this period resulted in several suicide attempts, and his family took the radical move of arranging for him to live with a London psychiatrist. Six months later, he returned home cured. In 1922, Greene entered Balliol College at Oxford University to study modern history. He received a Bachelor of Arts degree three years later, in 1925.

As an undergraduate, Greene began to pursue an interest in writing that had been sparked at the age of fourteen upon reading Marjorie Bowan's *The Viper of Milan*. While still at Oxford, he published his first book, *Babbling April*, a collection of verses. He also contributed articles and reviews to the school newspaper. One of his reviews elicited strong response from a Catholic young woman, Vivien Dayrell-Browning, who wrote to correct his erroneous statement that Catholics "worship" the Virgin Mary. Greene began dating Vivien and soon also commenced instruction in the Catholic faith. He entered the Church in 1926 and he and Vivien were wed the following year. The couple had two children,

Lucy Caroline, born in 1933, and Francis, born in 1936, before separating permanently, although never divorcing, in the 1940s.

After Oxford, Greene at first pursued a career as a journalist. However, while he was yet in his early twenties, his historical novel *The Man Within* (1929) achieved such critical acclaim that, securing an advance from his publisher, he quit his newspaper job to write fiction full time. The two historical romances that followed sold poorly. But then in 1932 came the contemporary thriller, *Stamboul Train* (released in the United States as *Orient Express*), a huge success and the first of many Greene novels to be made into popular films.

In 1934, at the age of thirty-one, Greene set out on a walking tour across Liberia. From the experience came a lifelong passion for travel, especially to remote, exotic, or dangerous locations. This African trip resulted in his first travel book, *Journey without Maps* (1936), and, thereafter, all Greene's major novels were set in foreign locales, situations that allowed the author to explore corrupt or oppressive political systems and examine tensions between native and western values. Among other countries, Greene's travels during his life took him to Argentina, Israel, Haiti, Cuba, Russia, China, and Vietnam.

Greene separated his writing into two distinct categories, "entertainments" and "novels," and he frequently worked on both types at the same time. Entertainments are less concerned with moral issues or character development than with telling a fast-paced, suspenseful story. Novels, on the other hand, are more serious fictions intent on studying the complexity and paradoxes of the human condition. Replete with issues of crime, guilt, pursuit, betrayal, and the possibility of redemption, Greene's novels all bear a certain religious overtone. However, beginning with *Brighton Rock* (1938), a story of a teenaged hoodlum, Greene produced a tetrology of works, including *The Power and the Glory* (1940), *The Heart of the Matter* (1948), and *The End of the Affair* (1951), that explicitly examines matters of the Catholic faith lived in contemporary society. Labeled a "Catholic writer" to the degree that he felt his artistic freedom jeopardized, however, Greene backed away after this time from overtly Catholic themes. He continued to write prolifically, travel to volatile areas of the world, and work intermittently as a journalist, correspondent, and even as a wartime intelligence agent. In 1966, he located permanently to Antibes, France, on the Riviera. He died in Switzerland in 1991.

A consummate storyteller and a disciplined author who for decades produced at least five hundred words each day, Greene's massive body of works includes novels, short stories, screenplays, literary essays, film reviews, plays, an autobiography, travel books, and even children's stories. His output is often difficult to classify because of its size and diversity and because his was the rare quality of appealing to both highbrow and lowbrow audiences. His corpus of writing still awaits definitive critical assessment.

CRITICAL OVERVIEW

In the late 1930s, Greene was commissioned by his publisher, Longmans', to investigate the situation of the Catholic Church in Mexico, then under attack by the revolutionary, socialist government of President Plutarco Calles. As he traveled through the country, Greene observed the suffering of the Mexican people at the hands of the oppressive forces, their deplorable physical condition, and the tenacity of their faith and courage. He recorded his impressions in the travel book, *The Lawless Roads* (1939; also called *Another Mexico*). As he explains in this book, while in Mexico he heard the story of a fugitive "whiskey" priest who was so inebriated that he insisted on baptizing a baby boy, Brigitta. He also heard about Father Miguel Pro, the newly ordained Jesuit priest who returned to his native Mexico in 1926, ministered secretly to the people for a year, and then was captured and executed for treason in 1927. Calles made a point of circulating graphic photographs of Pro's execution as a warning to those who attempted to continue practicing the Catholic faith. Both of these stories subsequently formed the basis of *The Power and the Glory*. But Greene's encounter with Mexico proved to be a deeply personal experience as well. Although he had converted to Catholicism as a young man, only now after witnessing valiant suffering for the faith did Christianity become alive for him: he understood first-hand the paradoxical truth that faith thrives on persecution. He later stated about this powerful experience, "I began to examine more closely the affect of faith on action. Catholicism was no longer primarily symbolic, a ceremony at an altar. . . . It was closer now to death in the afternoon."[1] *The Power and the Glory* was written to explore this new sense of the reality and immediacy of faith as it is challenged by the modern political and atheistic state. The novel sold extremely well, particularly in France where the Catholic writer François Mauriac enthusiastically endorsed it, and in the United States where it was adapted into a movie, *The Fugitive*, starring Henry Fonda. It ranks among Greene's best works.

As his epigraph for *The Lawless Roads*, Greene selected a passage from John Henry Newman that considers the tragic condition of human nature after the Fall: we are corrupt, fearful, alienated creatures. And it is precisely from among such fallen humanity that Greene typically chooses his protagonists. Modern antiheroes rather than traditional heroes, Greene's main characters are usually guilty, hunted, frightened, and alone. Moreover, in "Greeneland," as his characteristic settings have been called, everyday life is a struggle for survival in an alien environment depraved and seedy at best, and violent and hopeless at worst. Yet, despite appearances, another world beyond sordid reality is postulated. Greene often explores characters living double lives or those poised precariously on the edge of two such worlds. His complex, psychologically realistic protagonists are at once both pursued and pursuing, sinful and redeemed, Christlike and Judas-like. In attempting to summarize his vision, Greene himself proposed these lines from a Robert Browning poem:

> Our interest's on the dangerous edge of things.
> The honest thief, the tender murderer,
> The superstitious atheist, demirep
> That loves and saves her soul in new French books—
> We watch while these in equilibrium keep
> The giddy line midway.[2]

Although his works examine issues of good and evil, Greene's desire to explore the "dangerous edge of things" kept him from broad didacticism or overt moralizing. In his Catholic novels, in particular, he probes the gray areas and insists on complicating moral issues rather than soothing or edifying the conventionally religious. In fact, in Greene's world, the saint and the sinner come to resemble each other. The epitaph for *The Heart of the Matter,* taken from Charles Péguy, also applies to *The Power and the Glory*: "No one knows as much about Christianity as the sinner unless it is the saint."

The setting of *The Power and the Glory* is both realistic and symbolic. The central Mexican states of Tabasco and Chiapas, bordering on Guatemala, are desolate landscapes of exhausting heat, driving rain, hovering vultures, terror, and violence. But Greene's graphic depiction of a physical wasteland resounds metaphysically as well, becoming a metaphor for the secular world that, denying God, has turned into a Kafkaesque nightmare region of corruption and abandonment. This is the modern world without faith, Greene implies, as well as the state of the human heart—sinful and debased, yet stamped with God's impregnable image. In the harsh environment of persecuted Mexico, Greene studies the drama of human nature stripped of all the external niceties and comforts of civilization and caught up in the struggle between primal forces of good and evil.

We first encounter the unnamed priest–protagonist as he is attempting to flee Tabasco by means of the *General Obregon*, a ship that calls only infrequently at the port city of Frontera. A wanted man because he continues to administer the sacraments secretly, he is the last remaining cleric in the atheistic Mexican state. (Another surviving priest, Padre José, has abdicated his priestly office and, as the regime demands, taken a wife.) We soon come to realize that the unnamed priest is a renegade from the Church as well, a sinful, weak, and fearful man who drinks too much, has fathered a child, and searches, as we see him in the opening scene, for a means to escape his hard fate. On the one hand the obligation of his priesthood impels him to continue to bring the truth of the Gospel and the comfort of the sacraments to people in desperate need. But on the other hand he understands that he is in a state of serious sin and, an outlaw, knows it is only a matter of time before he is apprehended and executed. Is his duty, then, first to himself—to seize the opportunity to escape to a neighboring state where religious persecution is less extreme so that he can confess to a fellow priest and save his own soul? The priest's moral dilemma is agonizing, and his contradictory character—simultaneously weak and heroic—realistically portrayed. Despite his constant temptation to provide for himself first and his understandable longing to escape from such brutal conditions, the call to serve others proves stronger even if he sometimes answers it with bitter resignation. Thus the priest moves inexorably toward certain death.

The novel is structured on an episodic pattern of brief encounters between the priest and others as he runs from the police. In Frontera, hoping to make his escape, the priest meets the exiled dentist, Mr. Tench. We then follow him as he is harbored by young Coral Fellows at her parents' banana station; stays briefly in the village of his daughter Brigitta and her mother Maria; travels to the capital Villahermosa where he is arrested and imprisoned overnight; returns to the banana station for refuge but finds it deserted; follows an Indian woman and her dead child to an Indian burial ground; finds temporary rest in the neighboring state of Chiapas with the German-American brother and sister, Mr. and Miss Lehr; then returns to Tabasco to minister to the American outlaw James Calver where he is seized and brought back to Villahermosa to be put to death. In each encounter, we learn more about the priest and understand how his pursuit by the authorities also signifies his pursuit by God's grace. In fact, the book's American title, when first released, was, fittingly, *The Labyrinthine Ways*, a phrase from Francis Thompson's well-known poem "The Hound of Heaven," which dramatizes the relentless hunt of Christ for the renegade sinner.

Although Greene begins the novel in medias res, through his memories we can ascertain some aspects of the priest's past and thus infer his spiritual progress. The son of a storekeeper, he was raised in the Mexican town of Carmen. He chose the life of a priest because it seemed a comfortable, gentile one, involving simply a little discipline, "as easy as saving money" (82). An ambitious and popular pastor in his parish of Concepción and a feted guest in wealthy homes, he delayed acting when the revolution set in until all his fellow priests were gone. He then easily let his spiritual practices slip one by one, surrendered to drink, and, in a moment of weakness, fathered a child with a peasant woman. Deeply flawed, the priest initially seems to warrant only our disapproval. However, we soon begin to realize that in his present appalling situation both internal and external suffering has chastened him, bringing about great depths of meekness and charity. His continual abject guilt for his sins has humbled him: he now believes himself utterly unworthy of his priestly calling. Because he deems himself the worst of sinners, he judges others with more compassion than previously and extends charity even to those who betray and murder him. He goes to his death believing himself a complete failure in God's sight while miserably aware that "there was only one thing that counted—to be a saint" (210).

In keeping with Catholic teaching, the novel expresses an implicit hierarchy of sin. The priest's former pride, self-satisfaction, and ambition are viewed as far more spiritually crippling than his sins of the flesh committed in moments of loneliness and weakness. Now, increasingly purified through suffering, his failings paradoxically become the means of his salvation. We recall that Julian of Norwich attests to this Christian mystery when she states that sin is "behovely"—necessary. As a contemporary critic puts it,

> In sin, it would seem, is the priest's heroism nurtured. This is not a doctrine on which everyone agrees. Is not evil at the opposite pole from virtue? And if so, how is the one said to support and nourish the other? Could vice ever be "the manure in which salvation flowers"? This is a problem, even an enigma. However, an enigma is the soul of Christian experience. Believers call it the mystery of redemption. And on this mystery is founded the whole of the faith.

The Gospels express this sense of mystery by means of paradoxes. The grain of wheat, so long as it remains whole, is unproductive; dying, it yields fruit a hundredfold. So with human life. When life is outwardly full, rich and exciting, it is likely to inhibit the deeper awareness. Let the walls crash upon the senses, and a whole inner world is likely to open up. Death, Jesus warned, is a precondition for rebirth. Even the producing branch is subjected to the test of the knife. Through his sin, the priest is cauterized of the virulent effects of his egotism. Thus cleansed, he is made ready for the final laying down of his life. The new growth from his death is the rekindling of faith among the youth of Mexico.[3]

The novel thus places emphasis on the power and mystery of God's ineffable grace working through and in all things, even the most desolate and sinful. Greene illustrates here St. Paul's conviction that "where sin abounded grace did much more abound." In Greene's world, God's grace works through weak, chastened individuals who strive to do his will even though their actions may seem ludicrously inadequate. The suffering endured by a repentant sinner shatters self-complacency and reveals to him his need for redemption. In fact, sinners who are so humbled are, in Greene's vision, better off spiritually than externally devout but self-righteous believers. Understanding this, the priest is more severe to the pious but uncharitable woman in the prison than he is, for example, to his betrayer, the mestizo, or to the murderer James Calver. While the self-righteous may insist that they know how God thinks and judges, the priest at one point honestly admits, "I don't know a thing about the mercy of God" (200). Writing in *Men I Hold Great*, François Mauriac maintained that *The Power and the Glory* serves as "a great lesson" to those who are "obsessed with perfection": "those scrupulous people who split hairs over their shortcomings, and who forget that, in the last day, according to the word of St. John of the Cross, it is on love that they will be judged."[4]

Despite the extremity of his situation, the priest never loses faith in God nor in the efficacy of the priesthood. His is a quiet witness to Christian truths in a hostile, atheistic world—that God is love, that suffering has value, that individuals have great dignity. We watch him tenaciously adhering to belief while progressing through a type of purgation on earth, finally conforming to the pattern of Christ's *kenosis*, redemptive suffering, and death. While the priest, in his humility, never considers himself a holy man, the novel raises the question of whether, in the end, he is a saint and a martyr. Is it possible that sanctity looks like this?

By way of ironic contrast to the priest's life and death, Greene skillfully juxtaposes the fictional tale of the martyr Juan, read by another of Greene's pious but hypocritical believers, an unnamed Mexican mother to her children. The tale concerns a heroic young man who, strong, brave, never wavering in faith and piety, goes triumphantly to his martyrdom. Against such conventional sentimental hagiography are levied the weaknesses and faults of the priest. Unlike the saintly Juan, he does not shout, "Viva el Cristo Rey!" as the bullets fire, but feebly waves his arms while murmuring "excuse," an ambiguous word that may indicate a plea to God to have mercy on his own sins or a request to pardon his executioners in imitation of Christ's words of forgiveness on the cross. Greene skillfully shifts the actual scene of the priest's execution from the priest's limited viewpoint to that of several onlookers, including the dentist Tench and the mother who reads the story of Juan to her children. To all appearances, this comical, scandalous priest goes to his death a coward, dying outside of God's grace. His is merely another routine execution in a town inured to such sights. But the book argues that grace defies appearances. Through the mystery of grace, sin is turned into holiness and weakness into strength: the great sinner becomes the great saint. In fact, as one critic has stated, "In no other novel of our time . . . are the paradoxes of sainthood more expertly handled."[5]

The priest's spiritual progress is especially conveyed in the novel's central scene set in a prison cell. Arrested for carrying contraband liquor, the priest is thrown into jail with others who together represent a cross-section of sinful, wretched humanity. In the dark, dank, crowded cell stinking of human filth, the priest paradoxically discovers a sense of genuine peace and comradeship that he had never known as the complacent pastor of an affluent parish. Although when he is rudely shoved into the cell he inquires with some alarm, "Who are these people?" he comes to identify with his fellow prisoners, realizing that indeed, "he was just one criminal among a herd of criminals" (121, 128). There, in prison, it was "almost as if he had died," a telling phrase pointing to the new depth of spirituality that is born in him (147). From this night forward, the priest exhibits even greater humility and charity, and a complete dependence on God's grace. Now stripped of everything reminiscent of his past life—altar stone, prayer book, wine, even the bit of wadded-up paper that he had desperately tried to save—he clings to faith and hope alone and discovers the courage to continue to follow God's lead. Thus, even when he finds brief respite at the comfortable *finca* of Mr. and Miss Lehr, he realizes such luxury can no longer satisfy him and he abandons once again his plans to escape. Fully aware that God is now calling him to sacrifice his life for others, he finally surrenders to the Hound of Heaven and consequently "felt quite cheerful; he had never really believed in this [the Lehrs'] peace" (180).

The Power and the Glory is also structured around three meetings that occur between the priest and the lieutenant, the police officer who has made it his mission to capture the last remaining cleric in his territory. Like the priest, the lieutenant remains unnamed, a technique that helps elevate the two characters from the particular to the universal and symbolic. Determined to rid the country of religious superstition and given free reign by his superior to use any means to do so, the lieutenant decides to take hostages from the villages in order to force the people to betray the priest's whereabouts. The first encounter between the two men occurs in Maria's village, where Brigitta, a hardened, mocking child, truthfully identifies the priest as her father, thereby convincing the lieutenant that he is not the sought-after man. The second meeting takes place the morning after the priest is released from prison. Here, once again, the lieutenant fails to recognize the priest (although ironically his photograph hangs on the police office wall just a few feet away) and, upon dismissing him, charitably hands him five pesos. The final and decisive encounter occurs when the priest, betrayed by the half-caste, is arrested by the lieutenant after ministering to James Calver and is escorted back to the capitol to be shot. These three evenly spaced-out encounters serve to build dramatic tension. However, far more importantly, they operate thematically to illustrate one of the work's most important themes. At every point, the priest and lieutenant are paired. The lieutenant, for instance, is described in priestlike terms. "Something of a priest in his intent observant walk," he lives a celibate, austere life of self-sacrifice in his intense dedication to the cause of revolutionary reform (24). Like a man of God, too, he "was a mystic," although his mysticism leads only to a sense of "vacancy—a complete certainty in the existence of a dying, cooling world, of human beings who had evolved from animals for no purpose at all" (24–25). He is admirable in his zeal to eradicate all traces of the injustice he associates with a corrupt, avaricious Church so that the country's children may inherit a future free from oppression. In fact, in his altruism, discipline, and passionate pursuit of what he believes is a just cause, the lieutenant seems more morally upright than the priest, a slovenly alcoholic and fornicator. Here, then, we have no stereotyped "good" or "bad" figures, but realistically drawn human beings in whom good and evil are combined. Both the priest and lieutenant understand that, in many ways, they are more alike than unalike. "You're a good man," the priest tells the lieutenant when the lieutenant hands him the five pesos. And "You aren't a bad fellow," the lieutenant admits to the priest during their extended dialogue upon the priest's arrest (140, 201).

However, although doubles of each other in some ways, the priest and lieutenant contrast sharply in ideology and here Greene debates a highly relevant issue in today's world. Convinced that an atheistic, socialistic state will liberate people from injustice and alleviate all misery, bringing about a kind of heaven on earth, the lieutenant, ironically, does not hesitate to shoot as many innocent victims as it takes to accomplish his idealistic plans. His appalling inability to recognize human dignity makes him committed to a faceless charity that is implemented only at the end of a gun: he "indulges in brutality and murder without seeming to realize that a man untouched by grace can be no more than the sum total of his deeds, and that the purity of his intentions cannot compensate for the cruelty of his actions."[6] Once his mission to hunt down and kill the priest is accomplished, he finds that his life has become empty and meaningless—he dreams of mocking laughter echoing down a hallway from which there is no exit.

By contrast, the priest firmly believes in the afterlife. Because of this conviction, he finds he cannot refuse to enter treacherous situations to bring the sacraments to the sick and the dying. His trust in the existence of a world to come where ultimate justice will reign makes him distrust any political system that claims to conquer all suffering on earth. Since Christ chose to save humankind by the Cross, suffering, in the Catholic vision, has tremendous spiritual value. Rejecting the lieutenant's idealistic notion that given the right social order all suffering can eventually be eliminated, the priest encourages patience and self-sacrifice in anticipation of the joys to come. "It's not worth bothering too much about a little pain here," he maintains (195). He understands that, for a Christian, suffering and joy go hand in hand: "Never get tired of suffering," he urges, for "pain is part of joy" (69). As we observe throughout the novel, his own suffering is instrumental to his spiritual growth. Moreover, unlike the lieutenant, the priest respects the dignity of each individual human soul made in the image of God and insists that "hate was just a failure of imagination" (131). Thus, although flawed, the priest through his faith becomes an instrument of God's grace in forsaken Mexico. His example prompts religious inquiry in young Coral Fellows and reinvigorates belief in the boy Luis who, bored by the fictional Juan, discovers true heroism in the priest's death. Through the pairing of these two children, the novel suggests that renewal of faith in Mexico will occur among the young. In addition, it is not unlikely that the priest's influence may also extend in the future to the lieutenant whose inner desolation upon killing the priest is made clear. Thus, Greene's exploration of the dialectical struggle between two opposing ideologies emphasizes the ultimate defeat of the lieutenant's atheistic and materialistic humanism. As critics Brock and Welsh have observed,

> The novel demonstrates the deficiency of attempting to correct social ills by predicating their solution to a system of general "Truths" which may permit individual suffering and cruelty in the interest of what may be considered an ultimate good. It also shows the colossal presumption of the idealist who passionately believes that man— despite his flawed nature—can be made better than he is.[7]

While the memorable ending of the novel—the arrival of a new priest, also unnamed, just as the whiskey priest is executed—has been criticized as a *deux ex machina*, it aptly reinforces the book's continual insistence on the supernatural value of the sacraments and the continuity of the priesthood. Throughout the work, Greene gives prominence to the spiritual power of baptism, confession, the Eucharist, and Holy Orders. The Catholic Church teaches that, through the graces given in the conferring of the priesthood by Holy Orders, the sacramental work of a priest is disassociated from his personal spiritual state—*ex opere operato* and not *ex opere operantis*. Thus, despite his personal sins, the priest validly gives the sacraments to others and the outpouring of divine grace in the world continues. In the view of the revolutionary regime, however, positive social change depends solely on the moral strength and goodwill of human beings. Even the best laid plans can be undermined by the weakness or evil intent of individual leaders. The priest points this fact out to the lieutenant: "That's another difference between us. It's no good your working for your end unless you're a good man yourself. And there won't always be good men in your party.... But it doesn't matter so much my being a coward— and all the rest. I can put God into a man's mouth just the same—and I can give him God's pardon. It wouldn't make any difference to that if every priest in the Church was like me" (195). God has chosen priests as his means of spreading grace on earth, and the dramatic ending of *The Power and the Glory* highlights God's continuing providence in this regard.

A panoply of minor characters serves to set the priest–protagonist in relief. While realistically portrayed, each also takes on a certain symbolic value. The thematic issue of suffering is first raised in the opening scene in which the dentist Tench searches in vain for his ether cylinder, used to quell pain. Rotting teeth are rampant in Greene's Mexico—the *jefe* especially experiences constant toothache—and stand for both human corruption and the corruption of the land itself. The mestizo is revealed to be a Judas-like character who betrays the priest for money and who challenges him to love and forgive his enemy. The well-ordered Lehr homestead provides no true haven but rather represents the Lehrs's insular denial of reality: the sheltered Miss Lehr admits to being shocked by the reports in *Police News*, and the priest is puzzled by the "quick fixes" for spiritual ills listed in her Gideon Bible. Equally naïve are the banana station owners, Mr. and Mrs. Fellows, who avoid all responsibility and depend almost completely on their precocious thirteen-year-old daughter, Coral. By contrast to her parents, Coral matures both physically and spiritually: introduced to the human inheritance of pain by the onset of her first menstrual period, she is also led by the priest to think about matters of faith for the first time. Presumably having met some type of violent death, she figures significantly in the priest's last dream.

Other minor characters include Padre José, the priest who has apostatized by marrying and has consequently become a ridiculous, sad figure, dominated by his shrewish wife and surrounded by a chorus of children's taunts whenever he ventures outside his home. Although the lieutenant foregoes his principles by asking him to hear the confession of the condemned priest, Padre José refuses to do so out of fear, leaving the priest poignantly abandoned by all on his last night on earth. Besides Padre José, the priest is also paired with the Yankee outlaw James Calver (whose name sounds like "Calvary"). As Christ was associated at the Crucifixion with common criminals in the two thieves, so both the priest and Calver are wanted men, their pictures hanging side by side in the police station. And just as Pilate released Barabbas because he was less of a threat to the state than Jesus, so the lieutenant is much more eager to capture the priest than the murderer Calver whose violent actions don't threaten the ideals of the revolution. Lastly, serving as a kind of silent chorus, is the extraordinary faith of the Mexican people themselves, peasants and Indians who, though suffering terribly, walk fifty miles to hear Mass and courageously accept death as hostages rather than betray the priest. Such tenacious faith is especially seen in the haunting episode involving the Indian woman who, accompanied by the priest, bears her dead child to the Indian graveyard covered with crosses high on the plateau, a primitive, eerie sight that serves to deepen the priest's sense of the mystery of faith.

It is interesting to note that Greene's apparent lack of orthodoxy in *The Power and the Glory*—his depiction of a scandalous priest who achieves glory, a "sinful saint"—brought strong reaction from the Catholic hierarchy of his day. The Vatican's Holy Office, the tribunal for the protection of faith and morals, condemned the book in 1954 because it was "paradoxical" and "dealt with extraordinary circumstances." Some years later, however, when Greene met Pope Paul VI, the pontiff, who was well-versed in literature, confided to the author, "Mr. Greene, some parts of your book are certain to offend some Catholics, but you should pay no attention to that."[8] *The Power and the Glory* was, in fact, several decades ahead of its time, reflecting a more psychologically complex vision of the human condition than was acceptable in the pre–Vatican II era of Church triumphalism. Throughout his career and especially when trying to dodge the label of "Catholic author," Greene strongly defended his artistic independence. He insisted that artists had the right—even the obligation—to be disloyal to any institution, whether church or state, that tried to prescribe or censor artistic vision. Writers, he maintained, must claim the liberty to create characters who express all views, whether orthodox or dissident, and to play the devil's advocate in creating sympathetic portraitures of even the most heretical, depraved, or unlikable human beings.

Greene was convinced that the primary duty of a novelist was to tell the truth. And the truth he has to tell in *The Power and the Glory* is disturbing and consoling at once. In a book full of paradoxes, ironies, and ambiguities, his message is calculated to upset those who complacently believe they know how God judges. Greene forces the proud who, like the Pharisee, are assured of their own righteousness to consider God's overwhelming love and mercy for sinful, cowardly, and despised humanity. He also consoles by insisting on the great dignity of the individual and the triumph of God's love despite human sins and weaknesses. Moreover, he asserts the dynamic presence of God continually at work in a land where the Church seems all but annihilated, an important issue in his time due to the threat of Communism. Along the way, Greene raises provocative issues of the nature of true holiness, the value of suffering, and the vitality of the priesthood. A sort of "divine comedy" despite its overt tragedy, *The Power and the Glory* emphasizes, finally, that God's ways are not at all men's ways. Like the priest who enjoys a good card trick, God here is revealed to be the ultimate trickster, concealing his power and glory just behind the desolate Mexican landscape.

FOR FURTHER READING

Graham Greene, *Brighton Rock*
———, *The End of the Affair*
———, *The Lawless Roads (Another Mexico)*
Shusaku Endo, *Silence*. This contemporary novel can be viewed as a type of Japanese counterpart to *The Power and the Glory*.

QUESTIONS FOR DISCUSSION

1. Greene was interested in dreams and the subconscious as revelations of the inner life. Three important dreams end the novel: that of the lieutenant, of the priest, and of Luis. Analyze each of them, paying particular attention to their details; for example, to the Christian symbolism in the priest's dream of the banquet, wine from the father's house, the bleeding fish, and so on. In what ways do these dreams add to your understanding of the novel's themes or characterization?

2. Consider the novel's title. "The power and the glory" in many Christian traditions is a phrase at the end of the Lord's Prayer, and it is part of the Mass for Catholics. As the book opens, the "power" is literally in the hands of the lieutenant. How does the significance of the title change as the novel progresses?

3. Can the priest be considered a saint and/or martyr at the end? Defend your position by explaining what the Catholic Church teaches about the criteria for sainthood and martyrdom.

4. Greene builds his work on a series of contrasts. Discuss in detail his pairing of some of the following figures: Brigitta and Coral; Coral and Luis; the priest and the lieutenant; the priest and James Calver; the priest and Padre José. What other doubles exist?

5. The novel is replete with ironies. For example, here are several in the opening scene: the priest's breviary is hidden in the book, *La Eterna Mártir;* Tench mistakes the priest for a doctor; and Tench has a salvaged stained glass window with a picture of the Madonna in his dentist's office. What other ironies did you note in the novel?

NOTES

Graham Greene, *The Power and the Glory* (New York: Penguin Books, 1991). All references are to this edition.

1. Graham Greene, *Ways of Escape* (New York: Simon and Schuster, 1981), 79.
2. Robert Browning, "Bishop Blougram's Apology," cited in Greene's autobiography, *A Sort of Life* (New York: Simon and Schuster, 1971), 117–18.
3. K. C. Joseph Kurismmootil, *Heaven and Hell on Earth: An Appreciation of Five Novels of Graham Greene* (Chicago: Loyola University Press, 1982), 91.
4. Quoted in Paul O'Prey, *A Reader's Guide to Graham Greene* (New York: Thames and Hudson, 1988), 77.
5. R. W. B. Lewis, "The 'Trilogy,'" in *Graham Greene: A Collection of Critical Essays,* edited by Samuel Hynes (Englewood Cliffs, NJ: Prentice-Hall, 1973), 59.
6. D. Heyward Brock and James M. Welsh, "Graham Greene and the Structure of Salvation," *Renascence* 27 (1974): 33.
7. Brock and Welsh, "Graham Greene," 32.
8. Greene, *Ways of Escape,* 90.

BIBLIOGRAPHY

Gaston, Georg M. A. *The Pursuit of Salvation: A Critical Guide to the Novels of Graham Greene.* Troy, NY: Whitson, 1984.

Hynes, Samuel, ed. *Graham Greene: A Collection of Critical Essays.* Englewood Cliffs, NJ: Prentice-Hall, 1973.

McEwan, Neil. *Graham Greene.* New York: St. Martin's Press, 1988.

Mesnet, Marie-Béatrice. *Graham Greene and the Heart of the Matter.* London: Cresset Press, 1954. Reprinted, Westport, CT: Greenwood Press, 1972.

Miller, R. H. *Understanding Graham Greene.* Columbia: University of South Carolina Press, 1990.

O'Prey, Paul. *A Reader's Guide to Graham Greene.* New York: Thames and Hudson, 1988.

Sharrock, Roger. *Saints, Sinners, and Comedians: The Novels of Graham Greene.* Notre Dame, IN: University of Notre Dame Press, 1984.

EVELYN WAUGH
BRIDESHEAD REVISITED

BIOGRAPHY

The second of Arthur and Charlotte Raban Waugh's two children, Evelyn Waugh was born in 1903 in the middle-class London suburb of Hamstead, England. Arthur Waugh was an editor, writer, and literary critic, and reading and writing were important family activities. Both Evelyn and his brother Alec, who also became a successful author, began composing stories as small children. Evelyn was sent to Lancing for prep school, an institution known for educating the sons of clergymen but at which he lost his boyhood enthusiasm for the Anglican faith. In 1921, he matriculated at Hertford College of Oxford University where he was active in debate, wrote articles and provided sketches for school publications, and joined the Hypocrites Club, a group of pleasure-loving aesthetes whose colorful characters and indulgent activities provided seed material for the Oxford scenes of *Brideshead Revisited*. Saddled with debts and never particularly studious, Waugh left college in his third year without taking a degree. For awhile he floundered, making several desultory attempts at finding a career. Interested in painting, he attended a London art school but soon dropped out, and a stint at teaching school also proved unsuccessful. Finally, he turned to writing as a full-time occupation, publishing at the age of twenty-five his first major work, a biography of the pre-Raphaelite painter, Dante Gabriel Rossetti.

That same year, 1928, Waugh also produced the first of what was to become a steady stream of satires, the genre at which he excelled. Both *Decline and Fall* (1928) and his next work *Vile Bodies* (1930) burlesque the superficiality and amoral lifestyle of 1920s British society. *Black Mischief*

(1932) satirizes the imposition of modern civilization onto the fictional African kingdom of Azonia; *A Handful of Dust* (1934), the shattering effects of upper-class marital infidelity; and *Scoop* (1938), the blunders of journalists during the Italian intervention in Ethiopia. The combination of frantic pace, black humor, devastating social commentary, and memorable Dickensian-like characters Waugh created in his satires remains unparalleled. Meanwhile, throughout his career, the prolific Waugh also published numerous works in other genres, including short stories, travel books, biographies, and an autobiography.

In his midtwenties, just as his literary star was rising, Waugh wed Evelyn Gardner. But the couple, known to friends as "he-Evelyn" and "she-Evelyn," separated after only two years of marriage due to "she-Evelyn's" infidelity. Bitterly wounded, Waugh secured a divorce on the grounds of her adultery. About the same time, he began to explore the Catholic faith, attracted to the Church's universal character, historical continuity, and, most likely, the clarity of its moral teachings in the wake of his personal chaos. Oxford friends referred him to Father Martin D'Arcy, master of the Jesuit College at Oxford, Campion Hall, who instructed him and received him into the Church in 1930. Seven years later, his first marriage annulled, Waugh wed Laura Herbert, a Catholic; their union lasted until his death and produced six children.

In 1939, the increasing threat of Nazism brought out the patriot in Waugh who, despite being a family man in his midthirties, volunteered for the military and served courageously in active duty for four years. Difficult to get along with due to his restlessness and inability to obey authority, however, Waugh was pressured to resign from the elite Commandos in 1943, an experience that considerably soured his enthusiasm for war and is reflected in Captain Charles Ryder's weary cynicism in *Brideshead's* prologue. While recovering from a minor injury, Waugh completed the manuscript of *Brideshead,* which was published as a book in 1945 after first being serialized. It sold astonishingly well, particularly in the United States where it was chosen as a Book-of-the-Month selection. Metro-Goldwyn-Mayer invited Waugh to Hollywood to discuss the possibility of a film version although Waugh eventually turned the offer down because he felt he would not be allowed sufficient control over the material. His sojourn in California was not wasted, however, for he discovered a rich vein of material in his visit to Los Angeles's Forest Lawn Memorial Park, a cemetery so utterly given over to disguising the reality of death that, as Waugh put it, "the body does not decay; it lives on, more chic in death than ever before."[1] The satiric novel *The Loved One* (1948) was the result.

Notable books in Waugh's later career include *Helena* (1950), a fictionalized biography of the mother of Constantine who is credited with finding the True Cross of Christ, and a trilogy of war novels about the Catholic soldier, Guy Crouchback, later revised into the single volume *The Sword of Honor* (1965).

Waugh's last decade was marked by the depression of *acedia* coupled with deteriorating physical health. Like Jonathan Swift and Mark Twain before him, he seems to have suffered the satirists' fate, becoming embittered and despairing toward the end of his life. An ardent traditionalist, Waugh especially deplored the liturgical changes of Vatican II, sadly convinced that his beloved Church was merely giving in to modernity. He died on Easter Sunday, April 10, 1966, and is buried at his family home, Combe Florey, in Somerset, England. His tombstone bears a simple but eloquent inscription: "Evelyn Waugh, Writer."

CRITICAL OVERVIEW

With his quick mind and keen sense of the absurd, Waugh is viewed today as one of the greatest satirists in the English language. At once hilarious and disturbing, his satires expose the savagery and spiritual aridity of a modern world devoid of traditional values. Like many of his generation, Waugh found T. S. Eliot's epic poem *The Waste Land* to be an accurate summation of the modern condition, and he evokes it several times in his writing. The title *A Handful of Dust* derives from a line of the poem and, in an early scene of *Brideshead Revisited*, the decadent Anthony Blanche blares out verses from the work on a megaphone across the Oxford campus. While some critics were disconcerted when Waugh moved from the irreverence of his satires to the seriousness of *Brideshead*, the novel, his sixth, can easily be seen as a logical progression in his artistic sensibility. Like the earlier novels, *Brideshead* broadly satirizes the moral wasteland of contemporary society, and some of its comic scenes, such as Anthony Blanche's malicious dinner gossip, Charles's father's "revenge" party, and Rex Mottram's attempted instruction in the Catholic faith, are among the most brilliant Waugh ever composed. But in this work Waugh for the first time explicitly proposes an answer to the modern condition in the stability, continuity, and moral and spiritual truths of the Catholic faith. Thus he now turns from a negative to a positive approach to the issue. Commenting on the new sober tone entering his novels with *Brideshead*, Waugh maintained that he would continue in future works to represent human nature more fully than he had done in his satires, "which, to me, means only one thing, man in his relation to God."[2]

A complex novel in theme and structure, *Brideshead* is filled with memorable characters and scenes, and contains a fascinating if sometimes uneasy combination of moods: romance, satire, sentiment, nostalgia, comedy, and spiritual depth all rolled into one. Written with rich, sensuous images and elaborate prose, the book is meticulously crafted. It is, in many ways, also a *roman à clef* based on Waugh's Oxford memories and other significant events in his life. Primarily, *Brideshead* is a conversion story, a genre that portrays a person changing from the "old man" to the "new" and gaining new sight in the process. The narrative traces the mysterious workings of divine providence as Christ, the Hound of Heaven, relentlessly draws people to himself, even through the most unlikely of circumstances. While the novel focuses on Charles's conversion from agnosticism to Catholicism, it also depicts the reconversions of three members of the Marchmain-Flyte family, Lord Alex Marchmain and his children Sebastian and Julia. About his ambitious theme, Waugh wrote, "Grace is not confined to the happy, prosperous and conventionally virtuous. . . . God has a separate plan for each individual by which he or she may find salvation. The story of *Brideshead Revisited* seeks to show the working of several such plans in the lives of a single family."[3]

The intricate plot takes place largely by flashback and ranges over the decades between the two world wars. Narrated through the first person, limited viewpoint of Charles Ryder, it relates his progress from youthful innocence, through adult cynicism and loss, to Christian faith and hope. A brief prologue and epilogue, set in the present wartime year of 1944, frame the book. In the prologue, we meet the thirty-nine-year-old Charles who, an army captain, has grown disillusioned with military life. His unit transferred under cover of night to a new camp, Charles discovers upon awakening the next morning that they are now occupying Brideshead Castle, a wealthy country estate that he had visited numerous times as a young man through his friendship with Sebastian Flyte and other members of the Marchmain family. As he hears once again the name of Brideshead, a host of memories floods over him, memories he now relates to us in a series of sometimes disjointed flashbacks. Waugh structures Charles's memories into two major divisions. Book 1, "Et in Arcadia Ego" recounts his college days in the mid-1920s and his earliest associations with Brideshead, and book 2, "A Twitch upon the Thread," recalls the years of young adulthood and his growing spiritual awareness.

The narrative moves from the pagan to the Christian as indicated by the two parts' titles. An ambiguous phrase, "Et in Arcadia Ego," engraved on the skull Charles keeps in his room, traditionally was inscribed on pagan tombs and can mean "I (a person) too was once in the happy land of Arcadia" or "I (the tomb itself, therefore the presence of death) too was in Arcadia."[4] The second meaning somberly attests to the fact that even in the most fulfilling and joyful moments of human life, decay and death lurk close at hand. While Charles's early days with Sebastian are full of the insouciance of youth, this carefree time must soon give way to the responsibilities of adulthood.

A lonely child whose mother has died in the war and whose father is cold and eccentric, Charles commences his Oxford career predictably enough. Advised by his priggish cousin Jasper as to the best way to succeed academically and socially, Charles finds his first companions among a group of bookish, conventional young men. But a world of beauty, love, and spontaneity opens to him when he encounters the young lord, Sebastian Flyte, by chance when Sebastian inauspiciously vomits into his open window after an evening of carousing. The contrite Sebastian invites Charles to lunch the next day where Charles is introduced to his colorful set of friends. Although wary of the more flamboyant flank of these aesthetes such as the homosexual Anthony Blanche, Charles is naturally drawn to the winsome, charming Sebastian in whose company he experiences the happy childhood he had never known. When he's called away from an excruciatingly dull vacation at his father's London house to Brideshead by the "injured" Sebastian, Charles revels in the Arcadian life of languor, beauty, art, and friendship he discovers there. Only Sebastian's Catholic faith, glimpsed at rare moments, remains an enigma to him.

But the Arcadian existence soon proves fragile as Sebastian's drinking, earlier just a youthful indulgence, begins to turn serious. On a trip to Venice where Charles meets Sebastian's father who years before had left his wife to live with a mistress, Charles hears the truth about Sebastian's impending addiction to alcohol. In Charles's subsequent visits to Brideshead, Sebastian's behavior becomes increasingly monitored by his mother and eventually, suspected of abetting Sebastian's habit by giving him money for drink, Charles is dismissed from the family. Sebastian withdraws from Oxford, and Charles, too, leaves the university to attend art school in Paris. Summoned by the family when Lady Marchmain falls ill, however, he agrees to search for Sebastian in North Africa to which Sebastian has escaped as he was being escorted to a Zurich sanatorium. Charles locates him in Morocco; although weak and ill, Sebastian insists on remaining to care for his companion, the wounded German Kurt. Returning to London, Charles encounters Cordelia, the Marchmain's youngest child, and it is she who, while lamenting the closing of the Brideshead chapel and the spiritual disintegration of the family, also predicts that "God won't let them go for long," thus introducing the Chestertonian Father Brown theme that will be worked out in book 2 (220).

Book 2 takes place ten years later. Although he has become a successful architectural painter, Charles is an unhappy, emotionally dead man whose marriage has failed due to his wife's infidelity. We first see him returning from a two-year trip to Central America where he has sought artistic inspiration. On the ship back to England with his wife, he meets his old acquaintance Julia Flyte, sister to Sebastian, who herself has been in an unsatisfying marriage. Becoming lovers, Charles and Julia live together contentedly at Brideshead for the next two years while beginning the processes of obtaining divorces from their mutual spouses so they can marry each other. But when the oldest Marchmain son, Bridey, accuses Julia of living in sin, Julia's illusion shatters and she feels the sting of conscience. Still, plans for her and Charles's divorces and their eventual union continue.

Now a young woman working as a nurse in Spain, Cordelia, on a visit to Brideshead, informs Charles of Sebastian's fate: still in Morocco, he has returned to the Church and attached himself to a monastery where he is loved by the monks although often still inebriated. Then, a dramatic turn of events occurs as Lord Marchmain unexpectedly returns to his ancestral home to die. Although an apostate from the faith for twenty-five years, he makes the sign of the cross at his death, prompting Julia once again to heed the voice of conscience and renounce Charles. For his part, Charles, too, comes to religious conviction in this grace-filled moment. And here Charles's memories break off. The epilogue returns us suddenly to the gray, prosaic world of war with Charles's battalion now occupying Brideshead. The once magnificent house and grounds are despoiled; the family dispersed. But Charles discovers the old servant Nanny Hawkins still in her attic room and the chapel newly reopened. Beginning in the profane world of war, *Brideshead* concludes with Charles on his knees in the chapel, praying before the sanctuary light.

At the beginning of book 2, Charles announces that his "theme is memory" (225). As such, the work is modeled on St. Augustine's profound meditations on the power and use of memory in the *Confessions*. Told in retrospective, *Brideshead*'s structure imitates Augustine's autobiography, and Waugh even evokes the *Confessions* explicitly when Sebastian misquotes Augustine's famous prayer, "'Oh God, make me good, but not yet'" (86).[5] In fact, both Sebastian and Charles can be considered Augustine-like characters searching for love and fulfillment through a world of sensual pleasures yet finally realizing, with Augustine, that "our heart is restless until it rests in you."[6] Like Augustine, Charles, now middle aged, reviews his past life from the vantage point of faith and, through his reminiscences, seemingly disconnected emotions and events assume coherence and meaning. In the process of memory, Charles, similar to Augustine, comes to understand how all events of his life have been orchestrated by divine providence to lead him to God even though at the time of their occurrence he had no awareness of being so directed. Through the Arcadian days of beauty and leisure; the poignant loss of Sebastian's friendship; the reawakening of emotion in his affair with Julia; and the powerful moment of Lord Marchmain's death, Charles, the romantic artist, has been gradually but inexorably led to faith. In *Brideshead* Waugh, therefore, echoes Augustine in proposing that the God-given gift of memory can be of immense value in the spiritual life, revealing to us in hindsight the divinely guided pattern of our lives. As Frederick J. Stopp has stated about the value of such contemplation,

> Romance and eschatology are the natural home respectively of the artist and of the Christian; the lingering and meditative backward glance at the pattern of past experience, and the intuitive, forward discerning look towards things as yet unformed, but which lie in a pocket of the mind . . . are of the essence of both the poetic and the religious approach to reality.[7]

Through memory, Charles traces the convoluted steps of his spiritual progress. Raised an agnostic, "the view implicit in [his] education was that the basic narrative of Christianity had long been exposed as a myth . . . religion was a hobby which some people professed and others did not" (85–86). While still the detached observer, he becomes more and more aware of the depths of religious belief in Sebastian and the Marchmain family, although their eccentric practice or nonpractice of the faith alternately intrigues and repels him. Sebastian, for example, is unyielding in his belief in the basic truths of Catholicism ("Oh yes, I believe that" he insists when Charles teases him about the Christmas story) but puzzles Charles in his desire to flee from moral responsibility (87). But ultimately Charles's spiritual awakening doesn't come about as much through his perplexity about the Marchmains's faith as by his experience of human love and his growing appreciation for aesthetic beauty. Through his deep affection for Sebastian, he comes to understand that "to know and love one other human being is the root of all wisdom," and he is naturally left bereft when, inexplicably to Charles, Sebastian withdraws as his addiction increases (45). Similarly, Charles's subsequent love for Julia, while also vibrant and intense, proves short-lived. Neither love fully satisfies or endures. But through the pain of such love and loss, Charles begins to see that both Sebastian and Julia were merely "forerunners" in his restless search for a love that does not fail, the quest that was also Augustine's. The older, wiser Charles who narrates his story, now far more aware of God's secret action in the world, realizes that "perhaps all our loves are merely hints and symbols; a hill of many invisible crests; doors that open as in a dream to reveal only a further stretch of carpet and another door; . . . each [of us] straining through and beyond the other, snatching a glimpse now and then of the shadow which turns the corner always a pace or two ahead of us" (303). In addition, Charles's dawning religious sensibility is also nurtured by the world of beauty and art first revealed to him in the languorous Arcadian days at Brideshead where he is "conver[ted] to the baroque" from the narrow puritanism of his upbringing (82). The gaudy seventeenth-century Italian fountain on Brideshead's grounds that he spends hours contemplating and sketching fascinates him with its intricacy of design. This new aesthetic experience serves to open Charles's heart and spirit to the wonders and delights of creation. Moreover, it is also during this time at Brideshead that Charles has his first serious conversation with Sebastian about religion. The Arcadian days at Brideshead, while full of pagan pleasures, thus represent a crucial stage in Charles's spiritual development, giving him "implicitly, as in a seed-kernel, all he will learn in the book."[8]

But Waugh's narrative of Charles's conversion and his Augustinian theme of memory are even more complex than first meets the eye, for Charles actually experiences *two* conversions in the book, as critic Laura Mooneyham has perceptively pointed out.[9] While reviewing through memory the steps that led to his becoming a Catholic, Charles's faith is renewed in the process and he moves from the apathy and depression of the prologue to the greater peace and lightheartedness of the epilogue. Though a fairly recent convert (as we know only by Hooper's remark about the chapel at Brideshead, "more in your line than mine" [17]), the Charles we encounter in the prologue is going through a period of *acedia*, a condition to which he appears prone for we see it in him again later in the narrative. After losing Julia, he had evidently hoped that military life would bring him the fulfillment he craves. Bored and restless after four years of service, however, he poignantly compares this latest let-down to the feeling of a married man who has lost all love for a once-cherished spouse. But it is precisely in his recalling of his memories while observing the operation of grace in his life that his faith is quickened once again even in the midst of the monotony and brutality of war. The Charles of the epilogue is now, as a soldier remarks, "unusually cheerful" (351). The epilogue, therefore, doesn't just pick up where the prologue left off but is integral to the narrative's development by depicting Charles's further spiritual progress. The overall structure of the book is thus circular and progressive with the frame constituting important parts of the organic whole. Thematically, Waugh suggests here the ongoing need for renewal in the spiritual life, a renewal that may be effected through the use of memory.

Besides Charles's conversion, *Brideshead* also concerns the return to the faith of Lord Marchmain, Julia, and Sebastian. Descendents of an old Catholic recusant family, the Marchmains are now "half paganized," as Waugh referred to them.[10] Outward forms of piety dominate family life due to Lady Marchmain's insistence—Mass, rosary, visits to the chapel— and the oldest son Bridey and youngest daughter Cordelia represent unproblematic acceptance of the faith. But scandal hovers over the family because of Lord Marchmain's defection twenty decades earlier from his marriage and his faith for the sensual pleasures of Italy. Sebastian, too, is on the run, perhaps for the same reason as Lord Marchmain—to flee from the demands of conscience and maturity. Julia, unable as a Catholic to marry well in a Protestant society, renounces her faith in order to wed the man of her choice. The name "Flyte" thus aptly applies to these characters on the run from the Hound of Heaven.

In a candid conversation with Charles, Lord Marchmain's mistress Cara states that while Alex Marchmain despises his wife, he is in reality "hating all the illusions of boyhood—innocence, God, hope," and she warns Charles that Sebastian appears similarly unable to grow up (103). Indeed, the teddy bear carrying Sebastian's one desire is for a simple, unchanging existence. In love with his carefree youth, rebelling at the hovering presence of Lady Marchmain who stands for the demands of faith and duty, and perhaps guilty of indulging in homosexual practice (as the novel suggests but never states), Sebastian falls into alcoholism and despondency. When Charles finds Sebastian in Morocco, he stumbles upon "the key I lacked" when Sebastian reveals his deep need to care for someone even worse off than himself after a lifetime of being cared for

(215). But however he may disregard it in practice, Sebastian never fully leaves his faith behind. His comments to Charles early in their relationship consistently confirm the depths of his belief, and his Augustinian prayer—"Oh God, make me good, but not yet"—prefigures his later embrace of religion. When she relates the tale of Sebastian's return to the Church, Cordelia suggests that Sebastian has even become a holy man, purified by the physical and mental suffering of addiction. "One can have no idea what the suffering may be, to be maimed as he is—no dignity, no power of will," she tells Charles. "No one is ever holy without suffering. . . . It's the spring of love" (309).

Julia's story of reconversion is far different. Resentful of the restrictions placed on her because of her family's Catholicism and determined to rise in society, she defies her mother by marrying the divorced Rex Mottram, a marriage clearly doomed from the beginning due to Rex's persistent infidelity and complete lack of moral and spiritual sensibility. As Julia bitterly discovers soon after the marriage, Rex was only "a tiny bit of a man pretending he was the whole," a phrase which, interestingly, Charles also later applies to himself (200). Searching for fulfillment, Julia has followed a lover to New York, but that affair, too, has failed, and thus she eagerly accepts Charles's companionship, as he does hers, when they come together in a storm at sea on the return ship to England. During their two-year affair and with the threat of war looming, Julia urges Charles toward marriage. But it takes the utterly tactless yet honest remarks of Bridey to force her to confront the moral teachings of her youth, which she has tried for years to repress. Her near-hysterical outburst after Bridey's second major "bombshell" of the novel reveals just how deeply those teachings are embedded in her psyche: she envisions Christ dying for her sin and the possibility of an eternity cast out from heaven if she persists in it. When Charles, trying to comfort her, assures her she's merely recalling the "nonsense" of her childhood teaching, she exclaims, "How I wish it was!" just as Sebastian had long before (290). An unwonted tension between the two mounts, reaching its peak when Julia, although hesitant earlier, insists on calling a priest for the dying Lord Marchmain. Clearly sensing a decisive moment approaching and anticipating the end of this his second Arcadian interlude, Charles strongly attempts to dissuade her from summoning Father Mackay. But Julia prevails, and it is not surprising to Charles that, after the cataclysmic moment of Lord Marchmain's death, Julia renounces him in a type of atonement for her years of transgressions. As one critic puts it, "She has no illusions about herself: she knows that she is unlikely to live a wholly virtuous life, but within the Church sin may be pardoned, whereas in marriage beyond the Church's recognition she would be out-cast, and grace could not reach her."[11]

While some critics contend that the scene of Lord Marchmain's deathbed conversion seems too contrived, a similar event actually occurred in Waugh's life when an impenitent friend of his suddenly made the sign of the cross on his deathbed. It was Waugh himself who had summoned a priest to give his friend the sacraments over the objections of family members. What must have been a profoundly moving experience for Waugh was turned into the pivotal scene of *Brideshead*. While Lord Marchmain's returning to Brideshead after his long absence foreshadows his return to the faith, it is Julia's act of calling the priest that sets the chain of conversions in motion. Waugh makes the stocky, bland Father Mackay purposely unimpressive so as to emphasize the powerful force of the sacraments he administers. Unaccountably, despite his vociferous objections, Charles finds himself on his knees, praying that Lord Marchmain will die repentant if only for the comfort it will bring Julia. Although his prayer is at first tentative, Charles suddenly knows with full conviction that God exists when Lord Marchmain makes the penitential gesture of tracing the sign of the cross on his body. "Then I knew that the sign I had asked for was not a little thing . . . and a phrase came back to me from my childhood of the veil of the temple being rent from top to bottom," he recalls (338–39).

The title of the second part of the novel, "A Twitch upon the Thread," is taken from a line in one of the Father Brown stories read by Lady Marchmain on the "bad" evening of Sebastian's drunkenness during the Easter holiday. It suggests that while God permits his children at times to wander far from the faith, he eventually and inevitably draws them back. So-called Catholic guilt, which Lord Marchmain, Julia, and Sebastian exhibit in spades, is, to Waugh, merely another name for a well-formed conscience. *Brideshead*, in fact, demonstrates the importance of a solid Catholic upbringing, such as that provided to her children by Lady Marchmain. Yet while she can be viewed as instrumental to the reconversions of her husband and children, Lady Marchmain remains an ambiguous figure, respected but unloved. On the one hand, she is a controlling, demanding woman who succeeds in alienating her husband and children. On the other hand, she is consistently associated with the chapel and with the figure of the Seven Dolours, Our Lady of Sorrows, whose heart was pierced by the sorrows she endured for her child's sake. As Frederick J. Stopp points out,

[Lady Marchmain's] role of catalyst in precipitating spiritual processes, of instrument in leading back her husband and her wayward children

to the fold of an ancient faith, could hardly assure her of their affection. . . . But if the Chapel, closed at her death, but presumably reopened after the penitent end of Marchmain, can become, in the concluding passages, the keynote of a new hope, this is due not least to
her insistent, disturbing, infuriating presence, destroying all the immediate creature happiness of several of her family, but leaving them with
their essential spiritual instinct intact.[12]

Thus Lady Marchmain may even be considered a Christ-like figure,
despised on earth for preaching a message her wayward family members do
not want to hear but leading them finally back after her death to the Christian fold. Moreover, the nunlike Nanny Hawkins, saying her rosary high in
her attic room, also serves a role in these conversions through her constant
prayer. Thus does Waugh implicitly confirm in *Brideshead* the Catholic
teaching of the Communion of Saints—that both the living and the dead
are bound together in charity and can help each other toward salvation.

Waugh effectively employs a number of evocative symbols in the
novel. Brideshead Castle itself, reconstructed in the seventeenth century of
stones from a earlier building, represents the deeply embedded tradition of
the Catholic faith in England, evidence of which Waugh found meaningful in precipitating his own conversion. The name of the house itself
comes from its location at the headwaters of the river Bride, a word deriving from the phrase often used for the Church, "Bride of Christ."
Moreover, at Brideshead two major symbols intertwine, that of the fountain and that of the chapel. The magnificent fountain on the estate
grounds, transported from Italy, symbolizes not only the Catholic heritage
but, in its intricate design, the endless creativity and diversity of God's universe. In studying it and sketching it, Charles feels a completely new sensation within him, "as though the water that spurted and bubbled among
its stones was indeed a life-giving spring" (82). The baptismal imagery
here is clear. Several other significant scenes are also set at the fountain, including Julia's outburst when Bridey accuses her of sin. Decorated in os-
tentatious, outdated art nouveau, the Brideshead chapel is at first viewed
merely as an aesthetic piece by Charles. Since he attaches no religious importance to it, statements such as Cordelia's emphatic "I think it's *beautiful*," and, at its closing, "suddenly, there wasn't any chapel there any more,
just an oddly decorated room," mystify him (92, 220). At the end of the
novel, when the fountain is covered with chicken wire and desecrated by
soldiers' cigarette butts, attention becomes focused on the newly reopened
chapel and its sanctuary light signify God's constant love and presence

among us. There, as he prays before the altar, Charles understands that "something quite remote from anything the [chapel] builders intended has come out of their work"—his own conversion to the faith (351). While aesthetic experience has opened the door to spiritual realities, he now looks beyond such matters to the God at the center of all creation.

Another important and related motif in the novel is that of the Latin phrase, *Quomodo sedet sola civitas* ("How solitary doth the city sit"), repeated three times with increasing significance. From the Lamentations of Jeremiah, the phrase mourns the destruction of Jerusalem and the consequent exile of the Jewish people. For Christians, it has traditionally been viewed as foreshadowing Christ's death and is thus used during Mass in Holy Week. Cordelia first cites the phrase when she relates to Charles how the chapel at Brideshead was closed upon Lady Marchmain's death. It appears again as Charles contemplates his inner emptiness on the ship returning to England. Lastly, Charles recalls the phrase once more as he surveys the devastation of Brideshead in the epilogue. The phrase is rich in symbolism. For one thing, its incremental repetition provides an indicator of Charles's spiritual development. The first time he hears the phrase it means nothing at all to him; the second time, he applies it in self-pity to his own arid emotional state; but the last time, he understands the phrase fully in its profound Christian implications. For faith to reach fruition, one must often first experience the collapse of all illusions of earthly fulfillment. This is the paradox of losing one's life in order to gain it. For Charles, now "homeless, childless, middle-aged, loveless," as he tells Hooper, all hope of fulfillment in his career and his love life has dissipated while, paradoxically, he has gained supernatural perspective and a genuine, sustaining faith (350). At the end, too, Brideshead Castle, now empty and forlorn, is only a shell of its former glory. But at its core burns the sanctuary light just as Julia, Sebastian, and Charles retain the redeeming light of faith despite the seeming tragedy of their lives.

Perhaps Waugh's greatest achievement in *Brideshead* is that while it is not a preachy or didactic book, it leaves the reader with a profound sense of the mystery and enduring power of Catholicism. Waugh doesn't, in fact, depict individual Catholics in a good light here at all, and embracing the faith is not made particularly appealing. Even after his conversion, Charles, for example, as one critic has stated, "is hardly a strong recommendation for the faith he has embraced" for he can be uncharitable and arrogant.[13] Despite such criticism, Waugh, however, refused to be the kind of Catholic writer who "produce[s] only advertising brochures setting out in attractive terms the advantages of Church membership."[14] While the novel may put emphasis on less savory aspects of the faith, it clearly confirms that in the futility of the modern pagan wasteland and the sordidness of a world at war, the Catholic Church offers the only sure hope, a "light in the darkness" that alone makes sense of the chaos of existence.

FOR FURTHER READING (AND VIEWING)

Evelyn Waugh, *The Loved One*
———, *The Sword of Honor Trilogy*
Augustine of Hippo, *Confessions* of St. Augustine
T. S. Eliot, *The Waste Land*
In 1982, Granada produced a ten-hour film version of *Brideshead Revisited* starring Jeremy Irons that, because it is a faithful rendition of the book, is highly recommended viewing.

QUESTIONS FOR DISCUSSION

1. Consider the Augustinian theme of the "restless search of the heart" in *Brideshead* in more detail as it applies to both Sebastian and Charles. In what other ways is the *Confessions* echoed in this novel?
2. Comment on how, as outsiders to the Marchmain family, Rex Mottram and Charles Ryder are paired although they are very different in character.
3. What does Sebastian mean when he tells Charles on page 89 that being happy has little to do with faith and that Catholics have a much different view of life than most people? How does the overall theme of this novel support the idea that conversion is a matter of seeing things differently than others?
4. Charles views his impending conversion in the image of an avalanche, an image repeated several times. Of what significance is this image?
5. What is Waugh's point about Charles's experience of human love and aesthetic beauty preparing the way for him, so to speak, to conversion?
6. Comment on the effectiveness of one or more of the comic scenes in the novel, such as Charles's father's "revenge" dinner party.

NOTES

Evelyn Waugh, *Brideshead Revisited* (Boston: Little, Brown, 1973). All references are to this edition.

1. Evelyn Waugh, "Death in Hollywood," *Life* (September 29, 1947), 84.
2. Evelyn Waugh, "Fan-Fare," *Life* (April 8, 1946), 56.
3. Quoted in Jeffrey Heath, "*Brideshead*: The Critics and the Memorandum," *English Studies* 56, no. 3 (June 1975): 227.
4. Katharyn W. Crabbe, *Evelyn Waugh* (New York: Continuum, 1988), 95.
5. Augustine's actual prayer is "Grant me chastity and continence, but not yet," *Confessions,* translated by Henry Chadwick (Oxford: Oxford University Press, 1998), 145.
6. Augustine, *Confesssions*, 3.
7. Frederick J. Stopp, *Evelyn Waugh: Portrait of an Artist* (Boston: Little, Brown, 1958), 112.
8. Stopp, *Evelyn Waugh,* 118.
9. Laura Mooneyham, "The Triple Conversions of *Brideshead Revisited,*" *Renascence* 45, no. 4 (Summer 1993): 225–35.
10. Quoted in Stopp, *Evelyn Waugh,* 108.
11. Eric Linklater, *The Art of Adventure* (London: Macmillan, 1948), 52.
12. Stopp, *Evelyn Waugh,* 111.
13. Robert R. Garnett, *From Grimes to Brideshead: The Early Novels of Evelyn Waugh* (Lewisburg, PA: Bucknell University Press, 1990), 157.
14. Evelyn Waugh, "Felix Culpa?" *Commonweal* (July 16, 1948): 322.

BIBLIOGRAPHY

Carens, James F. *The Satiric Art of Evelyn Waugh.* Seattle: University of Washington Press, 1966.

Cook, William J., Jr. *Masks, Modes, and Morals: The Art of Evelyn Waugh.* Rutherford: Fairleigh Dickinson University Press, 1971.

Crabbe, Katharyn W. *Evelyn Waugh.* New York: Continuum, 1988.

DeVitis, A. A. *Roman Holiday: The Catholic Novels of Evelyn Waugh.* London: Vision Press, 1958.

Garnett, Robert R. *From Grimes to Brideshead: The Early Novels of Evelyn Waugh.* Lewisburg, PA: Bucknell University Press, 1990.

Lane, Calvin W. *Evelyn Waugh.* Boston: Twayne, 1981.

Stopp, Frederick J. *Evelyn Waugh: Portrait of an Artist.* Boston: Little, Brown, 1958.

Wykes, David. *Evelyn Waugh: A Literary Life.* New York: St. Martin's Press, 1999.

FLANNERY O'CONNOR
EVERYTHING THAT
RISES MUST CONVERGE

BIOGRAPHY

A brilliant and unique talent, Mary Flannery O'Connor was born in Savannah, Georgia, on March 25, 1925, the only child of Edward F. Jr. and Regina Cline O'Connor. Both parents were descended from old southern Catholic families. When Flannery was thirteen, her father was diagnosed with the rare, inherited blood disease, disseminated lupus. He quit his real estate job, and the family moved back to Regina's ancestral town of Milledgeville, Georgia, a rural, fundamentalist Protestant community. Edward died there in 1941. Flannery attended Georgia State College for Women (now Georgia College) in Milledgeville, earning her bachelor's degree in an accelerated three-year program. During her undergraduate years, she served as the arts editor of the student newspaper, edited the campus literary magazine, and was well known for her witty drawings and caricatures. Upon graduation in 1945, she received a fellowship to study at the prestigious Writer's Workshop at the University of Iowa. While working on a master's degree in creative writing, she published her first short stories and began early drafts of what would become her first novel, *Wise Blood*.

At the age of twenty-two, with an advanced degree in hand, O'Connor moved to New York City in the hope of launching a writing career. In the fall of 1949, she took up residence as a boarder at the rural Connecticut farm home of friends and fellow Catholics, Robert and Sally Fitzgerald. However, her stay in the east was cut short when, in 1950, she too was diagnosed with lupus. She subsequently moved back to her mother's farm in Milledgeville where she lived out the rest of her short life, leaving home only briefly to give speeches or to visit friends.

Over the years, O'Connor's writing won a number of awards, which she used in part to pay for her medical expenses. These included two *Kenyon Review* fellowships for fiction (1953, 1954); several O. Henry awards for first prize stories; a grant from the National Institute of Arts and Letters (1957); and a Ford Foundation grant (1959). Her productivity decreased sharply in her last years as the disease worsened. Typically, she spent two or three hours writing in the mornings, producing one or two pages of manuscript, and then spent the afternoons "recovering" from the effort by reading, entertaining visitors, and tending to her brood of peacocks, chickens, and swans. Her wry sense of humor, often directed toward herself, never abated. She died in 1964 at the age of thirty-nine.

O'Connor lived nearly thirteen years aware of her approaching death and increasingly dependent on her mother as her illness progressed. The two women's very different personalities and outlooks made their relationship, while loving and deep, strained at times. A perceptive visitor to the home described Regina O'Connor as "a small, intense, enormously efficient woman, who, as she fussed strenuously and even tyrannically over Flannery, gave off an air of martyrdom which was the exact opposite of her daughter's quiet acceptance."[1] The tensions and complexities of the mother–daughter bond fueled some of O'Connor's best work. Her fiction returns time and again to parent and adult child relationships, especially in terms of assertion of pride and position, and to matters of would-be writers and artists. Many of her stories also end in the death of the protagonist.

O'Connor's corpus of works includes thirty-one short stories, nineteen of which were collected in the two volumes, *A Good Man Is Hard to Find* (1955) and the posthumously published *Everything That Rises Must Converge* (1965). *Flannery O'Connor: The Complete Stories* appeared in 1971. She also penned two short novels, *Wise Blood* (1952) and *The Violent Bear It Away* (1960). Her letters, through which we can learn much about her artistic sensibility and personality, have been collected in *The Habit of Being*. Also highly recommended is a volume of her speeches and essays, *Mystery and Manners,* in which she reflects in a more formal manner on the purpose and themes of her writing, and addresses such issues as her use of the grotesque, her identification as a regional Southern writer, and the impact of her faith on her fiction.

CRITICAL OVERVIEW

Flannery O'Connor's strong Catholic faith influenced all of her writing. Rather than restrict art, she was convinced that belief in Catholic doctrine expanded a writer's vision for it allowed the exploration of both the natural and supernatural realms. Doctrine, she maintained, actually provides "an instrument for penetrating reality. Christian dogma is about the only thing left in the world that surely guards and respects mystery."[2] Throughout her life, she was constantly preoccupied by such basic Christian concepts as sin, grace, and salvation. "I see from the standpoint of Christian orthodoxy," she stated. "This means that for me the meaning of life is centered in our Redemption by Christ and what I see in the world I see in its relation to that."[3] With her deeply held religious convictions, one might expect that O'Connor focused her writing on Catholic topics. However, the opposite is true: overtly Catholic characters, situations, and themes only rarely appear in her work. Instead, she wrote about what she knew best, her Protestant fundamentalist neighbors in small southern towns like the Milledgeville she knew so well. The uniqueness of her vision arises from the fact that she observes her characters and their environment from an overarching Catholic perspective. O'Connor was intrigued by the dramatic possibilities of the southern evangelical imperative to decide unequivocally for or against Jesus. She found, however, the American Protestant tendency toward individualism not only inadequate but even, in its extreme expression, destructive. Still, her sternest eye is directed toward modern, secular agnostics and liberal Protestants who, in diluting the hard facts of salvation, have forgotten the immense cost of Jesus' sacrifice.

O'Connor's major theme in all her works is the operation of God's grace in the world as it touches human lives and leads persons to deeper conversion. She concentrates, therefore, on the important moments in her characters' lives where they are invited to respond to God's grace. And since Christ's sacrifice is one of immense consequence, grace in O'Connor's world never comes easily or cheaply. Rather, more often than not it comes through violent means, invading complacent lives in disquieting, sometimes even horrifying, ways. "I have found that violence is strangely capable of returning my characters to reality and preparing them to accept their moment of grace. Their heads are so hard that almost nothing else will do the work," she observed.[4] While the repeated use of violence marks her fiction as particularly modern, it is never used gratuitously. Although shocking to characters and readers alike, such violence is always consistent with the story's plot and usually results from a character's own making. More importantly, on a symbolic level, it points to the violence of Christ's Passion and death, bloodshed necessary in God's plan of salvation. As one critic has put it, O'Connor's fiction constantly "pushes us back to the agonizing scandal of the cross."[5]

Although each story's situation differs, O'Connor's typical protagonist is a person who prides him or herself on being, in some way, "better" than others: smarter, a harder worker, a nicer disposition, more tolerant, more virtuous. Many characters are enormously pleased with their independence, hard-won achievements, or ability to arrange and control their lives for maximum security or ease. Self-described "intellectuals" or "artists"—those who are especially smug because of superior education or supposed talent—abound in O'Connor's fiction. Yet another type of character is one who knows God but tries, Jonah-like, to flee from his call. But no matter what form of arrogance they exhibit, all of O'Connor's protagonists suffer from a grossly distorted perception of who they really are. Firmly situated at the center of their own universe, they scorn those who think or look different than themselves, and they regard all intrusions into their carefully constructed lives as personal threats.

Such radical self-deception is in desperate need of correction. In every O'Connor story, a reversal occurs with the sudden, violent influx of God's grace. The proud, hypocritical person is revealed and judged by the higher standards of truth and charity. The effect of this revelation is the complete shattering of the character's "old self" in order to make room for the new. God's grace alters these characters' self-satisfied views of themselves and gives them, for the first time, an understanding of how they actually appear in God's eyes. While extremely disorienting, this new sight may lead—although we never know for sure—to the humility necessary for greater charity. "The surest sign of spiritual progress in O'Connor's fiction is a character's recognition of her or his wretchedness," Richard Giannone has stated.[6] O'Connor exhibits a profoundly Catholic sensibility in her belief that self-knowledge must precede conversion. "To know oneself is, above all, to know what one lacks," she stated. "It is to measure oneself against Truth, and not the other way around. The first product of self-knowledge is humility."[7]

O'Connor viewed herself as a writer of realism, but this descriptor needs qualification. As a Catholic author, she found it a great advantage that she didn't have to "play God" by trying to disguise or, as she put it, "tidy up" reality. The Catholic writer, she maintained, is "entirely free to observe. He feels no call to take on the duties of God or to create a new universe. He feels perfectly free to look at the one we already have and to show exactly what he sees."[8] Although known as an astute critic of the pre–Civil Rights South poised on the brink of social and economic change and seething with racial tensions, O'Connor never intended to produce mere sociological realism but rather aimed at fidelity to moral and spiritual truth. While her situations and characters are grounded in the concrete, like Nathaniel Hawthorne and writers of the romance tradition she "claim[ed] a certain latitude" of the imagination in order to approach the "truth of the human heart."[9] Thus, even while recording the racial and class conflicts of her times, she is interested in such tensions primarily as manifestations of the human tendency toward pride, which, as the greatest sin, breeds all forms of injustice, bigotry, hypocrisy, and hatred.

A "realist of distances," O'Connor, then, distorts surface reality to point to a higher reality.[10] Many first-time readers are struck—and not a little put off—by the odd, even grotesque look of her fiction. But such purposeful distortions deeply reflect the author's religious beliefs. Her characters, often deformed physically or spiritually and rarely likeable, seem more like caricatures than fully rounded human beings. As such, they suggest the spiritual truth that all people, when measured against God, are crippled by original sin. Through the use of freakish characters, O'Connor thus calls attention to our warped state in need of healing. The whole mystery of salvation is indeed just that—a great mystery. Jesus' life and death, O'Connor believed, radically changed all human experience for all time. As her character, the Misfit, puts it in one of her stories, "Jesus thown everything off balance."[11] Her fiction explores a fallen world grotesque in its extreme need of salvation and the very strangeness of God's plan for that salvation. After all, "what could be stranger than a God who decides to suffer with us? What could be more uncomfortable or more violent than the cross? What could be more comically grotesque than an individual trying to escape his own identity as God's child and in his rush out the temple door, smacking straight into the Incarnation?"[12] The odd, wild look of O'Connor's fiction reflects her sense of a world seen from God's eyes, one fallen in sin and in dire need of righting again.

O'Connor's stories are challenging on many levels. Their tone, for example, can be disconcerting for it alters between darkly satiric, broadly comic, and deadly serious. In addition, O'Connor was a master at dramatic timing and the manipulation of readers' responses. Her stories present complex interplays between the author's, narrator's, and characters' points of view. These multiple and often incongruous viewpoints not only serve to create a story's irony but also contribute to the reader's sense of dislocation. Typically, O'Connor lulls us into identifying with one character's thoughts and judgments only to reverse our sympathies later in the story. Such shifting perspectives disrupt our expectations because, with the reversal, the character we thought was the "good" or "correct" one no longer seems so benign or trustworthy. As a consequence, we, the readers, are forced to reassess our own values and standards of moral behavior. Furthermore, we recognize ourselves in the protagonists and therefore must acknowledge our own capacities for pettiness, meanness, hypocrisy, and pride. As Dorothy Walters states about O'Connor's technique, "When one looks *with* her, he perceives the comic. When one looks *at* her, he is suddenly made aware that he—the *hypocrite lecteur*—is himself being looked at, for the fictional characters but mirror his own self-image."[13] Finally, O'Connor's open endings invite us to speculate on what we might do in such a situation. As one critic succinctly puts it, "[O'Connor] leaves us the beauty of paradox, which is a great gift."[14]

Above all, O'Connor is never sentimental or artificially consoling: salvation remains for her a difficult truth, and humans are free to accept or reject the grace of conversion. O'Connor often received letters from Catholic readers who were dismayed at the sordid look of her fiction: this was not what "Catholic literature" was supposed to be. But the author refused to satisfy those who merely wanted insipid, "feel good" religious fiction that soothed their own sense of self-righteousness. "I once received a letter from an old lady in California who informed me that when the tired reader comes home at night, he wishes to read something that will lift up his heart," she quipped. "And it seems her heart had not been lifted up by anything of mine she had read. . . . One old lady who wants her heart lifted up wouldn't be so bad, but you multiply her two hundred and fifty thousand times and what you get is a book club."[15]

A voracious reader of theology and philosophy, whose influences include Augustine, Thomas Aquinas, Jacques Maritain, Romano Guardini, William Lynch, and Edith Stein, O'Connor studied Pierre Teilhard de Chardin's (1881–1955) writings a few years before she died. In such works as *The Phenomenon of Man* and *The Divine Milieu*, the French paleontologist, philosopher, and Jesuit priest expresses his belief that humankind is progressing in an evolutionary process toward ultimate fusion with an Omega point, that is, God. O'Connor found intriguing de Chardin's thesis that charity drives this upward evolutionary movement, and that the closer one moves in love toward Christ, the more one grows in brotherhood with one's fellow humans. To de Chardin, the human tendency toward self-sufficiency and self-seeking is harmful and is checked by the force of such convergence. "It is impossible to love Christ without loving others (in proportion as these others are moving towards Christ). And it is impossible to love others (in a spirit of broad human communion) without moving nearer to Christ," he wrote.[16] As a Catholic believer, O'Connor's vision of community found resonance in de Chardin's statement for she understood that all believers, living and dead, are mystically united in the Body of Christ. In O'Connor's works, the grace offered in the moment of conversion is a call to an acknowledgement of our essential relationship to others in God. The fact that O'Connor derived the title of her last story collection *Everything That Rises Must Converge* from de Chardin is thus significant to our interpretation of this work.

In her final year of life, O'Connor carefully arranged seven stories into a sequence that illustrates de Chardin's theory of a constant rising toward consciousness and convergence with others. The first story, "Everything That Rises Must Converge," signals the entrance into that higher consciousness, and the last story, "Revelation," unusual in O'Connor's canon, presents an elaborate culmination of this spiritual ascent in the detailed final vision of the protagonist. Each of the five stories in between these two bookends—"Greenleaf," "A View of the Woods," "The Enduring Chill," "The Comforts of Home," and "The Lame Shall Enter First"—shows the main character achieving, through the action of grace, some degree of new insight into his or her spiritual and moral condition. Thus, the first seven stories in the volume can be read fruitfully as a type of short-story cycle, as critic Forrest L. Ingram has discussed in his perceptive article, "O'Connor's Seven-Story Cycle."[17] Ingram maintains that the selection of these seven stories was O'Connor's original intention, and that the last two pieces that now end the volume, "Parker's Back" and "Judgment Day," were added by her editors after her death and unfortunately upset the unity of the cycle. As Ingram notes, O'Connor arranged the seven stories not by the date they were written or initially published, but so that they complement and comment on each other. Each story employs similar character types, themes, and situations and thus, by a type of incremental repetition, contributes to the volume's dynamic movement of rising and converging. A number of stories concern racial relations as the New South with its growing social and economic power for Blacks meets the Old South of prejudice and stubborn resistance to change. Several stories revolve around property threatened, and others focus on the sensibility of the artist–intellectual. Four of the volume's works discuss mother–son relationships. All seven stories are linked by the overweening pride and hypocrisy of the protagonists and their lack of sincere charity for others. And, as we will see below in the discussion of "Revelation," O'Connor suggests that this lack of charity, when taken to its logical extreme, may result in true evil.

The first story, "Everything That Rises Must Converge," introduces the themes, characters, and symbols that will be repeated throughout the cycle. The young adult and would-be writer Julian despises his mother for her elitist and prejudiced attitudes in their small southern town where Blacks have only recently made advances. Determined to teach her a lesson about her blindness and pettiness, Julian persists in irritating his mother as he reluctantly accompanies her downtown to her YWCA weight-reduction class. O'Connor deftly sets up the interior of the bus as a kind of microcosm of society, with riders of both colors uneasily sizing up the seating arrangements and choosing their positions carefully to avoid contact. The fact that Julian's mother encounters—to her dismay and Julian's delight—a Black woman who owns the same high fashion (but ridiculous looking) hat suggests just how far Blacks and Whites have now "converged" in matters of taste and buying power.

Although exquisite in its evocation of racial tension, the story is primarily concerned with Julian's inner life. In the first part, we sympathize with his judgment about his mother: she *is* obviously prejudiced and patronizing, and the educated Julian does seem, by contrast, morally superior. However, by the story's middle what we thought were correct judgments become confused. As Julian's self-talk continues and as the narrator, observing the situation from a higher plane, comments, the young man is revealed to be utterly phony. Retreating, as is his wont, into an insular mental bubble, he fancies himself successful, when, as the narrator informs us, in reality he is a failure. He deems himself free of elitist attitudes when, in fact, he longs for the patriarchal southern mansion and elegant lifestyle his ancestors once enjoyed. He considers himself liberated from his mother, yet he is clearly all but helpless without her. And he believes he is broad-minded and prejudice-free when in fact, in his current revengeful mood, he views Blacks merely as tools with which he can further antagonize his mother. While the story doesn't excuse Julian's mother for her bigoted attitudes, they are shown to be products of her generation's socialization and thus more forgivable than Julian's calculated maliciousness. Despite the story's repeated warnings that his mother's blood pressure is dangerously high, Julian succumbs to the "evil urge to break her spirit" (8). But when she collapses of an apparent heart attack after being hit by the woman who wears the identical hat, Julian's entire façade crumbles in an instant, leaving him lost and forlorn. Only now does he recognize his deep childlike love of and need for his mother. At the story's end, he is poised to enter a "world of guilt and sorrow" (23). In O'Connor's Christian economy, this is actually a hopeful ending. His mother's sudden, tragic death forces Julian into a bitter but healing self-knowledge. For the rest of his life, he will have to live with the guilt of having treated her so shamefully despite all she sacrificed for him, and this guilt may lead him to greater humility, repentance, and charity.

In "Greenleaf," Mrs. May's overriding concern is for the smooth operation of her dairy farm. A rigid, controlling woman, proud of her ability to manage her farm as a widow despite two good-for-nothing adult sons, she struggles with her tenant, Mr. Greenleaf, whom she considers lazy and inept. Mrs. May constantly feels the victim of forces plotting against her, and her dreams reveal her fear of being attacked by some irrational thing she cannot control. Once when she comes across Mrs. Greenleaf, a self-styled prayer healer, prostrate on the ground in prayer, she is appalled at such an obscene display of emotion: "She thought the word, Jesus, should be kept inside the church building like other words inside the bedroom. She was a good Christian woman with a large respect for religion, though she did not, of course, believe any of it was true" (31). The story's plot revolves around the antics of the Greenleaf sons' bull, which has broken from its pen and is now running loose on Mrs. May's property. One of O'Connor's most complex symbols, the bull, described variously as a "wild tormented lover" and "some patient god come down to woo her," blends both pagan fertility imagery with Christian imagery (52, 24). Aggressive and spontaneous, a "violent unleashed force," it is equated not only with the force of sexuality and physical passion (Mrs. May especially worries it will get into her cow pen and upset the breeding schedule) but also with Christ and the power of the Spirit (it wears a wreathe reminiscent of the crown of thorns and has been lost three days) (30–31). But this symbolism is, of course, lost on Mrs. May who knows only that the bull belongs to the despised Greenleaf family and is thus a personal affront to her authority. It is no wonder, then, that she insists that Mr. Greenleaf shoot it. At the story's end, even as she gleefully envisions the possibility that her tenant might be gored by the bull, she herself receives the heart stabbing. In her dying moment, her sight is "suddenly restored," but the new vision, as the narrator tells us, is "unbearable" (52). Her eyes close against it, evidently rejecting it.

The third story in the volume, "A View of the Woods," also presents a tragic conclusion in which the protagonist seems unwilling—and is given little time—to accept the grace of self-knowledge. This story sets up a conflict between a prideful seventy-nine-year-old man, Mark

Fortune, and his nine-year-old granddaughter, Mary Fortune Pitts. Mr. Fortune lives with his daughter, her husband Pitts, and their children, but he has no use for any of them except little Mary whom he believes alone has inherited his good sense and in whom he has placed all his hopes. In order to spite his son-in-law Pitts, Fortune systematically sells off portions of the land he owns to outside developers in the name of "progress." His faith placed in urban development schemes (he envisions a town in the future named "Fortune"), he vehemently attacks any obstacle to his plans and revels in his ability to disappoint the Pitts family who would like to have the rural property for their own. Believing that he's formed his protégée, Mary, into his own image, Fortune is astonished when she sharply opposes his latest plan to sell off the lot called "the lawn" that lies between the family's home and the woods. In O'Connor's works, it should be noted, woods are usually associated with supernatural mystery or mystical vision. When Mary insists that, if the lawn is sold, they will not have a view of the woods, Fortune has no idea what she talking about, for he has no capacity whatsoever for spiritual insight. To him, the woods hold only an "uncomfortable mystery" from which he turns away (71). When Mary continues to resist, the old man's frustration turns to cruelty, and he decides to beat her into submission. But in his mounting rage, he kills his granddaughter. In a horrifying moment of recognition, he understands what he has done: murder the only person who has loved him and whom he loves. Even more frightening, in a blinding moment of truth before he succumbs to heart failure, he realizes the futility of his faith in "progress" to save him: as he lays dying, only the huge, inert bulldozer, a symbol of mechanized power and destruction, hulks at his side. As is typical in O'Connor's stories, we are not told whether or not Mark Fortune repents of his behavior in his last moment, but it appears that he does not, making this one of the author's most pessimistic tales.

In "The Comforts of Home," Thomas, whose name means "twin," is paired with a delinquent young woman, the "little slut," Sarah Ham (a.k.a. Star Drake). Although thirty-five years old, Thomas, like many of O'Connor's young adult protagonists, has never married, lives at home, and depends completely on his mother for an orderly domestic life and well-cooked meals. After many years of such a comfortable routine, he deeply resents change. Thus when his mother, a do-gooder whose heart is in the right place although her actions are naïve, brings Sarah Ham home in order to rehabilitate the wayward girl, Thomas's anger at the girl, who taunts him and threatens both his security and his sexuality, swells to the point of desperation. The more distressed he becomes, the more he "hears" in his mind the contemptuous voice of his dead father, a cruel man who had mocked his only son for not being assertive enough. In his overpowering urge to preserve his comfort, Thomas eventually succumbs to that evil voice. Seizing upon his father's gun, he shoots at Sarah but inadvertently kills his mother instead. Now, his mother's repeated phrase to her son throughout the story, "I keep thinking [Sarah Ham] might be you," becomes ironically true, for at the story's conclusion Thomas has turned criminal, something he never thought possible. Moreover, his crime, matricide, is far more heinous than Sarah's petty misdemeanors. In a final ironic twist, the sheriff who comes upon the appalling scene just as it occurs instantly leaps to the conclusion that Thomas intended to kill his mother in order to be with Sarah. We can surmise, therefore, that Thomas will have to spend years, if not life, in prison on an unfair conviction. Still, similar to Julian in "Everything That Rises Must Converge," whose entrance into the "world of guilt and sorrow" is, to O'Connor, a positive spiritual step, Thomas may accept the grace of remorse and the humility of recognizing that, before God, he too is a sinner in need of salvation.

"The Enduring Chill" features yet another of O'Connor's pretentious young intellectuals whose gods are art and their own minds. Unsuccessful as a writer and now ill from an unknown cause, Asbury Fox comes home to his mother's farm intending to die a romantic artist's death, which he hopes will deeply wound his mother. Although at first unconvinced of the gravity of her son's illness, Mrs. Fox grows worried when Dr. Block, the local physician, cannot locate the cause of the disease. To alarm his mother even further, Asbury suddenly decides he wants to see a priest. Some time ago, he had encountered a young Jesuit who had impressed him with his cool intelligence. Mrs. Fox reluctantly complies with Asbury's request, but the priest who shows up the next day is not at all what Asbury expected. Fat, slovenly, and with only one eye, Father Finn likewise proves "single-eyed" in his purpose, dismissing Asbury's desire to discuss intellectual topics with a wave of his hand and demanding whether or not Asbury says his prayers. Asbury gets rid of the old man as soon as possible. He continues his plans for a romantic death by next insisting that the farm help gather around his bedside in a type of sentimental deathbed tableau. But this gesture, too, proves futile. Finally, as he passively awaits "his god, Art" to bring him death, a triumphant Dr. Block announces he's discovered the cause of Asbury's sickness: a nonfatal though recurring fever usually found in cows (103).

Now, Asbury has even failed at dying. All his defenses gone and knowing that because of his disease he will always be dependent on the mother he scorns, Asbury has no choice but to confront his own failure and sterility. "Shocked clean" from self-delusion, he is, at the story's end, poised to receive the grace of the Holy Spirit, which O'Connor figures humorously as a bird-shaped water stain on the ceiling (114). While violent and fearful, its descent will transform Asbury spiritually. Asbury's physical illness, on the other hand, becomes a vehicle for God's grace, and the "enduring chill" that he will have to live with a reminder of his inner corruption and impending death. This constant awareness may prompt Asbury to live a better life. "The Enduring Chill" is one of several O'Connor stories about the inability of art to save. In its many images of the Holy Spirit, it suggests that God is the only source of true inspiration and creativity.

In the cycle's penultimate tale, "The Lame Shall Enter First," we at first identify strongly with the kindly social worker, Sheppard, whose young wife has recently died and who reaches out to save a troubled, homeless boy, Rufus Johnson. But in this tense work charged with religious confrontation, O'Connor explores just what the word "save" means. A liberal reformist and atheist, Sheppard believes in purely sociological and psychological means of "salvation," and he is confident in his thoroughly rational manner of perceiving the world. He invites Rufus into his home to provide the teenager with an education he hopes will expand his horizons, introducing him, for instance, to the science of the microscope and telescope (both of which become effective symbols for Sheppard's distorted vision). Moreover, Sheppard has convinced himself that if he can only fix Rufus's misshapen club foot with a specially fitted shoe, Rufus's transformation will be complete. But in confronting the Christian fundamentalist Rufus, both Sheppard's beliefs and self-image are sharply challenged. For one thing, Rufus refuses to be "fixed" by Sheppard, whom he mocks. Furthermore, he recognizes that there is only one Savior and that Sheppard is not it. Rufus quickly grasps that the way to antagonize his benefactor is to play up religion, and his talk of Jesus, the devil, and the Bible increasingly infuriates Sheppard who slowly comes to realize that his endeavor to reform the boy is in vain. Significantly, after his repeated attempts to help Rufus fail and the effort he thought would boost his self-esteem becomes self-defeating, Sheppard's "love" switches to hate. His repeated self-vindicating phrase, "I have nothing to reproach myself with; I did more for him than I did for my own child," takes on new meaning as, in a moment of clarity, he suddenly apprehends just how true this statement is. In spending so much time trying to "save" Rufus to feed his sense of righteousness, Sheppard has ignored his own little son Norton, who all the while has been grieving his mother's death. The knowledge of his negligence and the desire to rectify it, however, tragically come too late—Norton hangs himself—but at the end of this story, too, the protagonist receives the grace of self-knowledge and remorse that may lead him, in time, to recognize his own need for a Savior.

Purposely positioned as the final piece of the seven-story cycle, "Revelation" is one of O'Connor's best-loved stories due to its rich humor and the explicitly drawn final vision of its protagonist. As she sits with her husband Claud in the doctor's waiting room (similar to the bus interior in "Everything That Rises Must Converge" a microcosm of society), Mrs. Ruby Turpin's inner monologue furiously works to rank others in a moral hierarchy that, of course, positions herself and Claud, decent White hardworking landowners, near the top. Her image of herself as broad-minded, charitable, and a decent Christian woman is ludicrously false, for at every turn she is shown to be condescending, bigoted, and self-righteous. Moreover, in her hypocritical judgment of others, Mrs. Turpin exhibits a potential for evil that goes far beyond mere pettiness. Unable to classify all humans according to her moral scale (where to put that Black dentist who owns two Lincolns and a swimming pool?); that is, unable to secure fully her own position at the top, she finds herself resorting in her dreams to bundling off all such people in box cars to the gas chamber (196). This horrifying image equating Mrs. Turpin with Hitler and the Holocaust is well calculated by O'Connor to hit us with severe force. O'Connor insists here that the logical end of such myopic egotism is the annihilation of those persons one deems "undesirable." In pride is the origin of all hatred, of true evil.

Just when Mrs. Turpin's rapture over her own merits swells to a crescendo—"Thank you Jesus, for making everything the way it is!" she cries aloud—a girl sitting near her in the waiting room appropriately named Mary Grace literally "throws the book" at her (206). With tremendous force, it hits Mrs. Turpin, significantly, directly over the eye, and the blow has the immediate effect of altering her sight. The shock of this violent action—Mrs. Turpin could not conceive that such a thing might happen to her—and, even more so, Mary Grace's hissed words, "go back to hell where you came from, you old wart hog" launches Mrs. Turpin into an emotional and spiritual crisis (207). To her credit, she recognizes immediately that she has been given some type of divine message, and in anger and confusion she demands, Job–like, an explanation of God. Her anguished question, "how am I a hog and me both?" is both wonderfully comic and deeply metaphysical: how is she both a part of fallen nature yet also saved by God's grace? Fittingly, in a story replete with pig imagery (which here and elsewhere O'Connor uses to symbolize unredeemed human nature), Mrs. Turpin, like the Prodigal Son, begins to sense her own wretchedness and need of salvation while in a pigpen. But it is the final vision she is granted that truly shocks her. She sees a ladder stretching from earth to heaven with people of all races, classes, and conditions climbing up, and she is mortified to find that she and Claud are at the end and not the beginning of the procession. In fact, the very virtues she has staked her righteousness on—her proper behavior, common sense, and pleasant disposition—are not only useless for redemption but actually hindrances to it and must be burnt away before she can enter paradise. Mrs. Turpin's judgment has been wrong, her scale of values completely skewed. Now, she sees clearly the mystery of divine love, which judges far differently than humans do. She is no more worthy of God's grace than the "white trash," Blacks, freaks, and lunatics she has rated below her. In fact, they are entering the kingdom before her.

Like all of O'Connor's stories, "Revelation" hits us uncomfortably close to home. We all tend to make God into our own image, assuming that his way of judging is similar to ours. We all fall into complacent self-pride and the disparaging of others who don't meet our standards of "goodness" or "correct behavior." We echo Ruby Turpin in proclaiming, "I go to Church; I give money to the poor; I say my prayers; I treat others decently—I'm a good person. Thank you Jesus for making me who I am!" But this is the prayer of the Pharisee and not of the Publican. Flannery O'Connor found pride so entrenched in the human condition that only a violent disruption of some type could break through hard heads and offer her characters the grace of realizing their dependence on God and essential connection to all other people. For Mrs. Turpin as for all O'Connor's protagonists, this is indeed "abysmal" but "life-giving knowledge" (217).

FOR FURTHER READING

Flannery O'Conner, *A Good Man Is Hard to Find*
———, *Mystery and Manners*
———, *Wise Blood*

QUESTIONS FOR DISCUSSION

1. In "Everything That Rises Must Converge," Julian's mother, mourning the loss of Old South society, says "I tell you, the bottom rail is on the top" (6). How does this image of a ladder find its culmination in Mrs. Turpin's vision in "Revelation" and thus bring the story cycle to a conclusion?

2. According to Forrest Ingram, each story in the cycle comments on each other and incrementally accrues meaning by repeating certain motifs, symbols, themes, and characters. What are some of these repeated elements from story to story? How does such repetition not only unify the stories but further O'Connor's dominant vision of a fallen world in dire need of salvation?

3. Select one or two stories and comment on O'Connor's use of humor and irony to enhance theme. What type of humor is employed, and how effective is it? How is irony created by the author's manipulation of point of view?

4. Speculate on the ending of each story, citing evidence for whether or not the protagonist accepts his or her moment of grace or insight. Does O'Connor appear more of a pessimist or optimist in her conclusions about her characters' openness to conversion? What paradoxes remain at the end of each story?

5. One technique that O'Connor frequently uses is that of the doubling of characters. Consider the impact, for example, of the following "doubles": Julian's mother and the Black woman with the identical hat in "Everything That Rises Must Converge"; O. T. and E. T. Greenleaf and Wesley and Scofield May in "Greenleaf"; and Thomas and Sarah Ham in "The Comforts of Home."

6. Which of the seven stories appealed to you most, and why? Which made you most uncomfortable, and why?

NOTES

Flannery O'Connor, *Everything That Rises Must Converge* (New York: Farrar, Straus & Giroux, 1993). All references are to this edition.

1. Rosemary M. Magee, ed., *Conversations with Flannery O'Connor* (Jackson: University Press of Mississippi, 1987), 56.

2. Flannery O'Connor, *Mystery and Manners,* edited by Sally and Robert Fitzgerald (New York: Farrar, Straus & Giroux, 1969), 178.

3. O'Connor, *Mystery and Manners,* 32.

4. O'Connor, *Mystery and Manners,* 112.

5. Jill P. Baumgaertner, *Flannery O'Connor: A Proper Scaring* (Wheaton, IL: Harold Shaw, 1988), 13.

6. Richard Giannone, *Flannery O'Connor and the Mystery of Love* (Urbana and Chicago: University of Illinois Press, 1989), 209.

7. O'Connor, *Mystery and Manners,* 35.

8. O'Connor, *Mystery and Manners,* 178.

9. Nathaniel Hawthorne, preface to *The House of Seven Gables* (1851; New York: Penguin, 1981), 1.

10. O'Connor, *Mystery and Manners,* 179.

11. "A Good Man Is Hard to Find," in *Flannery O'Connor: The Complete Stories* (New York: Farrar, Straus & Giroux, 1971), 131. O'Connor intentionally misspells "thrown" to capture the Misfit's speech.

12. Baumgaertner, *Flannery O'Connor,* 16.

13. Dorothy Walters, *Flannery O'Connor* (New York: Twayne, 1973), 21.

14. John Hawkes, *Esprit* (Winter 1964), quoted in *Critical Essays on Flannery O'Connor,* edited by Melvin J. Friedman and Beverly Lyon Clark (Boston: G. K. Hall, 1985), 4.

15. O'Connor, *Mystery and Manners,* 47–48.

16. Pierre Teilhard de Chardin, *The Divine Milieu: An Essay on the Interior Life,* translated by Bernard Wall (New York: Harper and Row, 1960), 125.

17. Forrest L. Ingram, "O'Connor's Seven-Story Cycle," in *The Flannery O'Connor Bulletin* 11 (Autumn 1973): 19–28.

BIBLIOGRAPHY

Baumgaertner, Jill P. *Flannery O'Connor: A Proper Scaring.* Wheaton, IL: Harold Shaw, 1988.

Desmond, John F. *Risen Sons: Flannery O'Connor's Vision of History.* Athens: University of Georgia Press, 1987.

Driskell, Leon V. and Joan T. Brittain. *The Eternal Crossroads: The Art of Flannery O'Connor.* Lexington: University Press of Kentucky, 1971.

Feeley, Sister Kathleen. *Flannery O'Connor: Voice of the Peacock.* New Brunswick, NJ: Rutgers University Press, 1972.

Giannone, Richard. *Flannery O'Connor and the Mystery of Love.* Urbana and Chicago: University of Illinois Press, 1989.

Ingram, Forrest L. "O'Connor's Seven-Story Cycle." *The Flannery O'Connor Bulletin* 11 (Autumn 1973), 19–28.

Martin, Carter W. *The True Country: Themes in the Fiction of Flannery O'Connor.* Nashville, TN: Vanderbilt University Press, 1969.

McFarland, Dorothy Tuck. *Flannery O'Connor.* New York: Frederick Ungar, 1976.

Ragen, Brian Abel. *A Wreck on the Road to Damascus: Innocence, Guilt, and Conversion in Flannery O'Connor.* Chicago: Loyola University Press, 1989.

ANNIE DILLARD
HOLY THE FIRM

BIOGRAPHY

Born in Pittsburgh in 1945, Annie Dillard is the eldest of the three children of Frank and Pam Lambert Doak. Her parents encouraged their children to be unconventional, creative, and expressive, and the arts of storytelling and joketelling were cultivated within the family circle. Pam Doak, in particular, had a quirky, humorous side, and Frank Doak, a business executive, once left home to boat down the Mississippi in imitation of Mark Twain's steamboat voyage in *Life on the Mississippi*. Intelligent and precocious, young Annie collected rocks and insects, played sports, and read everything she could get her hands on. In her autobiographical narrative, *An American Childhood*, she recounts how she especially poured over *The Field Book of Ponds and Streams* and other such guides that opened the wonders of the natural world to her.

Dillard attended Hollins College in Roanoke, Virginia, where she took literature, creative writing, and theology courses. At the end of her sophomore year, she married her writing instructor, poet and critic Richard H. W. Dillard, whom she has credited with providing her important early instruction in the craft of writing. After graduating from Hollins in 1967 with a bachelor's degree, she continued on at the college for an additional year to earn a master's degree in English. For her thesis, she chose to write on Henry David Thoreau's symbolic use of Walden Pond in *Walden*, a natural image that, for Thoreau, mediates between heaven and earth and expresses the depth and renewal of the spirit. The influence of Thoreau is obvious throughout all of Dillard's writing.

Dillard published her first two books, *Tickets for a Prayer Wheel* and *Pilgrim at Tinker Creek*, in 1974. The former is a collection of poems with, as the title indicates, religious and spiritual overtones. But it was the release of the latter book that heralded the debut of a unique literary talent. In 1971, Dillard fell seriously ill from pneumonia. After she recovered, she determined, like Thoreau, to live life more deeply and contemplatively. She thus began a series of camping trips, spending four seasons in the woods at Virginia's Tinker Creek in the Roanoke Valley. There, she kept a meticulous journal of her experiences, just as Thoreau had during his two-year sojourn at Walden Pond, and she later transferred all her notes, carefully annotated and cross-referenced, to note-cards. As she relates in her book about authorship, *The Writing Life* (1989), the writing process from these notes was an extremely difficult one. But upon publication, *Pilgrim at Tinker Creek* proved to be an astonishing success and made the author, who was still in her twenties, widely known. In 1975, the book was awarded the Pulitzer Prize for general nonfiction.

Over the years, Dillard has published works in a variety of genres. *Holy the Firm*, a short but profound book about theology and aesthetics, was published in 1977. A collection of essays on the natural world, *Teaching a Stone to Talk*, appeared in 1982, as did *Living by Fiction*, a work of literary criticism. That same year, Dillard traveled to China as part of a government-funded cultural delegation of scholars, publishers, and authors, and she recorded her experiences in *Encounters with Chinese Writers* (1984). *An American Childhood*, a personal memoir that records the growth of the artist's mind, appeared in 1987. Most recently, Dillard has published *For the Time Being* (1999), a complex series of meditations on such religious and spiritual issues as time's relation to eternity and the worth and meaning of individual human lives.

Divorced from her first husband in 1974, Dillard married Gary Clevidence in 1980; their daughter, Cody Rose, was born a few years later. The couple divorced, and Dillard married again in 1988, to Robert D. Richardson, a Thoreau scholar. In 1979, she accepted a position as Distinguished Visiting Professor at Wesleyan University in Middletown, Connecticut, and in 1983, after a brief hiatus teaching at Western Washington University in Bellingham, she returned to Wesleyan to teach creative writing full time.

Always a spiritual seeker, Dillard rebelled against her Presbyterian upbringing in high school, but returned to belief in Christianity upon reading C. S. Lewis's *The Problem with Pain*. In their intense theological probing and frequent emphases on incarnationalism and the sacramentality of the natural world, Dillard's works show a distinctive Catholic sensibility. The author herself converted to the Catholic faith in the early 1990s.

CRITICAL OVERVIEW

Dillard is a conscious inheritor of the nineteenth-century American romantic transcendentalist tradition of nature writing, an important one in the development of our literary heritage. Similar to Ralph Waldo Emerson and Henry David Thoreau, she is concerned with using nature as a metaphor for the inner life. As Emerson's groundbreaking romantic document *Nature* (1836) stated, the natural world is a text full of spiritual meaning that can be read by the careful observer. Thoreau, Emerson's disciple, determined to put Emerson's theories into practice by living intimately with nature and deriving lessons from it during the time he lived alone in the Walden woods. Dillard's intent, too, is to learn from nature while cultivating a habit of contemplative attention. Like the Transcendentalists, she records in her works the intricacy, beauty, and paradoxes of nature, the inscrutability of the Creator God, and the changing moods of the individual perceiving consciousness. Like many Romantics, she is also concerned with matters of the artistic life such as the source and renewal of the creative imagination and the artist's role in society. In such books as *Pilgrim at Tinker Creek* and *Holy the Firm*, Dillard takes the stance of the typical romantic quester whose search for identity evolves into a process of perception and self-projection.

But Dillard differs from the Transcendentalists in significant ways. Although strongly influenced by the tradition, she is by no means reactionary. Rather, her temperament is thoroughly modern, even postmodern, characterized by a strong sense of the fragmentation of our times and by existential anxiety in the face of a world seemingly in chaos. Moreover, she departs sharply from the Transcendentalists in confronting the issue of the existence of evil with unflinching directness. Famously, in *Nature*, Emerson suggests that one can merely "think away" unpleasant things: "disagreeable appearances, swine, spiders, snakes, pests, mad-houses, prisons, enemies, vanish; they are temporary and shall be no more seen."[1] In denying the reality of the Fall, Emerson thus had no use for a Savior. Dillard, however, refuses to pretend that evil and human suffering are not stark realities. She is thus far less idealistic and more realistic—far more Christian—than the Transcendentalists. As such, she is more aligned with the romantic Gothic writers such as Herman Melville and Nathaniel Hawthorne who, as inheritors of Calvinism, insisted on probing the dark side of nature and, by extension, human nature. Dillard has, in fact, called Melville America's greatest writer.

Although often labeled as such, Dillard, then, is far more than just a "nature writer." Her most characteristic work might be described as metaphysical nonfiction. *Pilgrim at Tinker Creek, Holy the Firm,* and *For the Time Being* are replete with philosophical and theological speculation and present a type of pastiche of learning derived from mystical, religious, philosophic, literary, and scientific sources. Dillard's writings demonstrate her enormous range of reading in diverse areas. Hers is a singular, truly interdisciplinary and integrative voice that consistently strives to unite scientific with religious inquiry in a deeply meditative, open-ended manner. Closer to poetry than prose, her language is at once colloquial and complex, full of irony, paradox, wit, understatement, and elaborate use of symbol and metaphor. In fact, Dillard's work may also fruitfully be compared to that of Gerard Manley Hopkins who bridged romanticism and modernism in his poetry and who is also known for his rich and unconventional use of language. As Sandra Humble Johnson observes, "Both writers have committed themselves to the clear, objective observation of the natural landscape, and based on that objectivity have taken the further step of examining the inner landscape in a quest for meaning. The dynamic is the same: observe meticulously what lies about you and allow the spirit to invade via the avenue of those perceptions."[2] In addition, as Johnson notes, both Dillard and Hopkins employ the literary device of the "high" or epiphanic moment when a fleeting sense of the unity of all things in God is achieved, and both are identifiably Christian in their theology.

Throughout all of her writings, Dillard's search for God is intense and personal. The search begins in the concrete world, by observing reality closely. Both fascinated and perplexed by God's creation, Dillard explores the limits of its mystery and the paradoxes of existence. To Dillard, the quest to understand God's ways must begin with a *kenosis,* a humble, open stance that empties the self of preconceived judgments or overly simplistic explanations. This stance is especially necessary because, as humans, we often feel so distanced from the natural world that we immediately dismiss it or desire to impose our wills on it. In moments of human suffering, this sense of alienation from nature is often particularly acute. In an essay entitled "Sojourner" in *Teaching a Stone to Talk*, Dillard describes this feeling:

> We don't know where we belong, but in times of sorrow it doesn't seem to be here, here with these silly pansies and witless mountains, here with sponges and hard-eyed birds. In times of sorrow the innocence of the other creatures—from whom and with whom we evolved—seems a mockery. Their ways are not our ways. We seem set among them as among lifelike props for a tragedy—or a broad lampoon—on a thrust rock stage. It doesn't seem to be here that we belong.[3]

Dillard's major theme throughout her writing is the attempt to understand the dual face of nature, both its beauty and its horror, and thereby approach the issue of reconciling the mystery of evil and suffering with the existence of a loving God. Her work, therefore, consistently moves toward confronting the most difficult questions of life, and in searching for answers she considers truths found in all the world's great religions, including Islam, Judaism, Hinduism, and Christianity. Above all, however, she is concerned with probing less examined, and often uncomfortable territory, in order to bring her readers to increased awareness. She often, therefore, dwells on the contradictions and paradoxes of life, and on the border areas where the physical and spiritual meet. As she puts it in *The Writing Life*, this kind of exploration lends distinct energy to her writing: "The writer knows his field—what has been done, what could be done, the limits—the way a tennis player knows the court. And like that expert, he, too, plays the edges. That is where the exhilaration is."[4]

In following the progress of the seasons, *Pilgrim at Tinker Creek* considers the intimate cycle of beauty and violence, abundance and destruction, in the natural world. As the book's title announces, the narrator here adopts the pose of the pilgrim or religious seeker, and moves from close examination of the natural world, to meditation, and then to wonder or praise. Apparently effortless and organic in its many shifting moods—telling stories, recounting memories, expounding scientific facts, speculating on philosophy—each chapter is in reality highly organized and tightly structured. The first essay presents the book's most memorable and horrific image: the narrator observes a parasitic giant waterbug feeding on the insides of a still-living frog. Such a nauseating event, while a common occurrence in nature, prompts the author to consider whether or not the world is indeed created and sustained by a good God. Her challenge to reconcile the apparently negative attributes of God with the positive, the solution she arrives at postulates a third answer, that the positive emerges from the negative just as dark shadows help define light. Death and life, suffering and joy, pain and beauty, necessarily go hand in hand. The artist's job, Dillard concludes, is to bring about spiritual awakening in the apathetic and to point toward this mystical unity of all things.

Holy the Firm is a little book, only about sixty-five pages long, but one packed with meaning and even more metaphysical than Pilgrim at Tinker Creek. Dillard has stated that she likes it best among all her books despite the fact that the composing process was nothing short of excruciating:

> Once I wrote a favorite, difficult book, a true account of three consecutive days on an island on the northwest coast. I began the book on one island and wrote most of it on another island; it took a long time. Much of it I wrote as poetry. Its two subjects were the relation of eternity to time and the problem of suffering innocents. The prose—once I decided to print it as prose—was so intense and accented, and the world it described was so charged with meaning, that the very thought of writing a word or two further made me tired. How could I add a sentence, or a paragraph, every day to this work I myself could barely understand? Its tone was fierce and exhilarated. . . . This book interested me more passionately than any other.[5]

In this slender book, Dillard, as in Pilgrim, struggles with the meaning of evil in the world and with the artist's role, but here she confronts these issues even more forcefully. A kind of spiritual autobiography with universal significance, Holy the Firm speculates on the human condition, the need for faith, and the importance of living life with passion and dedication. Although her approach is somewhat unorthodox, Dillard's book may be classified as a Catholic work in its final Christian vision, stress on incarnationalism and sacramentalism, and emphasis on the role of suffering in salvation.

"Nothing is going to happen in this book," the narrator of Holy the Firm informs us, alerting us to the fact that what we will encounter here is not a plotted story with a linear trajectory but a series of circular and recursive meditations (24). Dillard has stated that the book's three parts, covering three sequential day's events, refer to the Creation, Fall, and Redemption, but they also correspond, as the book itself makes clear, to three ways of considering God's relationship to his creation, immanence, emanance, and Holy the Firm. Each of the three chapters evolves organically around a major metaphor, a moth in a flame in part I, an injured little girl in part II, and a vision of Christ's baptism in part III, and these metaphors merge at the end of the book.

Part I, "Newborn and Salted," is replete with images of creation and innocence. The narrator's location is breathtaking: alone in a small house with a huge window, on an island in Puget Sound, and surrounded by mountains that seem to be at the farthest end of the known world. Mountains, sea, earth, and sky mingle in a fantastical, almost surreal landscape, a fitting environment for the author's pondering of "the fringey edge where elements meet and realms mingle" (21). In this first part of her text, Dillard's philosophic approach is one of immanence, a stance she later defines as close to pantheism. It assumes that, since God is present in all created things, everything that exists is "god-like." Borrowing a quote from Emerson (which also opens *The Writing Life*), the narrator speaks of the "god" of each new day, who, "pagan and fernfoot," unrolls all events before her, one after the other, leaving her "dazzled in days and lost," in an almost dreamlike state (30, 24). With no focal point, no memory or consciousness, and all things equally godlike, the only appropriate reaction to each new thing that appears is "oh!" Even the cat, Small, has a blank look on its face.

Yet what, the chapter inquires, does such a panorama—the constant unveiling—of life's changing circumstances mean? How do the day's many gods relate to the one unchanging God? What is time's relation to eternity? Even within this chapter that focuses on innocent wonder at the glories of creation, Dillard begins to foreshadow the direction her book will take. In truth, all is not right in paradise. As the narrator observes a spider in her bathroom, capturing and devouring its prey of moths, she is reminded of a camping trip she once took. Hoping to regain artistic inspiration, she was rereading a biography about the poet Arthur Rimbaud one evening in her tent by candlelight when she was startled by a huge golden moth that flew directly into the flame. While its body burnt instantly, its head, eerily, continued to act as a type of wick and flamed for several hours, "glowing within, like a building fire glimpsed through silhouetted walls, like a hollow saint, like a flame-faced virgin gone to God, while I read by her light" (17). This scene and the narrator's interpretation of it, evoking images of inner fire, nun, and light, combined with the sickening horror of such a freak occurrence, introduces *Holy the Firm*'s major themes. A second flashback now ensues as the narrator recalls how she once attempted in vain to convey to a creative writing class the many sacrifices involved in becoming an author. As *Holy the Firm* will ultimately be a book about the necessity of living a dedicated life, she equates here nun, thinker (philosopher, or any person who embraces the life of the mind), and artist, all of whom must live with passion and sacrifice in the pursuit of higher aims: "A nun lives in the fires of the spirit, a thinker lives in the bright wick of the mind, an artist lives jammed in the pool of materials" (22).

But the "notion of immanence needs a handle," the narrator correctly informs us; as a way to understand God's relationship to the world, it is far too unfocused and elusive (70). In part II, "God's Tooth," therefore, a second philosophic approach is put forward, that of emanation or the notion that the world is far apart from and quite other than God. Suddenly, without warning, the dreamlike state of continually unfolding creation comes to a sharp, painful halt. A plane has fallen from the sky, we are told, and a terrible tragedy has occurred. A neighbor was flying in his small aircraft with his young daughter, Julie. Both survived uninjured when the plane malfunctioned and crashed, but as the father was hurrying Julie to safety, a piece of burning fuselage flew into the little girl's face, burning her horribly. Cruel, freakish reality catches the narrator up short. Pain is not an illusion; suffering, especially such seemingly random and senseless suffering, cannot be met with a mere "oh!" As she struggles to make sense of the event, the narrator experiences a crisis of faith. Is God's creation benign or malicious? Is God in control or not? Does God care about us at all? In her bleak mood, she examines the concept of emanation. Often called deism, this idea views God as a type of great clockmaker in the sky who, after winding up the mechanism of the world, retreated, leaving it to tick itself out alone. But the consequences of this understanding of God frighten the narrator, for it suggests that the Creator has "abandoned us to days, to time's tumult of occasions" (43). In this concept, all of creation is merely afloat, random, unconnected, "slash[ed] . . . loose at its base from any roots in the real" (45–46). In fact, "thought itself is impossible, for subject can have no guaranteed connection with object, nor any object with God. Knowledge is impossible," and thus all human endeavor is, by extension, ultimately useless (46).

In her musings, the narrator recalls the single time she met Julie two weeks earlier, at a neighbor's cider-making party. She recalls watching the little girl fondly as Julie chased the cat, Small, around the yard, attempting to dress her in an odd doll's dress that looked like a nun's outfit. The narrator remembers thinking that she and Julie resembled each

other—making the fact that, by sheer accident, one of them is now se-
verely injured seem a sick joke. Indeed, the God who would allow such
an occurrence is but a tyrant, a "brute and traitor" (46). And now, in the
narrator's darkened perception, the landscape that seemed so breathlessly
wonderful as it unfurled before her in part I looks downright menacing,
"staged . . . brittle and unreal" (49). Human encounter with suffering alters perspective, turning the natural world into a place of otherness, of
stony silence, where humans feel unwelcome. That evening, the narrator once again spies from her window a new island that appears on the
horizon. But rather than greet it with wonder, she now inquires wearily,
"How long can this go on?" Still, she forces out a hopeful note, "but let
us by all means extend the scope of our charts" (50).

The "charts' scope" is indeed extended in part III, which takes
place on the next and last of the three days and is entitled "Holy the
Firm." Julie is in the hospital, and although the narrator can obtain no
word about her condition, she is now more collected in her grief. This
third chapter begins, in fact, with an avowal of faith: "I know only
enough of God to want to worship him, by any means ready to hand"
(55). God exists, she knows, and is worthy of her praise. But the puzzle
still remains: what purpose, then, can such suffering as Julie's possibly
serve? An answer comes to her as she ponders the parable of the blind
man in the Gospel. Jesus is asked by his disciples whether the man's own
sin or that of his parents caused his affliction. To their surprise, he replies
that individual sin was not the direct cause, but that God had permitted
the blindness so that his works might be made visible in the afflicted one.
"Do we need blind men stumbling about, and little flamefaced children,
to remind us what God can—and will—do?" the narrator asks rhetorically. She answers her question, again with a strong affirmation of faith:
"Yes, in fact, we do. We do need reminding . . . that we are created, *created*, sojourners in a land we did not make. . . . We forget ourselves, pic-
nicking, we forget where we are. There is no such thing as a freak accident" (61–62).

In her new mood of humble acceptance and seeking to worship
God by any means at hand, the narrator attends the single church, a Presbyterian one, on the island. Asked by the congregation to provide the
communion wine, she walks to town, musing on the fact that she, an ordinary person, is going to an ordinary store to buy the wine that will convey God's presence to his people. Although not placed in the fullness of
a Catholic context, the sacramental and Eucharistic imagery here is clear
and points to *Holy the Firm*'s ending. This is just what a sacrament does:

uses the humble, concrete things of this earth and flawed human beings as conduits of God's grace. On the trip back after obtaining the wine, the narrator, perhaps because of her newfound affirmation of belief, experiences a dramatic vision of Christ's baptism as she mounts the hill toward home and looks over the sea. In the vision, Jesus, just baptized by John, rises from immersion in the Jordan, and each drop of water still clinging to his body seems to contain all the world—all people, all circumstances, all events, all time past and present. All creation, the narrator realizes in this epiphanic moment, is founded on and unified in the person of Jesus: "It is the one glare of holiness" (67). This mystical revelation confirms for her the spiritual base of all reality and God's constant presence in the world. Moreover, Christ's baptism marked the moment of his formal dedication to his ministry: it led directly to the Cross. And in God's great plan of salvation, Jesus' total acceptance of God's will transformed the meaning of suffering forever, tying it to our redemption.

Now, after reviewing the two philosophic approaches to God's relationship to his universe she's already considered, immanence and emanance, the narrator posits a third view, which she calls Holy the Firm. Immanence, the concept that God is in all created things, is too similar to pantheism, and emanance, the view that God has abandoned his world, is too terrifying in its consequences. By contrast to these extremes, Holy the Firm, a notion from "esoteric Christianity," states that there is a "created substance" beneath the elements that is in constant contact with the Absolute (68). This substance forms the basis of everything that exists. This idea, a middle ground between pantheism and deism, allows the author to rest in confidence and hope. If God undergirds all things that exist, both time and space are founded on him, as are matter and spirit and, indeed, all the mysteries of nature. Therefore, time's relationship to eternity is now clear, as is the relationship of subject to object: "God has a stake guaranteed in all the world. And the universe is real and not a dream, not a manufacture of the senses; subject may know object, knowledge may proceed, and Holy the Firm is in short the philosopher's stone" (71). Moreover, as *Holy the Firm* beautifully demonstrates, arriving at this depth of trust in God's loving and absolute control over his world emerges precisely from the crucible of a person's encounter with suffering. The structure of Dillard's narrative is an incarnational one: we must go through such suffering in order to experience the restoration and renewal of the spirit, to find redemption.

Now, in the book's final pages, the author returns to *Holy the Firm*'s primary theme, a consideration of the role of the artist. Here, the fire images of the first two chapters, that of a moth immolated in a flame and that of a little girl injured by burning debris, evolve into an elaborate metaphor that speaks of the necessity of living life with dedication and passion. In remembering her reading of the biography of Rimbaud, *The Day on Fire*, in part I, the narrator suggests that her current quest, too, will be for renewal of artistic imagination and commitment. The tragedy of part II, however, made all human work seem absurd, including— perhaps especially—art. But in part III, with the confidence that God is in touch with and upholds all of his creation, the artist comes to understand not only her place in the world but also the source of creative inspiration. If Holy the Firm exists, the artist, too, is in constant touch with the Absolute: "he is holy and he is firm" (72). Art renders the seeming chaos of the world intelligible as it mediates between physical reality and spiritual meaning. In connecting time with eternity through her craft, the artist thus serves as God's visionary, illuminating the way to the spiritual realm. In fact, the artist works in "flawed imitation of Christ," whose Incarnation and sacrifice bridged the gap between heaven and earth (72). Like the nun and the thinker, therefore, the true artist must be totally devoted to her chosen life, and such dedication necessarily requires sacrifice toward a higher end. Recognizing that God supports all things, the artist discovers new passion and energy. "Hoopla!" she cries with joy, her quest completed (72). Like Isaiah, whose lips were touched with a burning flame so that he might fearlessly speak of the things of God, the narrator recommits herself to a difficult but ultimately worthwhile vocation.

We can now understand Dillard's image of the moth's head burning like a wick in a flame, a rich metaphor indeed. A moth has traditionally been viewed as a symbol of the human soul. Moreover, fire itself has complex connotations, both negative and positive. Fire and burning can indicate purgation and suffering, or passion, illumination, and truth. On Pentecost, we remember, the Holy Spirit descended on the disciples as "tongues of fire" and gave them the courage to preach the Gospel fearlessly. A life lived in service to a higher cause, whether that of artist, nun, or philosopher, is always countercultural, entailing the pain of isolation, discipline, hard work, and self-sacrifice. But, Dillard maintains, it is precisely through such purging "fire" that the "fire" of higher insight and spiritual vision is achieved. Suffering purifies, and it is through purification of the ego, a "baptism by fire," that one encounters God. The images of nun, thinker, and artist merge at the end of *Holy the Firm* with that of the moth's head conducting flame and lighting the room so that the narrator can read by its light. It now becomes a positive image of the dedicated life, a life of both sacrifice and service—the only life worth living.

Thus, we see that the author's solution to the crisis of faith and vocation in *Holy the Firm* is not an attempt to transcend pain or, like Emerson, ignore it, but to go down through it to find the Absolute. Hers is thus an incarnational, Christian model of resolving humankind's most pressing question in all ages: what purpose does the existence of evil and suffering play in the world? In her book, Dillard names the little girl burnt in the accident "Julie Norwich" for a reason: it is a direct reference to the fourteenth-century English mystic, Julian of Norwich, whose visions of Christ's Passion led her to write of God's overwhelming love and care for all humankind. At one point, God dropped a hazelnut in Julian's hand, telling her that the little object contains everything that was ever made—all of creation. God assures Julian repeatedly that he is in complete control of all things, for he is their foundation and sustainer. Moreover, Julian learns from her visions that the existence of sin, evil, and suffering in the world is, despite how they appear to us, truly insignificant in comparison with God's love, and that in light of all eternity, they last but an instant. Even more profoundly, God tells Julian that sin and suffering are actually useful in God's great plan of salvation for they have the effect, like nothing else, of humbling us and making us realize our need for a Savior. Ultimately, however, why God has intimately tied suffering to sanctity remains a mystery. God tells Julian that she must accept it as such, and rest in the assurance that he will ultimately transform all evil into good: "all shall be well."[6] In thus naming the injured girl after Julian of Norwich, the narrator reminds us of this comforting conclusion, one that can, even in the midst of apparently senseless tragedy, be embraced in the light of faith.

In *Holy the Firm*, Dillard's vision, finally, is a holistic one. In her search for the hidden God in the natural world, she imparts a strong sense of the unity and meaning of all creation. Dillard, in fact, believes that we've lost our connection to the things of the earth through too much emphasis on rational, scientific materialism. We now tend to see the world as completely other than ourselves and subject to our control. But science ultimately falls short—as indeed some are realizing today—and a more creative approach to understanding reality is necessary. "Dillard is convinced that if there is one thing twentieth-century science has taught us, it is that we cannot believe our eyes," Susan M. Felch states.[7] Still, in *Holy the Firm*, both the conclusions of empirical science—that the world is completely knowable through observation and testing—and the suggestions recently put forth by modern physics—that the world is chaotic, random, and unknowable—are rejected as the one Creator God upon whom all is founded and interconnected is revealed. In combining empirical observation with spiritual searching, Dillard succeeds in bridging boundaries between science and theology. She approaches the natural world not with the intent of mastering it, but with the open and humble stance of the mystic. Blending science, religion, and art into a unified vision, her pluralistic approach brings all the faculties into play in seeking understanding. But in the end, mystery remains: the paradoxical awe and fear, closeness and otherness, of nature and of nature's God. Ultimately, like Job, we must trust God's love and rest in the wonders of his power.

In an interview given soon after *Holy the Firm* was published, Dillard disclaimed, "I don't know anything about God, any more than anybody else does. I do not live well. I merely point to the vision."[8] An intense book rich in theological and aesthetic meaning, *Holy the Firm* points the way for the attentive reader to contemplate the wonders of creation, the mystery of our salvation, and the importance of living a dedicated life in the service of God's kingdom.

FOR FURTHER READING

Annie Dillard, *For the Time Being*
———, *Pilgrim at Tinker Creek*
———, *The Writing Life*
Julian of Norwich, *Revelations of Divine Love*
Henry David Thoreau, *Walden*

QUESTIONS FOR DISCUSSION

1. Read Julian of Norwich's *Revelations of Divine Love*. In what other ways does *Holy the Firm* work intertextually with this medieval mystical text?
2. For Dillard, the search for God begins in the concrete, natural world. Find several passages where the author describes in detail a small part of nature and then broadens her empirical approach to include creative or explorative thinking in arriving at theological or philosophical understanding.

3. In each of the three sections of the text, the narrator observes the appearance of new islands on the horizon and attempts to name them. Find these sections, intercompare them, and discuss how they add to our understanding of the narrator's changing perception throughout the text.

4. Throughout *Holy the Firm*, Dillard uses several images of salt. For example, she mentions in part I that the Armenians, Jews, and Catholics use salt on infants for cultural or religious reasons. What do these images add up to and how do they support the book's themes? How might they comment on Jesus' statement in the Gospel about his followers being the salt of the earth?

NOTES

Annie Dillard, *Holy the Firm* (New York: HarperPerennial, 1988). All references are to this edition.

1. Ralph Waldo Emerson, *Nature,* in *Selections from Ralph Waldo Emerson,* edited by Stephen E. Whicher (Boston: Houghton Mifflin, 1957), 56.

2. Sandra Humble Johnson, *The Space Between: Literary Epiphany in the Work of Annie Dillard* (Kent, OH: Kent State University Press, 1992), 128.

3. Annie Dillard, *Teaching a Stone to Talk* (New York: HarperPerennial, 1982), 149.

4. Annie Dillard, *The Writing Life* (New York: Harper and Row, 1989), 69.

5. Dillard, *The Writing Life,* 47, 49.

6. Julian of Norwich, *Revelations of Divine Love* (London and New York: Penguin Books, 1998), long text, 79.

7. Susan M. Felch, "Annie Dillard: Modern Physics in a Contemporary Mystic," *Mosaic: A Journal for the Interdisciplinary Study of Literature* 22, no. 2 (Spring 1989): 2.

8. Philip Yancey, "A Face Aflame: An Interview with Annie Dillard," *Christianity Today* (May 5, 1978): 960.

BIBLIOGRAPHY

Felch, Susan M. "Annie Dillard: Modern Physics in a Contemporary Mystic," *Mosaic: A Journal for the Interdisciplinary Study of Literature* 22, no. 2 (Spring 1989): 1–14.

Johnson, Sandra Humble. *The Space Between: Literary Epiphany in the Work of Annie Dillard.* Kent, OH: Kent State University Press, 1992.

McClintock, James I. "'Pray without Ceasing': Annie Dillard among the Nature Writers," *Cithara: Essays in the Judeo-Christian Tradition* 30, no. 1 (November 1990): 44–57.

Messer, Richard E. "The Spiritual Quest in Two Works by Annie Dillard," *Journal of Evolutionary Psychology* 9, no. 3, 4 (August 1988): 321–30.

Peterson, Eugene H. "Annie Dillard with Her Eyes Wide Open," *Theology Today* 43 (July 1986): 178–91.

Smith, Linda L. *Annie Dillard*. New York: Twayne, 1991.

SHUSAKU ENDO
DEEP RIVER

BIOGRAPHY

Shusaku Endo, one of Japan's best-known contemporary authors, was born in Tokyo in 1923. His parents divorced when he was a young boy. After graduation from Keio University, he won a scholarship that enabled him to pursue graduate study in French Catholic literature in Lyon, France, one of the first groups of postwar Japanese allowed to study abroad. There, he found himself especially drawn to such authors as François Mauriac, Julien Green, and Georges Bernanos, and he was also attracted to the British Catholic novelist, Graham Greene. Returning to Japan in 1952, Endo commenced a writing career that spanned more than four decades. His first short story, "To Aden," was published in 1954. The following year, his story "The White Men" won the prestigious Akutagawa Prize for literature, a national recognition that helped establish him as an important author. Endo's reputation as a provocative Catholic writer rests on such novels as *Silence* (1966), *The Samurai* (1980), and *Deep River* (1993). Also recommended are two novels that feature characters who appear in *Deep River: Wonderful Fool* (1959) concerns the Frenchman, Gaston, and *Scandal* (1986), features the Japanese woman, Mitsuko Naruse.

Endo's mother converted to Catholicism when he was a boy and subsequently became a strong influence on his own development of faith. Baptized at the age of eleven, Endo embraced Catholicism even as he felt that its strong western inflection was somehow incompatible with Japanese sensibilities. As a Japanese Catholic, he found himself ostracized everywhere he went. His Japanese schoolmates ridiculed him for believing in an "enemy" religion, and to his surprise his exposure to European Catholicism during his three-year stay in France only exacerbated his feelings of displacement and alienation. Speaking of the accounts of the religious conversions of some of the Catholic authors he studied for his graduate degree, Endo once stated in an interview, "I got the impression that they felt they had 'returned home' when they accepted Christianity. Being Japanese, though, I could not feel inside myself that embracing Christianity was any kind of homecoming. . . . The more I studied Christian literature, the wider the gap between me and these writers grew."[1] He determined to become a writer from this time forward because he felt he had found a theme he could spend a lifetime exploring. Indeed, this topic proved fascinating to Endo. Throughout his literary career, he examined the possible reasons why, despite the phenomenally successful work of such sixteenth-century missionaries as St. Francis Xavier, Christianity has made virtually no inroads in Japan whereas the faith has spread considerably in other Asian countries such as South Korea and the Philippines. Today, only about 1 percent of Japan's population is Christian, and only a fraction of that, Catholic.

In another interview, Endo further declared that his Christian faith influenced his desire to become an author because "Christianity should not be performance but sincere intention. The most difficult but surest way to get to such Christianity is by being a novelist. A critic can variously write about how far Christianity has become his flesh and blood, but a novelist must verify Christianity by image after image."[2] Moreover, Endo maintained that he wrote with the intention of upsetting readers, shaking them from a comfortable detachment or passivity and forcing them to consider the "grey" areas of doctrine or morality.

Endo suffered for many years from the effects of the tuberculosis he contracted on a trip to Europe in 1959. He underwent three major operations on his lungs, and at one point spent nearly two and a half years in the hospital (similar to his character Numada in *Deep River*). He died in Tokyo on September 29, 1996.

CRITICAL OVERVIEW

Shusaku Endo focused his literary career on examining two major intersecting tensions: that between eastern and western cultures, and that between Japanese culture and Christianity. Whether set in contemporary times, as is *Deep River*, or in the historical past, as are *Silence* and *The*

Samurai, each of his novels probes broad issues of cultural and religious identity, alienation and individualism in secular society, personal commitment to faith, and nuances of human psychology. A high moral seriousness and an intense examination of the human condition mark Endo as a deeply religious writer. In addition, because he rarely attempts to resolve the tensions he explores, Endo's works are open-ended and thus often ambiguous and challenging.

The complex novel *Silence* studies the fate of Catholic missionaries in Japan in the era immediately following the work of Francis Xavier. Based on meticulous research and involving some actual historical figures, the novel, inspired by Graham Greene's *The Power and the Glory*, focuses on the period of persecutions against Christians and foreigners under a succession of notoriously brutal Shoguns. Such persecutions gained in intensity around 1614 during the rule of Ieyasu and reached their peak under the ruthless Inuoye who devised the infamous "test" for suspected Christians of the *fumie*, or trampling of a religious icon, and who also implemented the horrific torture of the pit, described in *Silence* with graphic realism. *Silence*'s plot follows the increasing psychological agony of a young Portuguese Jesuit missionary named Sebastian Rodrigues whose heroic image of himself as a soldier of Christ, fueled by Counter-Reformation evangelical zeal, is shattered by the grim reality of suffering. In arguing with Rodrigues, the Shogun Inuoye insists that no matter what effort the missionaries expend, something in the Japanese attitude will never allow Catholic teaching to flourish in that country unadulterated but will always persist in blending the faith with other beliefs such as Buddhism, Shintoism, and Hinduism until it is all but unrecognizable. According to Inuoye, Japan is a type of "mudswamp" where no single faith can survive undiluted.

While Endo was intrigued by the tendency of the Japanese toward religious syncretism—Inuoye's "mudswamp"—he never implied that his countrymen lacked religious belief. Rather, he maintained, whether they profess Shintoism, Buddhism, or no religious belief at all, the Japanese people have a strong sense of a supernatural life force at work in the world.[3] Nevertheless, given the existence of this inherent religious belief, Endo pondered what it was in the national character that has made Japan particularly hostile to Christianity. Certainly, part of the resistance can be explained by history: to the Japanese, Christianity was and still tends to be an unpleasant reminder of attempts at foreign control and domination, an attitude embodied by the scornful Mitsuko in *Deep River*. Due to the persistence of this historical association, Endo was convinced that, for

Christianity to attract the Japanese, the more "maternal" face of Christ must be emphasized rather than the triumphant, stern lawgiver and judge preached by western missionaries and which smacks of western arrogance, power, and colonial tendencies. He thus wrote *A Life of Jesus* (1973) expressly to present to his fellow Japanese a Christ of forgiveness, compassion, empathy, and unconditional love. As he explains in the preface to this work, "The religious mentality of the Japanese is . . . responsive to one who 'suffers with us' and who 'allows for our weakness,' but their mentality has little tolerance for any kind of transcendent being who judges humans harshly, then punishes them."[4]

Written nearly thirty years after *Silence* and completing Endo's long study of the Japanese religious sensibility, *Deep River* takes an improbable set of four thoroughly secular and largely agnostic Japanese tourists to India, ironically one of the most religiously pluralistic nations on earth. Structuring the first half of the book as a series of "case studies," Endo describes how each of his tourists has arrived at a place in his or her life where a disturbing spiritual or moral crisis must be faced. Although none would necessarily put it this way, each protagonist is on a pilgrimage to find some answer to his or her predicament, and each, in India, comes to a greater self-understanding or experiences some type of inner transformation. "Everyone seems to be going to India with different feelings," Mitsuko Naruse, one of the tourists, observes as the group gathers for an orientation before they embark upon the trip (32). And weaving throughout these four individual stories is the saga of the young man Otsu, a social outcast and virtual failure in nearly every aspect of life who becomes a Catholic priest and similarly discovers a deeper meaning to his vocation in India.

The first case study we encounter is that of the middle-aged businessman, Isobe, whose complacent, conventional life is violently uprooted when he learns that his wife, Keiko, has incurable cancer. A typical Japanese husband, he has taken Keiko largely for granted during their thirty-five-year marriage. Suddenly confronted with the prospect of her imminent death, Isobe is stunned as, for the first time, he realizes his impending helplessness without her. Not only must he now face her death, but he also must deal with the guilt of having neglected her for so long. As Keiko grows increasingly ill, she has a number of odd, prophetic dreams, most likely induced by painkilling drugs. Just before she dies, to Isobe's astonishment, she gasps "I know for sure . . . I'll be reborn somewhere in this world. Look for me . . . promise . . . promise!" (17). Haunted by her words, Isobe listens closely during the meal following Keiko's cremation service as a Buddhist priest explains that, in Buddhist teaching, the spirits of the dead are reincarnated in other bodies on earth. Although Isobe has no real faith in such belief, the priest's words seem to confirm Keiko's last request. Thus, when Isobe by chance hears of scholarly research being done at an American university on children's memories of previous lives, he writes a letter of inquiry and receives, in return, information about a girl living in a remote village in northern India who claims to have had a past life as a Japanese. Although skeptical of the outcome of his quest, Isobe joins the tour group to India with the vague intent of tracking down the child who he thinks may be his reincarnated wife.

A second case study is that of Numada, a well-known author of children's stories. Through a flashback, we learn that he was raised in Manchuria, at that time a Japanese colony. A lonely boy whose parents quarreled constantly, he sought comfort in the unconditional love and acceptance of his dog, Blackie. From that time on, Numada understood the power of animals to provide humans with consolation. As an adult, he chose to pursue a career as a writer of tales that featured an idealized natural world. But even though he subsequently married and had children, the haunting loneliness he experienced as a boy never left him. Over the years, he adopted several birds as pets. The first of these was a hornbill, a strange, comical-looking animal that, on its first evening in Numada's home, uttered such a plaintive cry that he instantly recognized in it a soulmate. Later, Numada's gnawing inner pain turned to fear when he fell seriously ill from tuberculosis and was forced to spend nearly two years in the hospital, undergoing several failed operations. Searching for a means to cheer her husband, at one point his wife purchased for him a myna bird to replace the hornbill that had to be sold. Again, Numada quickly bonded with the animal. Then, a third, risky operation was performed on his lungs which, to the doctors' surprise, finally cured him. While still in recovery, Numada learned, however, that his distracted wife had inadvertently left the myna outdoors where it had died of neglect. Grief struck, Numada can't shake the feeling that, in some mysterious way, the myna has died in his place. After regaining his health, he thus signs on to a trip to India to pay homage to the native land of the beloved birds that have provided him with so much solace over the years.

A third case study is that of the elderly Kiguchi, who, as a young man, fought in the Burma jungle and participated in the so-called Highway of Death, the ill-fated Japanese retreat from the enemy, which took place toward the end of World War II. We first meet Kiguchi on the plane bound for India, and it is quickly apparent that, even many years later, his wartime memories are still raw. As he recalls, the fleeing Japanese soldiers died rapidly, one by one, of starvation and malaria, so much so that the path was littered with corpses. Along the way, Kiguchi, too, fell ill. But his comrade, Tsukada, refusing to abandon him, secured shelter in a hut and somehow located meat with which he tried to sustain their lives. Against all odds, both Kiguchi and Tsukada survived the terrible experience. Many years later, they reunited in Tokyo. However, it was not long after their friendship was renewed that Kiguchi realized Tsukada was drinking himself to death from some deep inner pain. As he lay gravely ill in the hospital, Tsukada finally confessed to Kiguchi and to the Christian hospital volunteer, Gaston, that the meat he ate that dreadful day was taken from the body of a dead soldier. "Someone who's fallen that far into the hell of starvation—would your God forgive even someone like that?" Tsukada, racked by guilt, cried out to Gaston (101). By way of answer, Gaston related to the anguished man the true story of the Andes plane crash survivors who stayed alive by eating the flesh of their dead friends and who, after they were rescued, were readily forgiven by all. Gaston's consoling words and deep empathy seemed to absorb Tsukada's pain, and he was able to die in relative peace. For his part, Kiguchi never forgot Gaston's gentle compassion. Now, some years later, he is traveling to India to come to terms with his memories of the Highway of Death and its aftermath. He hopes to hold a private memorial service there in honor of his fallen comrades.

Of all his tourists, Endo is clearly most interested in the case study of the complicated woman, Mitsuko Naruse. As a student of French literature at a Japanese university, Mitsuko is particularly drawn to the female protagonists in two novels she is studying, Moïra in Julien Green's *Moïra*, and Thérèse in François Mauriac's *Thérèse Desqueyroux*, both of whom act on dark impulses within them to perpetrate evil acts on innocent men. In imitation of Moïra and egged on by her hard-drinking college friends, Mitsuko seduces the clumsy, foolish-looking Catholic student, Otsu. As she herself recognizes, part of her intent was to mock Otsu's God. Elated at her success, she scornfully informs the emaciated man on the crucifix hanging in the university chapel: "I win. . . . He's dumped you and come to my room" (48).

Later, fearful of the destructive elements in her heart, Mitsuko marries a businessman whose conventional interests go no farther than sports cars and golf games. The two have so little in common that, even on their honeymoon in Paris, they amiably part for a few days' separate vacations. Ostensibly to view the location where *Thérèse Desqueyroux* was set, Mitsuko travels to the south of France but then suddenly detours to Lyon where she has heard that Otsu is studying at the seminary. Over lunch, Otsu tells her that it was her rejection of him that spurred his vocation: after Mitsuko left him, he understood "just a little the sufferings of that man who was rejected by all men" (62). But while Otsu is now far more secure in his faith, transformed, as he explains, by Christ, Mitsuko still can't comprehend his religious convictions in the least. "It makes my teeth stand on edge just to think of you as a Japanese believing in this European Christianity nonsense," she seethes (64). But some years thereafter, the now-divorced Mitsuko has not found the emotional or spiritual peace she craves. Unable to truly love other human beings and feeling as if her life were merely a kind of play-acting, she continues to be intrigued by Otsu. When she hears by chance at a class reunion that he is now working in India as a Catholic priest, she joins the tour in the hope of once again seeking him out.

A superb structuralist, Endo brings together the stories of these four unrelated persons, each making a pilgrimage to India for private reasons. Through these characters, the author explores the psychology of modern, secular individuals with no coherent religious beliefs dealing, in quiet desperation, with the human problems of death, pain, loneliness, guilt, and inner turmoil. After touring various sites throughout the country, the group arrives at Varanasi, the Hindu sacred spot where the Ganges and Yamuna rivers converge. There, they learn of the Hindu belief that those who bathe in the river will be purged from sin, and those whose ashes are scattered in it after death will be released from the endless cycle of transmigration. Both fascinated and repelled by the human drama unfolding before them as throngs of people, many of whom are dying, enter the Ganges, Endo's protagonists find release from long pent-up emotions. Each reveals their secrets to the others and each discovers some type of healing or peace.

The sorrowing Isobe, after a futile attempt to locate the "reincarnated" Indian girl, realizes what a supreme egoist he had been toward his wife during the many years of their marriage. Only after he loses Keiko does he come "to understand the meaning of irreplaceable bonds in a human being's life," his wife's quiet goodness, and his own sincere love of her (188). The river absorbs his lonely cry, "Darling! . . . Where have you gone?" the first heartfelt tenderness for his wife he has ever expressed (189). When Mitsuko sympathetically tells him that Keiko lives on in his heart, her sentiment, while merely a platitude, is true, for Isobe will bear the burden of his love for his wife and the guilt of having neglected her all his life. It may make him a humbler, more sensitive man.

Numada, the writer of children's tales who comes to India hoping to visit a wildlife refuge, is dumbstruck when the tour guide Enami refers to the nature of India as "vulgar," and he quickly rejects that idea. Although he can hardly abide the close, almost suffocating mingling of elemental forces in India, he is nevertheless able to carry out his purpose of purchasing a myna bird and then releasing it in a gesture of gratitude toward the bird that gave its life for him. Endo views Numada's act of thanksgiving and his close ties to the natural world as positive traits in a culture in which men in particular strive to suppress all hint of vulnerability. But of all the tourists, Numada is perhaps the one that learns the least in India, for he quickly deems his outpouring of emotion of "no marketable value" and escapes back into the idealized world of his fictional *Märchen* (204).

Kiguchi, meanwhile, succeeds in fulfilling his plan to hold a Buddhist service in memory of his fellow soldiers on the banks of the river. He confides his secrets to Mitsuko, telling her of the mysterious figure of Gaston who comforted his friend Tsukada in his despair and whom he has never forgotten. Gaston had stated that one could discover God's love even in terrible circumstances, and now Kiguchi ponders his growing sense that "the seeds of salvation are buried in every act of evil" (200). The possibility that God may have been with them or that good could have derived from the horrible Highway of Death moves him to view suffering in a new light and to consider studying, evidently for the first time, Buddhist teaching. To Endo, any movement toward religious belief made by his thoroughly secular characters is a positive sign of spiritual growth.

Throughout most of the narrative, Mitsuko is so distanced from God that she even becomes upset by the mention of the name. Otsu, therefore, suggests they use the code word, "Onion," instead, which, as Robert Coles explains, evokes "the many layers of faith, the humility faith asks of the believer, the connection between belief and tragedy—all of that conveyed through the ordinary, lowly onion, which one can peel and peel, though with tears."[5] Yet despite her discomfort with religion, Mitsuko is the only one of Endo's tourists who dons a bathing suit and enters the Ganges, the river of cleansing and rebirth. For Mitsuko, the act is a gesture of newfound solidarity with humanity and an acknowledgement of participation in the universal quest for spiritual healing. In fact, Mitsuko discovers that she is far more comfortable in the confusion of India where good and evil, life and death are intimately combined than she ever was in the countries of western Europe. Drawn to both the Hindu goddess Kali, who combines mercy with brutality, and to the goddess Chamunda, the self-sacrificing, suffering mother, Mitsuko finds in these images reflections of the complexities of her own heart.

Accompanied by Numada, Mitsuko succeeds in locating Otsu, who is living on the banks of the Ganges and daily laboring to help the sick and dying to the river, their final destination. In response to her questions, he tells her that he has chosen this work because he believes God dwells in all people and in all religions. After the Crucifixion, Christ continued to love his disciples who had betrayed, denied, and deserted him, Otsu explains, and therefore he became so etched on the disciples' guilty hearts that they were inspired to imitate his actions. According to Otsu's testimony, Christ is similarly reborn in the hearts of all those who believe in him. Although Mitsuko finds Otsu's words convincing because they are supported by his actions, in the novel's final, dramatic scene, as Otsu is mortally wounded while saving the callous Sanjo's life, Mitsuko screams out in frustration, "You're really a fool! . . . You've thrown away your whole life for some Onion! . . . When it comes down to it, you've been completely powerless!" (212). We are left to ponder, at the novel's conclusion, whether Mitsuko will ever come to some understanding of the type of self-sacrificing love Otsu represents. What we *do* know is that she will remember him for the rest of her life.

Without doubt, the greatest of all human problems is the reality of death. To one who does not believe in an afterlife, death's apparent finality can seem a horrible truth indeed. It is not surprising therefore, that Endo begins his series of case studies in *Deep River* with the character Isobe who faces just this pressing issue. As he numbly watches his wife's body being cremated, his heart rages within him, "*What the hell is this? . . . This isn't her*" (18). The most basic of human longings is for life that does not end, for the possibility of rebirth and renewal. Thus it is easy to understand why Isobe is impelled by Keiko's enigmatic last words to journey across the world in the vain hope that she may have been reincarnated somewhere on earth. But in a larger sense, we see that, besides the obvious case of Isobe, each of the major characters in the novel is on a quest for rebirth. In each protagonist's life, in fact, someone or something seems to have died so that the character might come to a type of spiritual or emotional renewal or rebirth. A dutiful and patient wife, Keiko quietly served her husband for years, smoothly managing all aspects of their domestic life. Her death was necessary, it appears, in order for Isobe to come to an awareness of his own failure to love and to experience the humility of heartfelt repentance. Numada is convinced that his pet myna died in his place during the risky surgery performed on his lungs, and his act of gratitude in releasing a bird in the wildlife sanctuary acknowledges his indebtedness to the natural world that has provided him with so much comfort throughout the years. Kiguchi owes his life to his friend Tsukada, and both the memory of Tsukada and his mysterious comforter, Gaston, now bring Kiguchi to the realization, a profoundly religious one, that good can be found in even the worst of circumstances. And Mitsuko, fascinated by the self-giving love she observes in Otsu, will continue to carry his memory within her, just as Otsu stated that the memory of Christ constantly renews life within his disciples. Mitsuko has, in effect, discovered what she has longed for, the source of authentic love. Eventually, she may come to recognize and accept Otsu's God.

Throughout the novel, Endo skillfully weaves the great theme of the Christian God as a suffering servant. This is a God who enacts *kenosis*, coming not in triumph and judgment but in humility and poverty so that we do not fear to approach him. This self-emptying God understands the depths of human misery for he has suffered alongside us. The theme of the suffering servant is closely tied to that of the human desire for rebirth, for it is through the servant-God's agony that salvation is effected. The beautiful passage from Isaiah 53, which prophecies the coming of such a Savior, is cited explicitly several times in the novel beginning with Mitsuko's chance perusal of the biblical text in the university chapel. In that scene, Mitsuko equates Otsu with the image of the man hanging before her on the cross; like the suffering Jesus, Otsu "had no charm as a man, had nothing in his looks that might appeal to her" (116). And the Otsu we witness in the final chapter of *Deep River* has indeed become the embodiment of the suffering servant as he imitates Christ in compassionate, selfless love. Like Christ, Otsu even sacrifices his life to save one who doesn't appreciate what he has done for him. But besides Otsu, *Deep River* provides us with numerous other examples and images of the suffering servant. Chamunda, the mother-goddess who bears the pains of India, is such an image, as is Indira Gandhi. The various "pierrot" or clown figures throughout the novel, such as Numada's hornbill, the horse-faced Gaston, and the artist Rouault's sad-eyed clowns, are also types of suffering servants: although considered foolish or ugly, they seem uniquely able to sympathize with human misery. Throughout the novel, the accumulation of such images, culminating in the Christlike Otsu, suggests the human longing for a God who understands our sufferings and is able to absorb and transform them. Endo even takes the titles of two of the book's final chapters directly from Isaiah's text: "Surely He Hath Borne Our Griefs" and "He Hath No Form Nor Comeliness."

Together with the suffering servant theme, *Deep River* also examines the intimate comingling of all things—of death and life and of good and evil—a mystery witnessed in the natural world but which western thought in particular has attempted to ignore. In "Shusaku Endo's River of Life," Luke Reinsma maintains that the novel is about "that which cannot be 'sliced into categories,' about that which passes understanding—about crossing boundaries between humanity and nature, between the natural and supernatural."[6] Throughout the narrative, Endo explores a host of divisions, antagonisms, and contradictions inherent in human life: East versus West, the clash of cultures, the opposition of religious beliefs, sectarian and political violence, and the tensions between social classes. What, he questions, can possibly rise above such divisive attitudes and unite rather than separate humankind? What will bring peace, both within the human heart and between persons? In accepting both the living and the dead, people of all races, cultures, and social classes, the "great mother" Ganges becomes a powerful symbol of such unity. Like the suffering servant face of God, the river is not beautiful, "but there is a difference in this country between things that are pretty and things that are holy," Enami patiently explains to the culturally insensitive Sanjos (107). And to Otsu, the Ganges may be compared with Christ, a deep and flowing river of love, "accepting all, rejecting neither the ugliest of men nor the filthiest" (185).

In *Deep River*, as in many of his works, Endo focuses in particular on the cultural divide between eastern and western ways of apprehending the world. In the French seminary, Otsu is opposed by both his teachers and fellow students when he states that, to his way of thinking, "evil lurks within good, and . . . good things can lie hidden within evil as well" (65). He is deemed heretical when he suggests that, like a magician, God transforms even sin into good. And he is likewise condemned for insisting that "God has many different faces. I don't think God exists exclusively in the churches and chapels of Europe. I think he is also among the Jews and the Buddhists and the Hindus," a belief that, to the seminary officials, borders dangerously on religious relativism (121). But despite the scorn of his superiors and his apparently heretical beliefs, Otsu never loses his deep faith and trust in Jesus. As he poignantly tells Mitsuko, he has devoted his life to pursuing only one goal: "the love of that Onion... [Love] is all the Onion has imparted to us. The thing we are most lacking in our modern world is love; love is the thing no one believes in any more; love is what everyone mockingly laughs at—and that is why someone like me wants to follow my Onion with dumb sincerity" (119). Indeed, the search for an authentic and enduring love underscores all the individual quests in the book. As Endo wrote in his *Life of Jesus*, "The greatest misfortune that Jesus found in the stricken people was their having no one to love them. At the center of all their unhappiness was the wretchedness, fouled with their own hopelessness and loneliness, for want of being loved. What they needed more than miraculous cures was love."[7]

In the midst of all the conflicts it explores, *Deep River* poses, then, through Otsu, the possibility of a Christ-like, self-sacrificing love that rises above all cultural, racial, and religious prejudices and, like the Ganges, embraces all humanity. As John Netland notes, in achieving this love, Otsu relinquishes all entrenched cultural associations; he is "a Japanese Christian... rejected by the French seminary, living in an Indian ashram, dressing as a Hindu, and performing acts of charity to those whose co-religionists will not touch them."[8] "What emerges in [Endo's] novels," Netland concludes, "is a critique of culture that draws its moral power from the self-effacing ethic of the cross, in whose peculiar economy of power the weak are exalted and the mighty judged. . . . [Endo's] characters must in some measure be dispossessed of their cultural identity in order to meet Christ."[9]

In one of the novel's final scenes, Endo parallels Otsu's work on the banks of the Ganges with that of Mother Teresa of Calcutta's Missionaries of Charity, and, in doing so, he makes a powerful statement about Christian love and human dignity. When Mitsuko, who herself is just beginning to understand her solidarity with all humans, questions the nuns about why they are attempting to do what is seemingly pointless work, that is, attempting to save just a few out of the multitudes of the suffering around them, the answer she hears, albeit indistinct, suggests to her that the Christian God is somehow reborn in these women, just as Otsu has told her. As Endo wrote in *Life of Jesus*, "The God of love, the love of God—the words come easy. The most difficult thing is to bear witness in some tangible way to the truth of the words. In many cases love is actually powerless. Love has in itself no immediate tangible benefits."[10] Mitsuko has never fathomed that the authentic love she longs for might be born from voluntary self-denial and self-giving. It is interesting to note that, besides being equated with Mother Teresa, Otsu is also partially modeled on the modern saint,

Maximilian Kolbe. Endo was fascinated by Kolbe and wrote a number of short stories about him. A Polish priest, Kolbe worked as a missionary in Japan in the 1930s. Physically slight, bespectacled, and of lowly demeanor, he was derided by the Japanese who mockingly nicknamed him, "Mouse." Arrested by the Nazis during World War II and sent to Auschwitz, Kolbe offered his life in place of that of a condemned prisoner and was starved to death. In Endo's story, "Fuda-no-Tsoji," upon learning of the circumstances of Kolbe's death, the narrator marvels that such an unremarkable person found the courage to die in the place of another. What, he wonders, could possibly motivate such a man to sacrifice his life for a fellow human being? Throughout *Deep River*, Endo is intent on showing that, like Christ the suffering servant, true strength often lies in apparent lack of power, and that those the world scorns are often its true heroes. "A person begins to be a follower of Jesus only by accepting the risk of becoming himself one of the powerless people in this visible world," Endo stated in *Life of Jesus*.[11]

In the end, *Deep River* is by no means a "classic" Catholic conversion novel in the vein of, for example, Augustine's *Confessions* or Waugh's *Brideshead Revisited*. Endo never suggests that his contemporary Japanese characters are ready to accept Christian truths. But each person, Endo shows, is capable of a greater spiritual response, a response that modern, secular, agnostic society, which tends to foster only the type of selfishness seen in the Sanjos, fails to nurture. It is only on the banks of the "deep river" Ganges that the secrets of hearts are revealed.

FOR FURTHER READING

Shusaku Endo, *A Life of Jesus*
———, *The Samurai*
———, *Silence*
———, *Wonderful Fool*

QUESTIONS FOR DISCUSSION

1. Read Isaiah 53 and discuss in detail how Endo shapes all aspects of his novel to point to the image of Christ as a "suffering servant."

2. The tour guide Enami knows that the descent into the cave of the Hindu goddesses is a type of "test" of tourists' reaction to

India. Entering the stifling cave can be seen, in fact, as a metaphor for penetrating the recesses of the unconscious mind and heart. How do the reactions of each of the tourists to the cave predict their spiritual or emotional growth while in India?

3. In what ways does Otsu develop morally and spiritually throughout the course of the novel? Why does he take the name, "Augustine," in the French seminary?

4. Of what significance to the novel's plot and themes are such incidences as (1) the discussion of India's caste system at the upper-class wedding celebration; and (2) the assassination of Indira Gandhi and the resultant Hindu and Sikh violence?

5. Endo strongly criticizes the attitudes of the materialistic young couple, the Sanjos, throughout the novel. Describe Mr. and Mrs. Sanjo in detail. How do their attitudes toward India differ from those of the other tourists? How do the other tourists regard them?

NOTES

Shusaku Endo, *Deep River,* translated by Van C. Gessel (New York: New Directions, 1994). All references are to this edition.

1. Quoted in Van C. Gessel, *The Sting of Life: Four Contemporary Japanese Novelists* (New York: Columbia University Press, 1989), 240.

2. Kazumi Yamagata, "Mr. Shusaku Endo Talks about His Life and Works as a Catholic Writer," *The Chesterton Review* 12, no. 4 (November 1986): 500.

3. Yamagata, "Mr. Shusaku Endo Talks," 495.

4. Shusaku Endo, *A Life of Jesus* (New York: Paulist Press, 1973), 1.

5. Robert Coles, "The Great Tide of Humanity," review of *Deep River, New York Times Book Review,* May 28, 1995, 21.

6. Luke M. Reinsma, "Shusaku Endo's River of Life," *Christianity and Literature* 48, no. 2 (Winter 1999): 208.

7. Endo, *A Life of Jesus,* 80.

8. John T. Netland, "From Resistance to *Kenosis*: Reconciling Cultural Difference in the Fiction of Endo Shusaku," *Christianity and Literature* 48, no. 2 (Winter 1999): 192.

9. Netland, "From Resistance to *Kenosis,*" 179, 181.

10. Endo, *A Life of Jesus,* 71.

11. Endo, *A Life of Jesus,* 145.

BIBLIOGRAPHY

Christianity and Literature 48, no. 2 (Winter 1999). This edition of the journal is devoted to Endo and includes a number of articles that discuss *Deep River*, including the Netland (note 8) and Reinsma (note 6) articles listed in the notes.

Gessel, Van C. *The Sting of Life: Four Contemporary Japanese Novelists.* New York: Columbia University Press, 1989.

Yamagata, Kazumi. "Mr. Shusaku Endo Talks about His Life and Works as a Catholic Writer," *The Chesterton Review* 12, no. 4 (November 1986): 493–506.

DENISE LEVERTOV
THE STREAM AND THE SAPPHIRE

BIOGRAPHY

In her poem "Illustrious Ancestors," Denise Levertov points to her family heritage as the source of her inspiration and vocation as a poet. Hers, indeed, was a household rich in intellectual, cultural, religious, and humanitarian pursuits. Her Welsh mother, Beatrice Spooner-Jones Levertoff, claimed as a descendent the mystic tailor Angell Jones of Mold. Beatrice Levertoff especially shared her love of nature with her daughters Denise and Olga, teaching them to observe things closely. Levertov's Russian-Jewish father, Paul Philip Levertoff, was descended from the renowned Hasid, Schneour Zalman, known as the Rav of Northern White Russia. Having converted to Christianity as a young man, Levertoff became an Anglican priest and dedicated his ministry to efforts to reconcile Judaism and Christianity. Born in 1923 in Ilford, England, Denise Levertov (who changed the spelling of her last name to distinguish herself from Olga, also a writer) was largely educated at home. Reading and writing were frequent activities for all members of the family, and artists and intellectuals were often to be found at the dinner table. The family also reached out to help others in need, working, for example, to aid Jewish refugees during World War II. In the family circle, then, Levertov honed her literary skills while also absorbing the acute spiritual sensitivity and social consciousness that became hallmarks of her poetry.

As a teenager, Levertov sent some of her work to T. S. Eliot and received an encouraging reply. When at the age of twenty-three her first collection, *The Double Image,* appeared, she felt sure of her vocation as a poet. After serving as a nurse in London during World War II, she married Mitchell Goodman, an American studying in England under the GI bill. In 1948, the couple moved to New York where their son, Nikolai, was born the following year. That same year, Kenneth Rexroth included some of Levertov's poems in his volume, *New British Poets*. But it wasn't until 1957, eleven years after her first collection, that Levertov published her second volume, *Here and Now*. Influenced by the new sounds and rhythms of American life and speech and by her association with young, experimental poets such as Robert Creeley, Robert Duncan and, later, William Carlos Williams, Levertov had altered her poetic voice and style nearly completely by this time. Veering from the neoromanticism of her early works, she embraced the colloquial speech, organic form, and concrete images that characterize the modernist sensibility. From this time forward, Levertov considered herself primarily an American poet.

Levertov and her husband were divorced in 1974. For many years, she taught creative writing at such institutions as Brandeis, MIT, Tufts, the University of Washington, and Stanford where she nurtured numerous young poets. Levertov's own writing was prolific: five decades of disciplined work resulted in nearly two dozen major volumes of poetry, numerous translations, and several collections of essays. An astute literary critic and theorist, Levertov's essays on poetic form and process help define the modernist aesthetic. Perused side by side with her poetry, they are invaluable aids to understanding her artistic and spiritual sensibilities.

Her early poems quasi-spiritual in tone although not formally religious, Levertov found herself gradually moving from a position of skepticism to Christian belief throughout the late 1970s and 1980s. Her collections during the 1980s such as *Candles in Babylon* (1982), *Oblique Prayers* (1984), *Breathing the Water* (1987), and *A Door in the Hive* (1988) especially reflect this growth toward religious affirmation. Influenced in particular by the Catholic Church's commitment to social justice as exemplified by such figures as Dorothy Day and Archbishop Oscar Romero, Levertov converted to Roman Catholicism in the early 1990s. In 1997, she brought together poems from seven of her previously published volumes in *The Stream and the Sapphire*, a collection designed to illustrate the progress of her conversion from agnosticism to Christianity. A testimony to both her remarkable poetic talent and deep spirituality, *The Stream and the Sapphire* proved to be Denise Levertov's final book. She died in 1997, at the age of seventy-four, from complications due to lymphoma.

CRITICAL OVERVIEW

Over her long career, Denise Levertov composed poems on love, war, nature, the environment, politics, religion, and much more. Her writing has been praised for its profound sensitivity, acute insight, celebration of life, and respect for both nature and human nature. Moreover, Levertov's lyrics are superbly crafted, for she was a master technician. In a Levertov poem, subject matter and technical elements of form, meter, sound pattern, and word choice blend seamlessly to produce a unified effect. Most critics have responded positively to her work, and students tend to find her poetry, unlike that of some of the more "academic" poets, readily accessible. Today, Levertov's work can be found in nearly every anthology of contemporary poetry, and her lively and informative essays, collected in such volumes as *The Poet in the World* (1973) and *New and Selected Essays* (1992), are often studied in the writing classroom.

Levertov's multidimensional body of poetry is difficult to classify. In the early part of her career, she was often equated with the Black Mountain School of poets, a group of experimental writers that formed in the 1950s around poet Charles Olson who was teaching at the time at Black Mountain College in North Carolina. Revolting against the formalist standards of the New Critics, Olson's 1950 essay, "Projective Verse" called for poetry that registered immediate perceptions of consciousness in organic form. Black Mountain College sponsored the arts journal *Black Mountain Review* that, although short-lived, became a forum for Olson's followers. Along with other young poets who challenged New Critics' standards such as the Beat poets, the Black Mountain poets were included in Don Allen's *The New American Poetry* (1960), an anthology that defined modernist American poetry of the era. Although Levertov was only loosely associated with these groups—for one thing, she never taught at Black Mountain College—her poetry was influenced by these movements and, in turn, helped shape them.

Perhaps the greatest influence on Levertov as she remade herself into a contemporary American poet was William Carlos Williams. Throughout her career, Levertov often acknowledged her debt to him. Williams insisted that poetry be based on concrete images, reflect natural language, and speak authentically about the self to the reader. His poetry was primarily that of experience, not ideas, in which the perceiving narrator concentrates on describing things or events accurately and allows the reader to infer the emotion or significance behind the description. For Williams, in fact, there were "no ideas but in things," that is, meaning derives from intense focus on a particular aspect of reality. Although she eventually moved away from Williams's insistence on the concrete and became more introspective, Levertov continued to follow Williams's lead in writing what one critic has called "poetry of the immediate," that is, poetry that relies on the poet's own experience, what is close at hand.[1] Despite the influence of others, Levertov's poetry is unique, an organic combination of both romantic and modernist styles that the poet absorbed and transformed throughout her long career. By both combining and extending these traditions, Levertov is considered to be an important contributor to American postmodern poetry.

Denise Levertov was distinctly aware that she was called to be a poet. Conceiving of her life and art as a pilgrimage, a spiritual quest, she took her vocation seriously, viewing poetry as a means by which she could not only live her life fully and well but enable others to do the same. She was especially fond of a phrase from Rainer Maria Rilke who wrote of the "unlived life, of which one can die."[2] To Levertov, the act of writing poetry necessitated a heightened appreciation for life and an extraordinary attention to the things of the world. "All the thinking I do about poetry leads me back, always, to Reverence for Life as the ground for poetic activity," she stated. "Without Attention—to the world outside us, to the voices within us—what poems could possibly come into existence?"[3] In fact, the poet's enhanced sense of attentiveness and wonder renders all aspects of life, even the most mundane, relevant. No element of everyday life is beyond the poet's domain. As Levertov stated, because the artist engages the world so intensely, her life is a demanding one for there is no possibility of merely sleepwalking through existence.[4] For Levertov, then, poetry begins with an intense love of life derived from the poet's grounding in reality. The poet is then obliged to write truthfully about experience. And from an authentic description of *what is* arises a heightened sense of reality. Levertov conceived of poetry in largely Platonic terms: within all created things and events exists an essential form or order that the poet finds and reveals. As Thomas A. Duddy explains it, Levertov understood the poet as having a "two-fold obligation. First he must portray with verisimilitude the facts of his world . . . second he must discover that unexpected, illuminating detail."[5] Through the use of imagination, the poet achieves an epiphanic vision and thereby reshapes everyday circumstances to new significance. Levertov, in fact, sometimes invoked Gerard Manley Hopkins's "inscape" and "instress" to describe her concept of the "unexpected illuminating detail" present within all things. She also found John Keats's idea of "Negative Capability" ("when a man is capable of being in uncertainties, mysteries, doubts, without any irritable searching after fact and reason") to be operative in her poetry in its interplay of tensions and quiet waiting for illumination. As Jean Garrigue aptly put it, "Many of [Levertov's] poems seem to begin from the middle of reverie and end there, in a suspension of meanings. She is all for the undertone and the overtone and for that mystique of the arrangement of things whereby mysterious doors open briefly onto a view of other dimensions."[6] Given her aims in poetry, it's easy to see how Levertov's work has been consistently open to the metaphysical. With its strong sense of the sacramental—of matter and experience as signs of the spirit—Levertov's poetry perhaps naturally moved toward explicitly religious themes in the last decades of her career.

Levertov also had a strong belief in the social responsibilities of the writer. The poet's duty, she maintained, is to communicate what she perceives so that others may also see. While a poem is about the author's own experience, it is never merely confessional or subjective but extends that experience to the reader. Poetry has the ability to awaken those who sleep through life and give voice to those who lack the ability to express themselves. It can raise the consciousness of the reader, penetrating both mind and heart, and prompt the reader to take action to right wrongs in the world or, at the very least, to be more sensitive to the wonders of the universe and the dignity of human life. To Levertov, "The poet's essential task then is to rescue us from our own indifference and inhumanity by rekindling a sense of sympathy and reverence for our fellow creatures," as critic Kerry Driscoll has put it.[7]

While Levertov's poetry is wide-ranging in topic, certain themes recur. Many poems concern the need to live life more deeply and joyfully. The author's love of nature in shown in numerous poems celebrating the beauty and bounty of the things of the earth. Her human subjects, too, are treated with a sense of sacredness and compassion in deference to the mystery and uniqueness surrounding each human being. But Levertov also wrote poems about the trauma and horror of life and about man's inhumanity to man. Her politically charged poems, in particular, often explore feelings of hopelessness, alienation, fear, and doubt. Intent on facing the human condition honestly, Levertov recorded throughout her body of poetry life's essential paradox: both beauty and brutality coexist in the world.

Like many members of her generation, Levertov opposed American involvement in the Vietnam War during the 1960s and early 1970s. Because a few of her Vietnam-era poems are regularly anthologized, she is viewed by some as chiefly a "protest" poet although this is just one of her poetic stances. When her strident political voice emerged in such volumes as *The Sorrow Dance* (1967), *Relearning the Alphabet* (1970), and *To Stay Alive* (1971), some critics were dismayed at the difference between these poems and her early lyrics celebrating nature and beauty. Still, through the bitter and often disjointed tone of her Vietnam works, Levertov explored complex moral issues and reaffirmed hope and human dignity despite tragic circumstances. The well-known poem, "What Were They Like?" for example, explores with realism and compassion, in a catechism-like form, just who the Vietnamese are—people with fears and dreams just like any other people. With her strong commitment to social justice causes, Levertov continued her political activism throughout her life and wrote poems protesting war, Nazism, violence, nuclear threat, environmental crises, and human rights abuses throughout the world. In 1983, she penned the libretto for composer Newell Hendricks's oratorio, *El Salvador: Requiem and Invocation*, a tribute to Archbishop Oscar Romero and the three American nuns and one lay sister who were murdered in El Salvador because of their outcry against the country's oppressive regime. In all of her political poetry, Levertov confronted evil in the world and hoped to move her readers to greater understanding and action.

Trained as a young girl in the ballet, Levertov likewise conceived of a poem as a flowing unity in which the various parts work harmoniously with the whole. In organic art, form follows function. That is, a poem's form arises from the writing of the poem itself: the piece grows internally rather than having a certain structure imposed on it from the outside in a preordained way. In his influential essay, *The Philosophy of Composition*, Edgar Allen Poe laid out a mechanical, sequential process for the composition of a poem: the poet first selects the effect to be conveyed, then chooses a tone, then sounds, then words, etc. Organic poets, however, proceed in the opposite manner. To such poets, a work begins in an emotional response to an object or experience. The poem comes as a whole: the artist waits for the feeling to take shape and cannot force it. The process of writing the poem, then, becomes a process of discovery and not merely a record of what the poet already knows. Yet organic form does not imply merely random or spontaneous jottings. In several of her essays, Levertov wrote perceptively of the unique goals and challenges of organic composition. When writing organically, she maintained, the poet must tap into more areas of the self for the act of writing is always an adventure into unknown territory.[8]

In a Levertov poem, primary structural cues are conveyed through line arrangement. Indented lines and line breaks indicate how the poem is to be read and determine its pauses, pace, and tone. Frequently, the meditative silences and quiet observations of her poems derive from short lines, which slow the pace. Word choice and placement are, in addition, critical to the poem's overall effect. Levertov used colloquial, ordinary speech, but her placement of words and the emphasis given them often heightens or changes their meaning. She also made frequent use of echo words where meaning accrues and alters with each repeated use of the key word. While she often played with the ambiguity of words, exploring subtle shades of meaning, she avoided elaborate word play and complicated allusions. In addition, a key feature of her songlike lyrics is her well-developed sense of prosody. Highly attuned to the oral quality of her writing, she worked intently with the interplay of sound deriving from alliteration, repetition, assonance, and onomatopoetic effects. While complex, her sound patterns are nevertheless subtle, enhancing but never detracting from her poems' themes.

As she approached conversion to Christianity, Levertov's poetry increasingly expressed spiritual yearning, a sense of mystery arising from ordinary life, and the tensions of alternating doubt and belief. In fact, it was in the very act of composing poetry that she moved toward firmer faith. "By temperament I was disposed to assent," she stated, "and the experience, as a poet, of being at times a channel for something beyond my own limitations was . . . an open door to specifically religious experience."[9] While composing an "agnostic Mass" entitled "Mass for the Day of St. Thomas Didymus," a multipart poem based on the ritual of the liturgy, she found herself moving toward religious conviction. With St. Thomas Didymus as her patron—the doubting Thomas who required physical proof to believe—Levertov used her poetry to explore the nuances of faith, doubt, confidence, fear, longing, and joy that are familiar ground for any sincere Christian seeker. In some poems, she examined the faith of believers such as Jacob, Tobias, St. Thomas, St. Peter, Julian of Norwich, Thomas Merton, Brother Lawrence, and Dom Helder Camara, and in others strove to "enter" certain biblical scenes, attending to all sensory details before meditating on the meaning arising from them.

In this regard, she found the practice of Ignatian meditation quite similar to the poetic process.

Hers a "poetry of engagement," as one critic has called it, Levertov did not abandon that engagement with the world when she converted to the Christian faith.[10] In fact, with its clear incarnational and sacramental emphases, Catholicism offered Levertov a strong reason for continuing to ground her work in daily realities and quotidian experiences. As she moved toward belief, she was surprised to discover that "an avowal of Christian faith is not incompatible with my aesthetic nor with my political stance."[11] In fact, what primarily drew her to Catholicism was the activism of Catholics who grounded their politics in their beliefs, protesting against abuses while yet maintaining faith and hope. But because she still found herself with doubts, her conversion ultimately took the form of a Pascalian wager, a leap of faith: "If a Romero—or a Dorothy Day . . . or a Thomas Merton—or a Pascal, for that matter!—could believe, who was I to squirm and fret, as if I required more refined mental nourishment than theirs?"[12]

In her final year of life, Levertov designed her last volume, *The Stream and the Sapphire*, to trace her spiritual path. As you read the poems in this slender volume, it is best to do so aloud, slowly and meditatively, with appropriate pauses. Read each poem at least twice. Here are some notes on a few of the poems you'll encounter.

Section 1, "The Tide"

This section groups poems that express the interplay of faith and doubt. As in the keynote poem, "The Tide," faith is depicted as a dynamic process, ebbing and flowing throughout the course of life. Several poems here, such as "The Avowal," "Standoff," and "To Live in the Mercy of God," express the poet's great longing to relax in full acceptance of God's love and the difficulty of doing so. In a number of poems, such as "Suspended," the poet pictures herself in a limbo or in-between state, waiting in darkness for light, sustained only by a slender thread of faith.

"AGNUS DEI"

While this poem is only one part of the six part "Mass for St. Thomas Didymus," it proved to be an important turning point for Levertov in her faith journey: it was while writing these verses that she moved from agnostic to believer. You may wish to read the entire poem, found in the collection *Candles in Babylon*, to explore the function of this part of the poem within the whole "Mass." The doubting Thomas, from John 20:24–29, probed Christ's wounds before emphatically proclaiming, "My Lord and my God!" Thomas represents the human need to prove the existence of God and, his name meaning "twin," the alteration between skepticism and belief. Levertov's "Mass" in honor of St. Thomas ends with the "Agnus Dei," which meditates on the image Christ chose for himself: a lamb. Considering how timid and foolish sheep are, the poet explores in detail just what such an image might lead us to conclude about God's nature. The poem ends with the startling conclusion that, in the reciprocal communion of love, God has deigned to have us—human beings—love, nurture, and shelter him, the defenseless lamb. Somehow, God needs us as much as we need him: he wants us to respond to him freely in love. Yet, fearful of involvement and responsibility, more often than not we reject the offer as too demanding, too terrifying. Still, the poet invites us to a commitment, however tentative: "Let's try."

"FLICKERING MIND"

A poem about the vicissitudes of human emotion, this piece explores in first person the narrator's wandering attention to God. Although in the early stages of newfound faith she experienced joy in belief, now she finds herself running from God, unable to focus her thoughts on him for more than a moment. Levertov took the title of her collection, *The Stream and the Sapphire*, from this poem. To the poet, God is both "stream" and "sapphire," the unchanging center of all that is dynamic and fluid in the universe. As a believer, the poet realizes that the call of faith—and its constant challenge—is to live fully immersed in the reality of the world even while keeping her attention on the "jewel" in its midst. The poem ends with a open-ended question that invites us to meditate on just how this may be accomplished.

"ON A THEME BY THOMAS MERTON"

This poem concerns the condition of Adam in the Garden of Eden immediately after the Fall. Now separated from God because of sin, Adam has lost his ability to focus, falling from a singleness of vision to multiplicity. Pulled in many directions, as a child is confused and mesmerized by the lights and sounds of a carnival, Adam becomes disoriented. His lack of focus creates a dark chasm separating him from God so that God must search for man and man, in turn, cannot see God's love and care. This poem can be read in light of Augustine's theme of the restless and fragmented self in the *Confessions*.

"Variations on a Theme by Rilke"

As this poem opens, its narrator, a monk, has just finished showing to his listener a book of paintings of Christ. Among others, the book contains artwork by the fourteenth-century Italian, Giotto; the fifteenth-century Van Eyck and seventeenth-century Rembrandt, both Dutch; and the twentieth-century French modernist, Rouault. Although very different in conception and technique, each portrait of Christ, the monk avers, is truthful, for each resulted from the wellspring of the artist's faith. As a church's stained glass windows are lit only when light pours into the building from the outside, so the artist who lives in grace, no matter his time, place, or culture, will produce an image of God that captures some authentic aspect of the divine countenance. In her ending lines, Levertov evokes Hopkins's lovely phrase in the poem, "As Kingfishers Catch Fire": "For Christ plays in ten thousand places, / Lovely in limbs, and lovely in eyes not his / To the Father through the features of men's faces." Although God does not change, his image, revealed to the faithful through grace, is stamped on all creation. Creativity, the poem attests, is a God-given light that allows the artist to portray the divine and also to join in a community of faith-filled artists that transcends the limitations of time and space.

Section 2, "Believers"

Here, Levertov groups poems that study historical, biblical, and mythical figures who may serve as models of unwavering Christian belief.

"Caedmon" and "St. Peter and the Angel"

In telling the story of Caedmon, Levertov relies on Venerable Bede's account of the first English Christian poet's awakening to his vocation, a movement from silence to song. Narrated in the first person, Caedmon presents himself as a peasant, awkward and tongue-tied when among others. Miraculously, through the offices of an angel, he receives the gift of speech. As she often does, Levertov examines here the origin of artistic inspiration, which is revealed to be a type of fire coming from the divine, an image drawn from Isaiah. In her notes to the *The Stream and the Sapphire*, Levertov states that "Caedmon" is a companion piece to the previous poem "St. Peter and the Angel," which likewise relates the story, derived from Acts, of a prisoner freed from captivity by the intervention of divine grace. Set free, Peter finds his situation even more frightening than the chains of captivity for freedom necessitates the continual decision to follow Christ wherever he leads. But freedom also brings joy and reunion with others: at the end of "Caedmon," the poet is liberated from his isolation and enters the circle of dancers. Now joined in harmony with others, he is yet set apart by his unique vocation.

"THE SERVANT-GIRL AT EMMAUS"

This poem finds its inspiration in a painting by the seventeenth-century Spanish artist Velázquez concerning the biblical story of the risen Christ who accepted an invitation to dine with the two travelers he met on the way to Emmaus. When cleaned in 1933, the painting revealed the scene, previously obscured, of a young black female servant listening intently to the men as they converse at the table behind her. She is startled, in hearing his voice, to recognize Jesus whom she had once heard preach and had later learned was crucified. Thus, she already understands what the men who accompany Jesus do not but will momentarily discover as he breaks the bread she has served to them: that the Lord is indeed risen from the dead.

"THE SHOWINGS: LADY JULIAN OF NORWICH, 1342–1416"

In this long poem, Levertov dialogues with Julian, the fourteenth-century mystic whose *Revelations of Divine Love* explores the mystery of the coexistence of evil and God's power and love in the world. Opening with a direct address to Julian, the narrator notes the fact that in the modern, scientific world, our understanding of the immense size and complexity of the universe and of all we do not know, symbolized by black holes, produces cosmic anxiety and doubt. Is there really a God in control of all this vastness? The poem thus opens with the "doubtful fear" that Julian found so crippling to spiritual progress. The poet then recalls the scene in which God places a hazelnut in Julian's hand, a tiny object representing all that exists. Julian learns of God's tremendous love and care for all created things and that, indeed, he is keeping us very safe. But can Julian be trusted, or were her visions merely the product of a neurotic mind? To explore this question, the narrator recreates Julian's life imaginatively, conceiving of her as a normal quick-witted young girl full of wonder at all about her. And Julian, like ourselves the narrator observes, lived in difficult, fearful times. Still, she maintained faith and trust in God, clinging to the promise of his protection and mercy like a performer in a circus swings from the high wire by her teeth. The poet discovers in Julian a model of strength and confidence in God's power and love and in the ultimate triumph of good over evil.

"ANNUNCIATION"

In this moving piece, the poet first disassociates us from the familiar scene of room, lectern, book, and lily depicted in countless paintings of Mary's Annunciation by quickly glossing over these physical details. She thus prepares readers to go a step farther, bidding us move from the usual notion of Mary as utterly meek and obedient as she responds to the angel Gabriel to an image that, instead, lays emphasis on her astonishing courage as she freely deliberates on and then accepts the angel's request. As she also does with Julian in the above poem, the poet imagines Mary as a normal girl in all ways but possessing an unusual degree of intelligence, empathy, and charity so that, when the angel suddenly bursts into her life, she understands fully the astonishing vocation to which she has been called. The poet sees Mary as a model of courage and dignity for us who, when we experience "annunications" in our lives, more often than not close the door to inspiration out of weakness or fear.

Section 3, "Conjectures"

In the third and shortest section of the volume, Levertov groups three poems that speculate on theological matters. Two examine the meaning of obscure Gospel passages and a third, appropriately entitled "A Heresy," considers the possibility that purgatory may be a type of reincarnation.

"What the Figtree Said"

The story of Christ cursing the fig tree is told several times in the Gospels (Matthew 21:18–22; Mark 11:12–14) yet remains a puzzling one. In this poem, the poet intriguingly locates the point of view in the fig tree itself. Christ's odd behavior, cursing a tree for not bearing fruit, disturbed some of his followers who turned away in scorn or sheer embarrassment for him. But unlike those literal-minded folk, the fig tree perceives that Christ was speaking metaphorically: that is, that the tree's presence served merely as a convenient vehicle for Christ to condemn those among his followers whose hearts refused to produce the "fruit" of understanding and love he sought from them.

Section 4, "Fish and a Honeycomb"

The six poems in the concluding section of the book each focus on scenes from Jesus' Passion and Resurrection. Thus a volume that begins with the tension of faith and doubt ends with avowals of belief in the reality and efficacy of Christ's sacrifice. The title of this section is taken from the last phrase in the poem "Ikon: The Harrowing of Hell" and points to both Christ's humility in accepting sustenance from human beings while on earth and his feeding us with his own body and blood in the Eucharist.

"Salvator Mundi: Via Crucis"

Here, the poet considers that the worst suffering Christ endured during his Passion was not physical torment nor the betrayal and desertion of his friends but the horrible temptation to give up, to "renege," on that which he had been incarnated on earth to do: save humankind by means of the Cross. The poet sees in this very human emotion—the sickening realization that one has taken on too much to bear—both Christ's courage and love, for despite this temptation he accepted God's will completely and bore with his pains to the end.

"Ikon: The Harrowing of Hell"

This poem begins in the state of limbo, according to Dante a type of vestibule of hell where Christ, as is traditionally believed, descended after his death to free those prophets and other just persons who had died before his coming. One of those he rescues is Didmas, the Good Thief, to whom just a short while before as they hung next to each other on their crosses Christ had promised, "This day you will be with me in paradise." Christ now sets all these good souls on the road to heaven. But he himself must still complete his mission on earth, assuming once more his human body. The poet imagines that the act of entering once more the limitations of time and space and walking among those who had betrayed him must have been excruciatingly difficult. For now Christ's resurrected and glorified body longs only for the home of Father and heaven. But with supreme patience and love, Jesus returns to the earth to give his followers the comfort of his presence and renew their hope for eternal life with him.

"ST. THOMAS DIDYMUS"

In this poem, Levertov creatively combines several Gospel stories to imagine how the Apostle Thomas may have secretly harbored doubts as he accompanied Jesus on his ministry, only coming to belief when he is able to probe Christ's wounds after the Resurrection. Thomas here narrates his own story. He recalls the incident when a man brought his possessed son to Jesus to be healed; in anguish, the man wrestles with the question of why the innocent often suffer cruelly in this life. Observing the scene, Thomas recognizes in the man his twin, for Thomas, too, has had such doubts about God's love and mercy but has been wary of expressing them in the company of Jesus and the other disciples. Even after Jesus heals the boy, Thomas's uncertainty persists. By juxtaposing these Gospel scenes, Levertov thus builds a case for why, then, Thomas refused to believe the news that Jesus was alive three days after his Crucifixion: similar to the case of the sick boy now miraculously healed, he cannot accept the fact that the suffering of the innocent can result in triumph and glory. But as he touches Jesus' hands and side, a light of understanding penetrates his heart. While it does not answer his question—the age-old question of why we must suffer—he realizes through grace that God has a magnificent plan, mysterious until the end of the world, in which pain and suffering play a profound part and at the center of which is the Passion, Resurrection, and Glorification of Christ. This poem is one of many Levertov works that grapple with the problem of evil in the world and resolve it through the light of faith.

FOR FURTHER READING

Denise Levertov, *New and Selected Essays.* The following essays in this collection are especially recommended: "Work that Enfaiths," "A Poet's View," "The Poet in the World," and "Poetry, Prophecy, Survival."

Brother Lawrence, *The Practice of the Presence of God.* This well-known spiritual text will lend insight to the poem, "Conversion of Brother Lawrence."

Julian of Norwich, *Revelations of Divine Love.*

QUESTIONS FOR DISCUSSION

1. Select several poems to read aloud and explicate. To explicate a poem, first come to an understanding of its meaning by working through it according to its natural division into line, sentence, or verse paragraph. How does each part of the poem contribute to the whole? What kind of movement is present in the poem—from idea to idea and from beginning to end? Who is narrating the poem and why is the choice of narrator important? What is the poem's tone—the speaker's attitude to the subject? What elements of prosody—meter, rhyme, and other technical aspects—are present and how do they contribute to the poem's effect? Finally, after examining all its parts, evaluate the poem critically as to whether it is successful or not.

2. Levertov carefully arranged the poems in this volume. Consider how the various poems in each section, and the four sections of the book itself, contribute to her stated purpose of showing her "slow movement from agnosticism to Christian faith, a movement incorporating much of doubt and questioning as well as of affirmation."

3. What kind of Christian believers does Levertov single out for examination, and why? Why, for example, is she attracted to such figures as St. Thomas Didymus, Julian of Norwich, Caedmon, Brother Lawrence, and Dom Helder? What do these figures have in common?

4. Read and discuss Levertov's essays, "A Poet's View" and "Work that Enfaiths" in *New and Selected Essays.* In what ways can her thoughts here on faith and the artistic process add to an understanding of her poetry?

NOTES

Denise Levertov, *The Stream and the Sapphire* (New York: New Directions, 1997). All references are to this edition.

1. Ralph Mills, Jr., "Denise Levertov: Poetry of the Immediate," *Tri-Quarterly* 4, no. 2 (Winter 1962): 34–35.
2. Denise Levertov, *Light Up the Cave* (New York: New Directions, 1981), 98.
3. Denise Levertov, "Origins of a Poem," in *The Poet in the World* (New York: New Directions, 1973), 54.
4. From "The Craft of Poetry" seminar. Quoted in Linda W. Wagner, *Denise Levertov* (New York: Twayne, 1967), 19.
5. Thomas A. Duddy, "To Celebrate: A Reading of Denise Levertov," in *Critical Essays on Denise Levertov,* edited by Linda Wagner-Martin (Boston: G. K. Hall, 1991), 111.
6. Jean Garrigue, "With Eyes at the Back of our Heads," in *Denise Levertov: Selected Criticism,* edited by Albert Gelpi (Ann Arbor: University of Michigan Press, 1993), 15.
7. Kerry Driscoll, "A Sense of Unremitting Emergency: Politics in the Early Works of Denise Levertov," in *Critical Essays on Denise Levertov,* edited by Linda Wagner-Martin (Boston: G. K. Hall, 1991), 150.
8. Wagner, *Denise Levertov,* 94.
9. Denise Levertov, "A Poet's View," in *New and Selected Essays* (New York: New Directions, 1992), 242.
10. Audrey T. Rodgers, *Denise Levertov: The Poetry of Engagement* (Cranbury, NJ: Associated University Presses, 1993).
11. Levertov, "A Poet's View," 243.
12. Levertov, "A Poet's View," 250–51.

BIBLIOGRAPHY

Gelpi, Albert, ed. *Denise Levertov: Selected Criticism.* Ann Arbor: University of Michigan Press, 1993.

Little, Anne Colclough, and Susie Paul, eds. *Denise Levertov: New Perspectives.* West Cornwall, CT: Locust Hill Press, 2000.

Marten, Harry. *Understanding Denise Levertov.* Columbia: University of South Carolina Press, 1988.

Renascence (Fall–Winter 1997–1998). This edition is devoted to Levertov and contains a number of articles on her religious themes.

Rodgers, Audrey T. *Denise Levertov: The Poetry of Engagement.* Cranbury, NJ: Associated University Presses, 1993.

Wagner-Martin, Linda, ed. *Critical Essays on Denise Levertov.* Boston: G. K. Hall, 1991.

APPENDIX:
ADDITIONAL WORKS
OF CATHOLIC LITERATURE

These works of Catholic autobiography, fiction, and poetry are also highly recommended.

Hilaire Belloc, *The Path to Rome*
Willa Cather, *Death Comes for the Archbishop*
Geoffrey Chaucer, *The Canterbury Tales*
Dorothy Day, *The Long Loneliness*
Isak Dineson (Karen Blixen), *Babette's Feast*
Andre Dubus, *Voices from the Moon*
T. S. Eliot, *Four Quartets*
Rumer Godden, *In This House of Brede*
Ron Hansen, *Mariette in Ecstasy*
Jon Hassler, *North of Hope*
John of the Cross, *The Dark Night of the Soul*
Gertrud Le Fort, *Song at the Scaffold*
Thomas Merton, *The Seven Storey Mountain*
Thomas More, *Utopia*
John Henry Newman, *Apologia Pro Vita Sua*
Kathleen Norris, *The Cloister Walk*
Walker Percy, *Lancelot*
Katherine Anne Porter, *Ship of Fools*
Jessica Powers, selected poetry
J. F. Powers, *Morte d'Urban*
Christina Rossetti, selected poetry
Dorothy L. Sayers, *The Man Born to Be King*
Henryk Sienkiewicz, *Quo Vadis?*

Muriel Spark, *Memento Mori*
Jean Sulivan, *Eternity, My Beloved*
Teresa of Avila, *The Interior Castle*
Thérèse of Lisieux, *Story of a Soul*
J. R. Tolkien, *The Lord of the Rings*

ABOUT THE AUTHOR

Mary R. Reichardt is a professor of literature and Catholic studies and the director of the master's program in Catholic Studies at the University of St. Thomas in St. Paul, Minnesota. She received her Ph.D. in English from the University of Wisconsin–Madison. Her teaching and research interests include Catholic literature, American literature, women's literature, autobiography, and the short story. This is her sixth book.